Quantitative Data Analysis in Education

This book provides a refreshing and user-friendly guide to quantitative data analysis in education for students and researchers. It assumes absolutely no prior knowledge of quantitative methods or statistics. Beginning with the very basics, it provides the reader with the knowledge and skills necessary to be able to undertake routine quantitative data analysis to a level expected of published research.

Rather than focusing on teaching statistics through mathematical formulae, the book places an emphasis on using SPSS to gain a real feel for the data and an intuitive grasp of the main concepts and techniques involved. Drawing extensively upon up-to-date and relevant examples, the reader will be encouraged to think critically about quantitative research and its potential as well as its limitations in relation to education.

Packed with helpful features, this book:

* provides illustrated step-by-step guides showing how to use SPSS, with plenty of exercises to encourage the reader to practice and consolidate their new skills;
* makes extensive use of real-life educational datasets derived from national surveys in the US and UK to illustrate key points and to bring the material to life;
* has a companion website that contains all of the educational datasets used in the book to download as well as comprehensive answers to exercises and a range of other useful resources that are regularly updated.

The book will therefore appeal not only to undergraduate and postgraduate students but also to more established and seasoned educational researchers, lecturers and professors who have tended to avoid or shy away from quantitative methods.

Paul Connolly is Professor of Education at Queen's University Belfast and has gained extensive experience researching and publishing in education. He has taught quantitative methods using SPSS for the last ten years to undergraduate sociology students and, more recently, students on masters programs in education as well as the taught doctorate program (Ed.D.).

Quantitative Data Analysis in Education

A critical introduction using SPSS

Paul Connolly

 Routledge
Taylor & Francis Group

LONDON AND NEW YORK

First published 2007
by Routledge
2 Park Square, Milton Park, Abingdon, Oxon OX14 4RN

Simultaneously published in the USA and Canada
by Routledge
711 Third Avenue, New York, NY 10017

Routledge is an imprint of the Taylor & Francis Group, an informa business

© 2007 Paul Connolly

Typeset in Times New Roman by
Florence Production Ltd, Stoodleigh, Devon

British Library Cataloguing in Publication Data
A catalogue record for this book is available from the British Library

Library of Congress Cataloging in Publication Data
Connolly, Paul, 1966–
    Quantitative data analysis in education: a critical introduction using SPSS/
    Paul Connolly.
        p. cm.
    Includes bibliographical references.
    1. Educational statistics. 2. SPSS (Computer file) I. Title.
    LB2846.C66 2007
    370.2'1–dc22   2006039709

ISBN10: 0–415–37297–6 (hbk)
ISBN10: 0–415–37298–4 (pbk)
ISBN10: 0–203–94698–7 (ebk)

ISBN13: 978–0–415–37297–8 (hbk)
ISBN13: 978–0–415–37298–5 (pbk)
ISBN13: 978–0–203–94698–5 (ebk)

Contents

List of figures		viii
List of tables		xii
List of boxes		xiii
Acknowledgments		xiv

Introduction   1

Who is this book for and what is it about? 2
What makes this book different? 3
Key themes underpinning the book 4
Structure of the book 7
Companion website 8
Differing versions of SPSS 9
And finally, what this book expects of you! 9

1 Getting started with SPSS   13

Introduction 13
Understanding what a dataset is 13
Opening an existing dataset in SPSS 16
Creating your own dataset 25
Conclusions 34

2 Exploring, displaying and summarizing data   35

Introduction 35
Different types of variable 35
Displaying and summarizing scale variables 43
Displaying and summarizing nominal and ordinal variables 62
Conclusions 66

3 Analyzing relationships between variables   68

Introduction 68
Preparing variables and the dataset for analysis 68
Analyzing relationships between two variables 76

Analyzing trends over time 103
Conclusions 111

4   Good practice in presenting findings   **112**

Introduction 112
Generating and editing tables in SPSS 112
Generating and editing charts in SPSS 122
Chart Builder 134
Conclusions 139

5   Confidence intervals and statistical significance   **142**

Introduction 142
Sources of bias in samples 143
Confidence intervals 145
The concept of statistical significance 158
Testing for statistical significance 163
Conclusions 170

6   Conducting statistical tests and calculating effect sizes   **175**

Introduction 175
Selecting the appropriate statistical test 175
Chi-Square test 178
Mann-Whitney U test 189
Kruskal-Wallis test 194
Independent samples t-test 200
One-way ANOVA 208
Spearman and Pearson correlations 214
Wilcoxon test 217
Related samples t-test 220
Analyzing experimental research designs 223
Dealing with weighting variables 236
Conclusions 242

7   Where next?   **243**

Introduction 243
*Develop your understanding of the nature of quantitative data
    and how they are generated 243*
*Face your demons and have a closer look at the statistics behind
    the concepts covered in this book 244*
*Move onto more advanced quantitative data analysis techniques
    involving three or more variables 245*

*If you're still keen for more, think seriously about enrolling on an advanced
    statistics course or program 246*
Above all, make sure that you enjoy yourself! 246

Appendix 1 Defining variables in SPSS Version 9.0 and earlier   247
Appendix 2 Editing charts in SPSS Version 12.0 and earlier   251

References   260
Index   263

Figures

1.1 The bullying dataset as it appears in SPSS 15
1.2 Save As window 17
1.3 Opening SPSS in Windows XP 18
1.4 SPSS 15.0 for Windows window in SPSS 19
1.5 Open Data window 19
1.6 Options window in SPSS 20
1.7 Value labels icon in SPSS 20
1.8 Viewing summaries of variables 21
1.9 Variable View in SPSS 21
1.10 Value Labels window in SPSS 22
1.11 Frequencies window in SPSS 23
1.12 SPSS Output window 24
1.13 Defining variables in SPSS 26
1.14 Variable Type window in SPSS 27
1.15 Value Labels window in SPSS 29
1.16 Missing Values window in SPSS 29
1.17 Completed Variable View for the international.sav dataset 30
1.18 Data View for international.sav dataset 31
1.19 Explore window in SPSS 31
1.20 Simple Scatterplot window in SPSS 32
1.21 Scatterplot showing the relationship between school life expectancy
 and female adult illiteracy rates in 20 countries 33
2.1 Histogram window in SPSS 45
2.2 A histogram showing school life expectancy for 20 developing countries 45
2.3 Interpreting a stem and leaf display 47
2.4 Properties of the normal distribution 50
2.5 Weight Cases window in SPSS 52
2.6 Age distribution of mothers in the earlychildhood.sav dataset 53
2.7 Descriptives window in SPSS 54
2.8 New variable representing the standardized scores from the
 "MOMAGE1" variable as seen in Data View in SPSS 55
2.9 Distribution of per capita GDP among the 20 countries in the
 international.sav dataset 56
2.10 Sort Cases window in SPSS 59
2.11 The median, interquartile range and range 59

2.12 Define Simple Boxplot window in SPSS   61
2.13 Boxplot showing the distribution of per capita GDP for the 20 countries
      in the international.sav dataset   62
2.14 Output window in SPSS   64
2.15 Define Pie window in SPSS   65
2.16 Pie chart and bar chart showing ethnic breakdown of the
      earlychildhood.sav sample   66
3.1   Recoding variables in SPSS   70
3.2   Select Cases window in SPSS   73
3.3   Main SPSS window indicating that the "Select Cases" procedure is
      being used   73
3.4   Split File window in SPSS   75
3.5   Crosstabs window in SPSS   78
3.6   Define Clustered Bar window in SPSS   85
3.7   Two different ways of presenting gender differences in school grades
      achieved using a clustered bar chart   86
3.8   Histogram showing the distribution of GCSE point scores for the
      youthcohort.sav dataset   88
3.9   Define Simple Boxplot window in SPSS   89
3.10 Racial/ethnic differences in the GCSE scores obtained by Year 11
      pupils in England in 2002   90
3.11 Bivariate Correlations window in SPSS   94
3.12 Relationship between levels of truancy and GCSE scores among
      Year 11 pupils in England in 2002   97
3.13 Relationships between male and female illiteracy rates and between
      male illiteracy rates and school life expectancy in 20 countries 99
3.14 The relationship between the simple measure of school performance
      taken by the percentage of pupils gaining five or more GCSE grades
      A*–C and the more complex value added measure of school performance 101
3.15 Relationship between female illiteracy and per capita GDP (US$) in
      20 countries   102
3.16 Define Simple Line window in SPSS   104
3.17 Percentage of Year 11 pupils in England achieving five or more GCSE
      grades A*–C (or their equivalent) between 1974/5 and 2003/4   105
3.18 Define Multiple Line window in SPSS   106
3.19 Percentage of Year 11 pupils in England achieving five or more GCSE
      grades A*–C (or their equivalent) between 1974/5 and 2003/4 by sex 107
3.20 Compute Variable window in SPSS   108
3.21 Data View showing timeseries.sav dataset with new computed
      variables added   109
3.22 Sex differences in the percentage of Year 11 pupils in England
      achieving five or more GCSE grades A*–C (or their equivalent)
      between 1974/5 and 2003/4   110
4.1   Changing the title of a table in SPSS   115
4.2   Selecting a cell in a table in SPSS   116
4.3   Selecting a row in a table in SPSS   116
4.4   Altering borders in a table in SPSS   117

4.5	TableLooks window in SPSS	118
4.6	Cutting and pasting a table directly into a report	119
4.7	Altering the order of rows in a table in SPSS	121
4.8	Cell Properties window in SPSS	122
4.9	Comparison of a clustered bar chart and a stacked bar chart as means of displaying gender differences in school grades achieved by young children in America	123
4.10	Clustered bar chart as it first appears in SPSS, comparing the school grades achieved by boys and girls as reported by their parents	124
4.11	Chart Editor window in SPSS	126
4.12	Adding a title to a chart in the Chart Editor window in SPSS	127
4.13	Adding a footnote to a chart in the Chart Editor window in SPSS	128
4.14	Changing the color of bars using the Properties window in SPSS	129
4.15	Categories view in the Properties window in SPSS	130
4.16	Text Style view in the Properties window in SPSS	131
4.17	Selecting and moving the legend in the Chart Editor window in SPSS	132
4.18	Selecting and changing the chart size in the Chart Editor window in SPSS	133
4.19	The clustered bar chart as it finally appears	133
4.20	Initial Chart Builder dialog window in SPSS	135
4.21	Chart Builder and Element Properties windows in SPSS	135
4.22	Selecting a chart type in the Chart Builder window in SPSS	136
4.23	Selecting variables in the Chart Builder window in SPSS	137
4.24	Element Properties window in SPSS	138
4.25	Population pyramid showing sex differences in GCSE scores attained by Year 11 pupils in England in 2002	139
4.26	Example of a "Gee Whizz" chart	141
5.1	Selecting a random sub-sample of cases in SPSS	146
5.2	Distribution of the means of 20 random samples selected from a population of 13,201 cases	148
5.3	Explore: Statistics window in SPSS	150
5.4	Define Simple Error Bar: Summaries of Separate Variables window in SPSS	151
5.5	Error bars showing 95 percent confidence intervals for the means of 20 samples randomly selected from a population with a mean of 49.29	151
5.6	Define Simple Error Bar: Summaries for Groups of Cases window in SPSS	153
5.7	Error bars showing differences in mean GCSE point scores between different racial/ethnic groups for Year 11 pupils in England	154
5.8	Options window for Define Clustered Bar window in SPSS	157
5.9	Clustered bar chart with 95 percent confidence intervals added	158
5.10	Standardized distributions illustrating one- and two-tailed tests	168
6.1	Running a Chi-Square test in SPSS	179
6.2	Creating a 2×2 contingency table in SPSS	187
6.3	Defining categories for the variable "SEGRADES" as "Missing" in SPSS	190
6.4	Running a Mann-Whitney U test in SPSS	191
6.5	Running a Kruskal-Wallis test in SPSS	195
6.6	Distribution of the "gcse" variable in the valueadded.sav dataset	201

6.7   One-Sample Kolmogorov-Smirnov Test window in SPSS   202
6.8   Running an Independent-Samples T Test in SPSS   203
6.9   Running a one-way ANOVA in SPSS   209
6.10   Correlation between the ages of a young child's mother and father
       from the earlychildhood.sav dataset   215
6.11   Two-Related-Samples Tests window in SPSS   218
6.12   Paired-Samples T Test window in SPSS   221
6.13   Examples of experimental research designs (or randomized controlled
       trials)   224
6.14   Distribution of the post-test reading scores from the experiment.sav
       dataset   227
6.15   Relationship between pre-test and post-test reading scores in the
       experiment.sav dataset   228
6.16   Linear Regression window in SPSS   230
A1.1   The main data view window as it appears in SPSS Version 9.0 and earlier   247
A1.2   Define Variable window as it appears in SPSS Version 9.0 and earlier   248
A1.3   Define Variable Type: window as it appears in SPSS Version 9.0 and
       earlier   248
A1.4   Define Missing Values: window as it appears in SPSS Version 9.0 and
       earlier   249
A1.5   Define Labels: window as it appears in SPSS Version 9.0 and earlier   249
A1.6   Define Column Format: window as it appears in SPSS Version 9.0 and
       earlier   250
A1.7   The main screen showing a variable that has been defined as it appears
       in SPSS Version 9.0 and earlier   250
A2.1   The initial clustered bar chart as it appears in SPSS Version 12.0
       and earlier   252
A2.2   Chart Editor window in SPSS Version 12.0 and earlier   253
A2.3   Titles window in SPSS Version 12.0 and earlier   254
A2.4   Text Styles window in SPSS Version 12.0 and earlier   255
A2.5   Category Axis window in SPSS Version 12.0 and earlier   256
A2.6   Footnotes window in SPSS Version 12.0 and earlier   257
A2.7   Colors window in SPSS Version 12.0 and earlier   257
A2.8   Bar/Line/Displayed Data window in SPSS Version 12.0 and earlier   258
A2.9   Final version of the clustered bar chart created using SPSS Version 12.0
       and earlier   258

Tables

1.1   Educational and economic indicators for 20 countries   26

2.1   Calculating the position of a case within a normal distribution using Z scores   51

2.2   The extent to which parents in America stated that they read to their young children (aged 0–6) in the past week   64

3.1   Average GCSE point scores by racial/ethnic group for school leavers in England, 2003   88

3.2   Percentage of boys and girls gaining five or more GCSE higher grade passes in England in 2004/5   108

5.1   The means of 20 samples (n = 200) selected from a population of 13,201 cases   147

5.2   Scenario 1: Proportions of male and female university students indicating that they would use podcasts of lectures if they were made available (Total sample = 10)   159

5.3   Scenario 2: Proportions of male and female university students indicating that they would use podcasts of lectures if they were made available (Total sample = 20)   160

5.4   Scenario 3: Proportions of male and female university students indicating that they would use podcasts of lectures if they were made available (Total sample = 40)   161

5.5   Percentage chances of events occurring expressed as probabilities   162

5.6   Percentage chances and probabilities that findings derived from a sample may have occurred by chance assuming that there are no such differences in the population as a whole   162

5.7   Type I and Type II errors   166

6.1   Proportions of male and female school leavers in England achieving five or more GCSE Grades A*–C or their equivalent, 2002   185

6.2   Results of linear multiple regression from an analysis of the results of the pre-test/post-test control group experimental design   232

Boxes

0.1   Summary of datasets used in the book   10
1.1   Amended extract from the Northern Ireland Young Life and Times
Survey 2005   14
2.1   Examples of ordinal variables   37
2.2   Example of an interval variable   42
2.3   Summary guide for distinguishing between different types of variable   44
2.4   Examples of normal distributions   49
2.5   Summary guide as to the appropriate way to display and summarize a
variable   67
3.1   Examples of expressions to select cases and their meanings   75
3.2   Details of the variables "SEGRADES" and "MOMGRADE" from the
afterschools.sav dataset   91
3.3   Summary guide as to the appropriate way to analyze the relationship
between two variables   111
4.1   Summary guide: good practice in presenting data in tables and charts   140
6.1   Summary guide for selecting the appropriate statistical test   177

Acknowledgments

There are a number of people and organizations I would like to thank for making this book possible. I am grateful to SPSS Inc. for granting me permission to use screen shots of SPSS Version 15 in the book. I would also like to thank the National Center for Education Statistics (NCES) within the US Department of Education for giving me permission to use and make available reduced versions of two datasets derived from their National Household Education Surveys Program. I am also grateful to the Department for Education and Skills (UK) for kindly preparing and providing me with a specially adapted dataset from the first sweep of Cohort 12 of the Youth Cohort Study of England and Wales to use and make available for this book. I would also like to thank the Northern Ireland Young Life and Times Survey for granting me permission to use and make available a reduced version of their 2005 dataset.

In addition, I am extremely grateful to Ian Schagen and Karen Winter for reading and commenting on various sections of the book. I would also like to thank everyone at Routledge and especially Philip Mudd and Amy Crowle for their help and support and above all their patience! I am also grateful to the countless undergraduate sociology students at the University of Ulster and masters and doctoral students at Queen's University Belfast to whom I have taught quantitative methods for the last 10 years. It is only because of their openness and honesty that I have gained the many insights that have made writing this book possible. Finally, and as always, I would like to thank my partner, Karen, and our children—Mary, Orla and Rory—for making my life worthwhile.

This book is dedicated to my mum, Brenda Connolly, who I know is very proud of me.

Introduction

I should really start this book with a confession—there was a time when I didn't do numbers. To be really honest, there was a time when I was actually very critical of quantitative research. To explain, one of my main areas of research was (and still is) concerned with the effects of race and ethnicity on young children's identities and peer cultures. When I first began reading around this area I waded through quantitative study after quantitative study that attempted in different ways to measure the levels of racial prejudice found among young children. Most of these studies used what I felt were simplistic methods, often taking the form of highly structured, experimental designs and recording children's reactions to photographs of black and white children or their preferences for differently colored dolls (see Milner, 1983; Aboud, 1988). My main concern was that it was just not possible to put a number on children's prejudices. Children's racial attitudes are not fixed and quantifiable; rather they are complex, contradictory and context-specific. I argued strongly that the only way we can fully understand the impact of race in young children's lives is through qualitative research that is able to capture the complexity of children's attitudes and identities and place these within their specific contexts (see Connolly, 1996, 1997, 2001). At the time my own research was therefore qualitative, drawing upon in-depth ethnographic methods to study young children's social worlds (see Connolly, 1998). Moreover, my criticisms of quantitative research in relation to race and young children soon became generalized to a criticism of all quantitative research that I too easily dismissed as simplistic and positivist.

Over time, however, I have progressively come to question this position. In ignoring quantitative methods altogether I came to realize that there was a significant body of research that I could barely understand, never mind critically engage with. Moreover, I realized that my dismissal of all things quantitative meant that there were many research questions that I simply could not ask as I did not have the research skills to address them. Indeed, some of these were important questions of direct relevance to my own research interests and were concerned with identifying broader patterns in terms of children's racial and ethnic awareness as well as differences in educational opportunities and attainment between boys and girls from differing racial, ethnic and social class backgrounds. While my qualitative ethnographic methods proved to be extremely effective in identifying particular social processes and practices of exclusion and discrimination, without quantitative methods I had no way of even beginning to understand how common or generalizable these patterns were.

With all of this in mind I eventually began to face my demons and started to explore, learn about and use quantitative methods. Over time I came to realize that the problem is not with quantitative methods as such but with how they are sometimes used. While the use of quantitative methods can lead to the production of crude and simplistic generalizations it does not have to be this way. There is actually a wide range of techniques in quantitative data analysis that can show the variety and complexity of social life extremely effectively. In fact, and as I have come to find out, at the very heart of statistics is a concern with recognizing uncertainty and understanding variability. If done properly, therefore, quantitative data analysis can provide a powerful and extremely critical tool to use in educational research that can complement and expand the understandings gained through qualitative research.

Over the last ten years my interest in quantitative methods has grown to the extent that I enrolled and successfully completed a Master's degree in applied statistics and also began to teach quantitative methods to undergraduate and postgraduate students. Moreover, with the advent of software programs such as SPSS and my direct experience of using it to teach quantitative data analysis, I came to realize that every student (even those who are adamant that they have a phobia of statistics and just cannot do anything with numbers) is capable of acquiring the necessary knowledge and skills to do routine quantitative research to a high level. As this book will show, so long as you can understand intuitively what is going on, there is no longer the need to get bogged down with mathematical formulae. Moreover, the key theories and concepts underpinning quantitative data analysis are actually pretty simple and straightforward and are likely to be considerably easier to understand than many of the theories you are expected to confront in courses on education, philosophy, psychology and sociology.

Today, I am still involved in undertaking qualitative and ethnographic research and remain as convinced as ever of its value and importance. However, I have also acquired a mission in life and that is to convince as many people as possible that they can do quantitative data analysis to a high level and that it also has so much potential if done properly and appropriately. This, then, is the reason for writing this book. What I hope to do through the chapters to follow is to demystify quantitative data analysis for you and, hopefully, to not only give you the ability to handle and analyze quantitative data but to also give you some of the interest and passion that I have developed over the last few years for quantitative research.

Who is this book for and what is it about?

This book is for anyone undertaking and/or using educational research. Drawing upon my own experience of learning quantitative data analysis for myself and then having to teach it to successive cohorts of (extremely apprehensive) students, it is a book that assumes no previous knowledge of statistics whatsoever and has been written purposely with the goal of demystifying the analysis of quantitative data and making it accessible. The book should therefore appeal not only to undergraduate and postgraduate students but also to more established and seasoned educational researchers and lecturers who have tended to avoid or shy away from quantitative methods. Moreover, the book is also written for those skeptics out there who are critical of quantitative research, just as I once was.

The specific aim of the book is to provide you with the knowledge and skills necessary to be able to undertake routine quantitative data analysis to a level expected of published research. By routine quantitative data analysis I mean those methods that one would expect any competent and well-rounded educational researcher to have. As such they include:

- the ability confidently to handle quantitative data; including data derived from large, national and international datasets;
- the ability to summarize data, not just in relation to the production of appropriate summary statistics but also in relation to the display of those data in tables, bar charts, scatterplots or using a range of other graphical techniques;
- the ability to use your data from a sample to generalize about the wider population from which the sample was taken (and thus to understand and apply concepts such as "confidence intervals" and "statistical significance");
- through all of this, an ability to read, understand and critically evaluate the quantitative research of others.

What makes this book different?

There are clearly many textbooks already out there that focus on quantitative methods and statistics and that all promise to be accessible and user-friendly. What makes this book different is the way that it draws together a number of key elements. While you will find books out there that successfully address one or two of the following elements, there is none to date that includes all them as in this book:

- The book is written specifically for students, researchers and academics in education and makes extensive use of examples from education involving a range of high quality real-life educational datasets from the US and UK.
- The book assumes absolutely no prior knowledge of statistics and begins with the very basics to then build up a clear and comprehensive understanding.
- The book avoids mathematical formulae almost completely and, instead, focuses on providing you with a solid intuitive grasp of the key theories and concepts underpinning quantitative data analysis.
- The book takes a grounded and realistic approach, aiming to provide you with a comprehensive set of skills that will give you the versatility to deal with problems you will encounter when handling real data. As such the book focuses much more attention on the basics rather than rushing you through a wide range of techniques, including advanced statistical techniques such as multiple regression, factor analysis and log-linear analysis. While it may be tempting to get a book that covers all of this it usually leaves you with just a taster of these differing techniques but also insufficient knowledge and skills to be able to then apply these independently to your own real data.
- Finally, the book takes a critical approach to quantitative data analysis. Rather than just mechanically and unquestioningly showing you how to use a range of quantitative techniques with SPSS, this book continually makes you think about what it is exactly that you are doing, what the limitations are of the methods you are using and what conclusions you can reasonably and appropriately draw from your findings.

Key themes underpinning the book

It is this critical approach to quantitative data analysis that makes this book particularly distinctive. Partly reflecting my own critical past (and present) perspective, as well as my sociological background, there are three key messages in particular that run throughout the chapters to follow.

Quantitative data are not better than qualitative data

While talk of mixed-method designs has now become very fashionable in educational research (Gorard with Taylor, 2004), you only have to scratch beneath the surface to still find the type of entrenched positions that used to characterize my own thinking and that are based upon claims that quantitative methods are better than qualitative methods or vice-versa. We have all heard it at one time or another (and I still read it each year in Master's dissertations); that qualitative methods are subjective and anecdotal or that quantitative methods are crude and simplistic and thus unable to capture the realities of social life. However, it is only when you step back from these arguments to consider them properly that you can see just how nonsensical they are. For example, it is equivalent to a builder arguing that hammers are better than screwdrivers. It just does not make any sense. The point is that both tools are useful but for different jobs. Imagine if the builder advertised his or her services but stated that whatever the job, he or she would only ever use a hammer. How many of you would invite them into your house to re-tile your bathroom? It may sound silly but how is this any different from someone in an educational research context claiming that they only do quantitative (or qualitative) research?

Therefore, while this book is all about quantitative data analysis, this focus should not be interpreted as privileging quantitative methods over qualitative, or even entering this rather sterile and meaningless debate. As in the analogy of the builder and her or his tools, quantitative methods simply represent one set of tools that can do certain tasks really well but are likely to be limited in their ability to address others. It is only when you have access to the full range of research tools that you are likely to be able to do the job properly. This is a message that I hope is clearly made throughout this book as you are encouraged to reflect upon and interrogate the uses of quantitative methods in relation to different issues and topics in education and their strengths and limitations.

All quantitative data are socially constructed

Another unhelpful product of the "quantitative versus qualitative" divide has been the artificial distinctions that tend to be made between the two methods. It is often argued, for example, that quantitative data are all about numbers whereas qualitative data are all expressed in words. Similarly, quantitative methods are all about hypothesis testing while qualitative methods are associated with grounded theory. The list goes on (see Hammersley, 1992). Perhaps one of the most sustained arguments is that quantitative data are objective whereas qualitative data are subjective. There is certainly something really seductive about tables full of numbers or fancy charts and diagrams that give the air of authority and objectivity. After all, a statistic speaks for itself, doesn't it? 15.6 percent is 15.6 per cent. It is therefore all very open and clear, so the argument goes, and does not require the type of detailed critical reflection that qualitative researchers must go through in order to assess what influence they are bound to have had on what their respondents said or did in their presence.

However, 15.6 percent may be 15.6 percent but what is it a percentage of? Moreover, what measure(s) were used to calculate that percentage and what are these measures supposed to represent? A second key message running throughout this book, therefore, is that quantitative data are as much socially constructed as qualitative data. However, whereas many qualitative researchers have come to acknowledge and accept this and incorporate a consideration of this in their analysis, there is still a tendency for those using quantitative methods to hide behind their numbers and the air of objectivity that surrounds them. Through the many examples used in this book, therefore, you will be encouraged to recognize and assess the socially constructed nature of the quantitative data you are dealing with. As will be argued, subjective decisions are made as soon as you make a decision to focus on a particular issue and collect quantitative data on it. Moreover, the measures that are actually used to represent the issue at hand all reflect the values and assumptions of the researcher.

It is here, therefore, that the book will keep issues of reliability and validity at the heart of the analysis. When considering issues of reliability we are basically concerned with whether the measures used are consistent and trustworthy. A steel ruler would be an example of a reliable measuring instrument, as each time it is used to measure the length of a particular object it should always result in the same answer. In contrast, a ruler made of elastic would be unreliable. Given that it is highly malleable it is quite likely that even if you are measuring the same object you will come out with slightly different results each time. In quantitative research, and particularly the use of questionnaires, one of the most common ways in which reliability is undermined is through poorly worded questions that, for example, are difficult to understand or ask two questions in one. Take the following question for students: "Is your teacher helpful and accessible?" The problem of reliability here is that we simply do not know whether someone answering "yes" to this question is agreeing that their teacher is helpful or that they are accessible (or both). Moreover, if asked the same question again the next day the student may answer differently simply because they are now focusing on how accessible their teacher is whereas the day before they answered it with how helpful they are in mind.

Similar problems of reliability arise when words are used that are either quite specialist, and thus difficult to understand, or that have potentially multiple meanings. In both cases, and as before, we simply do not know what the respondent has in mind when they answer the question. Take, for example, a question for teachers: "Have you ever experienced sexual harassment while in school?" There is a problem with reliability here simply because different teachers will have different interpretations of what constitutes sexual harassment. In addition to question wording, there are also potential threats to reliability posed when interviewers are used to collect survey data. In this sense there is always the possibility of interviewer effects. For example, a respondent may answer a question differently if it was a woman interviewing them compared to if it was a man. This may be especially relevant to sensitive questions such as the one above relating to sexual harassment.

In all these cases, therefore, we need to be aware of, and reflect upon, the basic reliability of the measures used to produce the quantitative data we are dealing with. Moreover, we also need to think extremely carefully about issues of validity. When we consider issues of validity we are assessing whether the measure that we are using is actually measuring what it is supposed to be measuring. By definition, if the measure is unreliable then it is also not going to be valid. In the case of the illustrations used above, for example, if we are dealing with poorly worded questions then we can never be sure what it is the respondent had in mind when they answered that particular question. As such we can never be sure whether the answers given do actually reflect the specific issue we are concerned with or not. However, validity is much more than this.

It is possible to have a reliable measure but one that is simply not valid. For example, if we take the issue of assessing quality in early child care then one simple measure we could use is the ratio of staff to children. The more staff there is per child, the more it could be seen as indicating a quality environment. This would certainly be a reliable measure as we would be able to accurately count the number of staff and children in each setting. However, the question is whether this is also a valid measure of a quality early child care setting? The staff-to-child ratio would certainly tell us something. We could assume, for example, that if there is only one member of staff for every 20 children then this is likely to suggest a poor-quality environment. However, an assessment of quality in early child care includes much more than this (Sylva et al., 1999). It also involves the physical environment itself and what opportunities this provides children to play and learn. It would include what resources are actually available within that environment, as well, crucially, as the nature of the relationships between staff and children. Any truly valid measure of quality in relation to early child care settings would therefore need to incorporate all of these dimensions. However, this only raises more questions regarding validity. For example, how precisely (if at all) can the nature of staff–child relationships be measured? Moreover, if we want to create one overall measure of quality for each setting how do we combine all of these separate measures? Do we weight them all equally or give additional weighting to some over others? Is it actually meaningful to have a simple and singular numerical indicator of quality for a setting rather than, possibly, a "quality profile"? (Dahlberg et al., 1999).

What should be abundantly clear from this example is that while it may be possible to produce some form of numerical indicator or indicators for quality of early child care settings that are reliable, we should never be seduced by the numbers themselves into assuming they are in any sense objective. Whatever numbers are produced they are clearly the products of a series of value-judgments and thus in this sense are socially constructed. Now there is nothing wrong with this in and of itself but it does place a clear onus on us to always question the quantitative data we have and to identify the values and assumptions on which they are based.

Quantitative data analysis is much more than just the production of summary statistics

The third and final key message underpinning this book is that quantitative data analysis is far more than just summary statistics. In fact, it will be argued throughout the book that the simple reliance upon summary statistics is not only misleading but can be potentially dangerous. In this sense the book draws upon, and is influenced by, what is known as "exploratory data analysis" (or EDA) that has been associated with the work of John Tukey (1977) and others since (see: Hartwig and Dearing, 1979; Marsh, 1988). EDA can be understood partly as a response to concerns with the way in which quantitative data analysis has become equated simply with statistics and thus the use of statistical summaries and of significance testing (Hartwig and Dearing, 1979). For Tukey (1977), EDA should be seen as detective work with an emphasis being placed on gaining as much information about the data and how they are distributed as possible. This, in turn, places a particular emphasis on the use of graphical methods to display the data in as many different ways and formats as possible so as to gain a true feel for what is going on and also to see the unexpected. With this in mind, and as Hartwig and Dearing (1979: 9) contend:

> One should be sceptical of measures which summarize data since they can sometimes conceal or even misrepresent what may be the most informative aspects of the data, and one should be open to unanticipated patterns in the data since they can be the most revealing outcomes of the analysis.

While summary statistics are not dismissed as such, an EDA approach has tended to emphasize the necessity of understanding the data and what is to be summarized first, before then generating appropriate summary measures (Hoaglin *et al.*, 1983). Moreover, and emanating from this, there is a concern with the extremely limiting nature of significance testing that, for proponents of EDA, seems to have become the dominant mode of quantitative data analysis. As Hartwig and Dearing (1979: 10) explain:

> In this confirmatory model of analysis, a model for the relationship (often linear) is fitted to the data, statistical summaries (such as means or explained variances) are obtained, and these are tested against the probability that values as high as those obtained could have occurred by chance. Not only does this mode of analysis place too much trust in statistical summaries but it also lacks openness since only two alternatives are considered. The data are not explored to see what other patterns might exist.

This, then, is a theme to run throughout the book. As will be seen, there is an underlying emphasis on displaying and exploring data and on the need to accompany summary statistics with such displays wherever possible. It is through this that we will begin to appreciate and understand the full complexity and variability contained in the data. Ironically, part of my call in this book is for the need to begin describing quantitative data more qualitatively through the use of appropriate charts and diagrams.

Structure of the book

The book begins in Chapter 1 with an overview of SPSS. It describes what a quantitative dataset actually looks like and how this is managed through SPSS. Moreover, it takes you through the entire process of creating a new dataset, conducting some analysis of it and then saving it and the results. What I hope to do through this first chapter is to show that quantitative data analysis need not be difficult and, thus, to give you the confidence to continue through the rest of the book. Chapter 2 then takes you right back to all of the basic ideas and concepts associated with descriptive statistics and how to calculate these with SPSS. It is here that you will learn about the different types of variable that exist and the importance of being able to distinguish between them. You will also learn about the differing and most appropriate ways to summarize various types of data in terms of calculating averages and variations and also how best to display all of this. Having been introduced to all of these core concepts, Chapter 3 takes this a stage further by focusing on how best to summarize and display relationships between variables while Chapter 4 then examines how to display data effectively through tables and charts using SPSS and covers the key elements of good practice in relation to this.

The book then moves on, in Chapter 5, to what is commonly known as inferential statistics. While you will wish to describe and summarize the data you have, you will often also want to do more than this. Typically you will want to use the data you have from a sample to generalize or *infer* things about the wider population from which the sample is taken. This takes us into the area of confidence intervals and statistical significance and the use (and often abuse) of significance levels as reported in research reports (often noticeable by the appearance of strange references to "$p < 0.05$" or "$p = 0.032$"). While the mathematics behind these concepts and statistical calculations can get quite complex, with the use of SPSS we can conveniently side-step all of this and concentrate instead on gaining an intuitive and critical feel for what is going on. As mentioned earlier, the actual concepts underpinning inferential statistics are not difficult to understand and are definitely much easier to grasp than some of the theories you are probably encountering elsewhere in education and related fields such as philosophy, psychology and sociology.

Having dealt with the key concepts and ideas associated with statistical significance, Chapter 6 then runs through some of the most popular significance tests you are likely to use in educational research such as the Chi-Square test, t-test, Pearson correlations and one-way analysis of variance (ANOVA). Again, while the mathematics underpinning each of these can be a little difficult to follow, this need not concern us here. Rather, the emphasis is simply upon gaining a proper sense of what each test is doing, in lay person's language, how to actually do the tests with SPSS and, most importantly, how to interpret the results. Chapter 6 also includes a consideration of how best to analyze and report findings from simple experimental research designs in education.

Chapter 7 concludes the book by looking forward in terms of providing you with guidance as to where to go next should you wish to broaden and deepen the understanding of quantitative data analysis provided in this book.

Companion website

Throughout this book the emphasis is upon learning the key concepts and skills associated with quantitative data analysis through practice and the use of real-life and high-quality educational datasets. The datasets to be used include large-scale national datasets from surveys in America and the UK and a brief summary of each is provided in Box 0.1. All of these can be accessed and downloaded from the companion website for this book that is located at: www.routledge.com/textbooks/9780415372985. Alongside the ability to access and download the datasets themselves you will also find a wealth of further information on the website including:

- further details on each of the datasets used including a full description of the variables contained in each as well as the methods used to collect the data, including copies of questionnaires where relevant;
- full, step-by-step explanations relating to all of the exercises suggested in the book for you to use to check your own answers by;

- updated links to a range of websites from which you can access and download additional datasets for secondary analysis;
- guidance that will be regularly updated as to how to access and download some of the major educational datasets that exist;
- any step-by-step guidance that is needed in order for you to deal with any additional features that later versions of SPSS (for Windows and for Macs) may include compared to the one that provides the focus for this book (Version 15.0).

Differing versions of SPSS

This book focuses on the latest version of SPSS (Version 15.0) available at the time of going to print. If you are a student or researcher or an academic at college or university, your institution is likely to have a site licence for SPSS and you should be able to access this latest version through them. However, this book is also fully compatible with any version of SPSS for Windows from Version 8.0 onwards. There are actually only a very small number of differences between this version and earlier versions of relevance to the issues covered in this book. Where these occur they are identified and alternative step-by-step guides are provided in the appendices. This book is also compatible with equivalent versions of SPSS for Macs, including the latest one currently available (Version 13.0 for Mac OS X). All you will notice in the Mac versions is that while the windows and dialog boxes contain exactly the same information as those shown in the chapters to follow, some tend to be laid out slightly differently.

Of course, there will come a point when SPSS releases a newer version of the software package either for Windows or Macs. In anticipation of this, any differences between Version 15.0 and newer versions will be explained on the companion website and, where necessary, additional step-by-step guides will be provided to help you undertake the analyses in this book using any new features contained in these later versions of SPSS.

Finally, the book is also compatible for those of you who have student versions of SPSS. The student versions actually have most of the features of the full versions of SPSS and the only difference of relevance to this book is that they cannot be used on very large datasets. As some of the national datasets used in this book are large, reduced versions have been specifically prepared and are ready to download from the companion website for those using a student version of SPSS so that you can still follow all of the examples and exercises.

And finally, what this book expects of you!

Finally, there are only two expectations of you as a reader of this book. The first is that you put any existing concerns or preconceptions about quantitative data analysis to one side and approach the book with an open mind. If, for example, you are afraid of statistics and/or have little confidence in your ability to do quantitative data analysis then please try to put all this to one side and start afresh with this book. You should forget any past experiences of being taught maths and statistics. Instead, you should start reading this book with an open mind and with the confidence that you will actually be able to understand and do what is covered in the chapters to follow. I have taught quantitative data analysis for nearly ten years now and have had to work with students just like you

Box 0.1 Summary of datasets used in the book

afterschools.sav   This dataset consists of a small number of variables selected from the After-Schools Programs and Activities Survey (2005) that consisted of a nationwide telephone survey of a random sample of households in the United States (n = 11,684). As the name suggests, the survey focused on activities and programs that elementary and middle school-age children participated in during after-school hours. The variables selected for this dataset focus on the children's academic performance and levels of suspension and exclusion from school.

bullying.sav   This dataset consists of a small number of variables selected from the Young Life and Times Survey (2005) that consisted of a random sample of 16 year olds in Northern Ireland (n = 819). The survey runs annually and covers a wide variety of topics relating to young people's attitudes and social activities. The variables selected for this dataset focus specifically on the young people's experiences of bullying in school.

earlychildhood.sav   This dataset consists of a small number of variables selected from the Early Childhood Program Participation Survey (2005) that consisted of a nationwide telephone survey of a random sample of households in the United States (n = 7,209). The survey itself gathered a wide range of information largely focusing on the non-parental care arrangements and educational programs of preschool children. The variables selected for this dataset focus on the types of educational activities that parents/guardians undertake at home with their preschool children.

experiment.sav   This is a fictitious dataset containing data on 60 elementary/primary school-aged children, half of which attended an after-schools Reading Club and the other half attended an after-schools combined Reading and Drama Club. Two measures were taken of the children at the start of the school year and then again at the end: a standardized reading score and also a rating of how much they said they liked reading.

international.sav   This dataset contains data taken from the website of the United Nations Statistics Division (http://unstats.un.org). It focuses on a randomly selected sample of 20 countries and provides information on their per capita GDP, levels of male and female illiteracy and also the average number of years children in each country are expected to attend school.

timeseries.sav   This dataset focuses on the performance of young people in public examinations during their final compulsory year of schooling in England over a 30-year period between 1974/5 and 2004/5. The data were provided by the Department for Education and Skills (UK) and contain the percentages of boys and girls who achieved at least five GCSE examination passes graded A*–C or their earlier equivalent in each year.

valueadded.sav   This dataset consists of data taken from the Department of Education and Skills (UK) website (http://www.dfes.gov.uk/performancetables/) and focuses on school-level performance data for 124 schools located in 4 local education authorities in England. These data were originally reported and analyzed elsewhere by Gorard (2006a).

youthcohort.sav   This dataset consists of a small number of variables selected from the Youth Cohort Study of England and Wales that consisted of a longitudinal study of a random sample of young people who had reached their school leaving age in 2002 (n = 13,201). The survey tracks the young people over the next few years and focuses on their education, training and career pathways. The variables selected for this dataset focus specifically on the young people's performance in public examinations (GCSEs) at the end of their final compulsory year of schooling.

20samples.sav   This is a specially-created dataset for use in Chapter 5 to illustrate the concept of statistical significance. It contains data from 20 samples of 200 young people each randomly selected from the youthcohort.sav dataset.

Further details on all of these datasets, including a full list of all of the variables contained in each dataset and how they are coded can be found on the companion website.

each year. I have never come across a student yet that has not been able to pick up and learn the core knowledge and skills covered in this book. You just need to trust me. And for those of you who are skeptical or critical of quantitative research more generally, just as I was, then please give this book a go. Again, all you need to do is to approach it with an open mind.

The only other expectation of you as a reader is that you do put the effort in and work through the book carefully. While the book can be used as a source of reference, it is meant to be read initially in logical sequence. Especially if you are new to quantitative data analysis, therefore, you do need to work your way through the book chapter by chapter. In particular, you need to actually follow the practical examples and further exercises suggested and do them yourself with SPSS. You will only ever develop confidence and competence in quantitative data analysis with practice. Moreover, while I honestly believe that the core concepts and ideas covered in the book are pretty straightforward, you may need to persevere with some of them; possibly having to read a chapter twice or even three times. However, this is no different from any other academic book you are required to read. The difference for many people is that while they are willing to persist in terms of reading and understanding general educational theories, there seems to be a reluctance to do so with statistical concepts. It is almost as if there is a belief that if you cannot understand it the first time then you will never understand it and so there is no point continuing to try. While this is likely to reflect your previous experiences of being taught maths or statistics, it is an unrealistic approach to take. All this book expects of you is to forget it is a book about quantitative data analysis and to read and try to understand it as you would any other.

Chapter 1

Getting started with SPSS

Introduction

The aim of this first chapter is to give you an overview of SPSS and, through this, to show you that handling and analyzing quantitative data need not be difficult. In particular, by the end of this chapter you will:

- understand what a dataset is;
- be able to open an existing dataset with SPSS and also create your own dataset;
- understand the SPSS environment and be able to navigate your way around it;
- have gained some experience of undertaking simple analyses with SPSS;
- be able to save a dataset and also the output of the analyses you have undertaken.

Understanding what a dataset is

At the heart of quantitative data analysis is the dataset. A dataset is actually just an array of numbers organized into rows and columns. Perhaps the best way to explain it is to start with a real-life example. You will see in Box 1.1 an amended and reduced version of a self-complete questionnaire used as part of the Northern Ireland Young Life and Times Survey 2005. The full questionnaire is much longer than this. All I have done here is to keep two basic questions (what sex the young person is and then what type of school they went to) and then the eight questions in the questionnaire on bullying in school. The layout for the bullying questions is almost exactly as it appears in the original questionnaire.

There are two key things to note from this questionnaire. The first is that each question is given an abbreviated name (i.e. "RSEX," "TYPESCHL," "SCLOTBUL" and so on). As will be seen shortly, each question basically equates to a single **variable** and these abbreviated names are the names used by SPSS for each variable. Many questionnaires of this type do not actually include the variable name like this but simply add them in afterwards. The other thing to note is that there is a number assigned to each of the boxes that the respondent is able to tick. These represent the **values** that each of the variables can take. Thus for the first question—"Are you male or female?"—the variable name is "RSEX" and this variable only has two values: either "1" or "2," indicating that the respondent is male or female respectively.

The actual dataset derived from this questionnaire, as it appears in SPSS, is shown in Figure 1.1. You will shortly be asked to open this dataset and explore it. However, for now it is useful just to draw out and highlight two key points from this. First, each row (i.e.

Box 1.1 Amended extract from the Northern Ireland Young Life and Times Survey 2005

RSEX
1. Are you male or female?

                  ✓
Male   [ ] 1
Female   [ ] 2

TYPESCHL
20. What type of school do you (did you last) attend?

                         ✓
Planned integrated [ ] 1
Grammar   [ ] 2
Secondary   [ ] 3
Other   [ ] 4

The next few questions are related to bullying in school.

SCLOTBUL
22. Would you say that students at your school get bullied by other students?

A lot   [ ] 1
A little   [ ] 2
Not at all   [ ] 3
Don't know [ ] 4

STFBULJB
23. Are there particular staff at your school whose job it is to deal with bullying?

Yes   [ ] 1 (Please go to next question 24)
No   [ ] 2 (Please go to next question 25)
Don't know [ ] 3 (Please go to next question 25)

GOTOSTAF
24. Do you think that most people – if they were bullied – <u>would</u> or <u>would not</u> go and talk to one of these members of staff?

Would talk to them   [ ] 1
Would not talk to them [ ] 2
It depends   [ ] 3
Don't know   [ ] 4

SCHLBUL
25. In general, do you think your school provides real help for people who are bullied or not?

Yes   [ ] 1
No   [ ] 2
Don't know [ ] 3

UBULLSCH
26. Have you yourself ever been bullied in school?

      ✓
Yes [ ] 1 (Please go to the next question)
No   [ ] 2 (Please go to question 28)

OFTENBUL
27. How often have you yourself been bullied at school in the last two months in school?

             ✓
A lot   [ ] 1
A little   [ ] 2
Not al all   [ ] 3

UBULLOTH
28. Have you yourself ever taken part in bullying other students?

      ✓
Yes [ ] 1 (Please go to the next question)
No   [ ] 2 (Please go to question 30)

OFTENUB
29. How often have you taken part in bullying other students at school in the last two months in school?

             ✓
A lot   [ ] 1
A little   [ ] 2
Not at all   [ ] 3

horizontal line) represents what is called one case. A **case** is the term used to refer to the unit of analysis. In this example each case represents one young person who completed the questionnaire. Only the first ten cases are actually visible in Figure 1.1. However, this questionnaire was completed by 819 young people and so there are a total of 819 cases (i.e. 819 rows) in this dataset and they could be viewed simply by scrolling down using the right-hand scroll-bar. The second thing to note is that each column (i.e. vertical line) represents a variable. The name of each variable can be seen at the top of each column and they correspond to and appear in the same order as the variables in the questionnaire itself (Box 1.1). The only additional variable that does not appear in the questionnaire is the first one—"ID"—which is the unique number given to each questionnaire (and thus is a unique number that can be used to identify each case).

All of the numbers that appear in the middle of the screen are basically the values for each of the variables (i.e. the values corresponding to what boxes each respondent ticked). To take the first case as an example (i.e. the first row) then reading across horizontally we can see that their unique ID number is "1," their sex ("RSEX") is coded as "2" and the type of school they attend ("TYPESCHL") is coded as "3" and so on. If we refer back to the original questionnaire we can see that these values mean that this person is therefore female and attends a secondary school. If we continue we can see that the value for the next variable ("SCLOTBUL") is "2". Again, referring back to the questionnaire we can see that this means that when asked "Would you say that students at your school get bullied by other students?" this respondent answered "A little." You can easily continue across the rest of the line to find out how she answered the remaining questions.

The only other thing that needs to be explained are the values of "-1" for the variables "GOTOSTAF" and "OFTENBUL." These are values added in afterwards by the researcher to indicate that these two questions were skipped by the respondent. To understand this, have a look again at the questionnaire in Box 1.1. For Question 23— "Are there particular staff at your school whose job it is to deal with bullying?"—the respondent is given differing instructions depending on how they answer this question. Thus if they answer "yes" (there is a particular member of staff) then they are asked to go onto the next question (Question 24) which asks how approachable that member of staff is. However, if they had answered "no" or "don't know" to Question 23, as our first respondent has, then there is no point asking them this next question and so they are instructed to skip it and jump directly to Question 25. In such circumstances, rather than

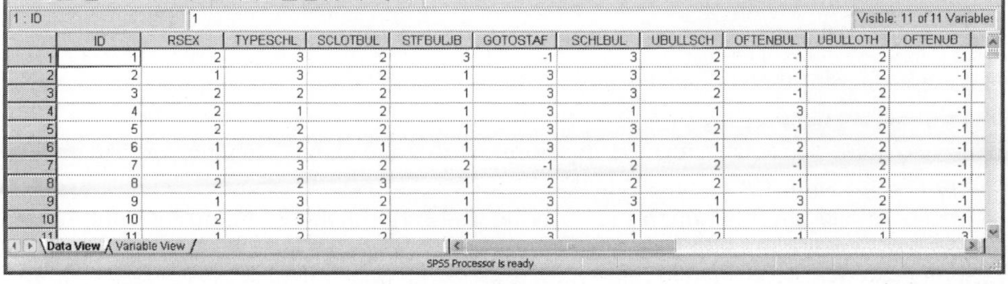

ID	RSEX	TYPESCHL	SCLOTBUL	STFBULJB	GOTOSTAF	SCHLBUL	UBULLSCH	OFTENBUL	UBULLOTH	OFTENUB
1	2	3	2	3	-1	3	2	-1	2	-1
2	1	3	2	1	3	3	2	-1	2	-1
3	2	2	2	1	3	3	2	-1	2	-1
4	2	1	2	1	3	1	1	3	2	-1
5	2	2	2	1	3	3	2	-1	2	-1
6	1	2	1	1	3	1	1	2	2	-1
7	1	3	2	2	-1	2	2	-1	2	-1
8	2	2	3	1	2	2	2	-1	2	-1
9	1	3	2	1	3	3	1	3	2	-1
10	2	3	2	1	3	1	1	3	2	-1

Figure 1.1 The bullying dataset as it appears in SPSS

just leaving this variable ("GOTOSTAF") blank for this respondent a special value, "-1," is typed in to indicate that this question has been legitimately skipped.

Before we get you to actually open up and explore this dataset there are three general points to draw from what you have seen so far. The first is that all data need to be translated into numeric form for SPSS to work with (with the exception of descriptive "labels" that we will get onto later). Thus, while the categories that a respondent can choose from for each question are all described in words (e.g. "A lot" or "A little"), we have had to assign them numbers so that they can be entered into the dataset. An important lesson from this is that you should, therefore, think very carefully about how you design your questionnaire to ensure that, as far as possible, the data you gather can be coded in this way. This usually means trying as far as possible to restrict yourself to using **closed questions** (i.e. questions where there are only a fixed number of response categories to choose from). There will obviously be times when you need to include **open-ended questions** (i.e. a question that is followed by a space where the respondent writes down their answer in their own words). However, you need to bear in mind that you will have to go back and translate these qualitative answers into codes at some point if you want to analyze them quantitatively.

The second key point following on from this is that while numbers have been used for convenience to represent these different categories they may not actually mean anything numerically. Thus while males are coded "1" and females "2" for the variable "RSEX" this has no significance whatsoever. It does not mean, for example, that females are twice as much as males. It could easily have been coded the other way around or using other numbers (i.e. "0" and "1" or whatever). What this means is that we need to be extremely careful in terms of understanding precisely what type of variable we are dealing with and what the values associated with each variable actually represent. This is something we will return to in the next chapter.

The third and final key point to draw from the questionnaire and dataset shown is the usefulness of what is called **precoding** your questionnaire. Precoding a questionnaire basically means including where possible the variable names and values for each response category on the questionnaire itself. Box 1.1 shows just one of the possible ways that this can be done. The benefit of doing this is in terms of helping to reduce errors that can occur when entering data into SPSS directly from the questionnaire. Imagine, for example, that you have 500 questionnaires of four pages in length and the questions are not precoded and neither are the response categories. In such circumstances it would be very easy to make mistakes typing in the data. If you can precode your questionnaire then whatever box has been ticked you can see immediately which variable it relates to and also what the value is that you need to type in.

Opening an existing dataset in SPSS

Having been introduced to the bullying dataset it is now time to open it up and explore it in a little more detail. First of all you need to download the dataset from the companion website. All the datasets featured in this book are downloadable from the website and you can follow the same routine in each case.

To download and then open the bullying dataset you should begin by going to the companion website and finding the list of datasets. Right click on the link to download the **bullying.sav** dataset. Select "Save Target As. . ." and this will open the Save As window shown in Figure 1.2. Select an appropriate place to save the dataset using the "Save in:"

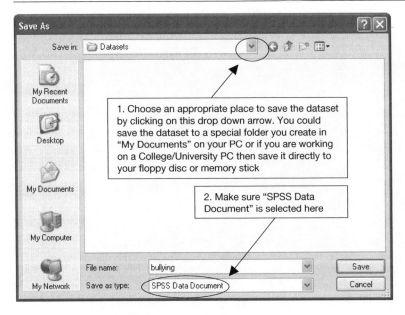

Figure 1.2 Save As window

drop-down menu as shown and also make sure you select "SPSS Data Document" using the "Save as type:" drop-down menu. When you have done this click on the "Save" button. When the download is complete another dialogue box will appear and you should click the "Close" button.

Open SPSS as you would any other program. For those of you using Windows XP operating system you can do this by clicking on the Start button located at the bottom left of your screen as shown in Figure 1.3. This will bring up the initial **SPSS 15.0 for Windows** window as shown in Figure 1.4. Make sure that the option "Open an existing data source" is selected and that "More Files. . ." is selected within this and then click "OK." This, in turn, opens up the **Open Data** window as shown in Figure 1.5. Make sure you select "SPSS (*.sav)" for "Files of type:" as shown and then use the "Look in:" drop-down menu to navigate around your PC to find the "bullying.sav" dataset where you saved it. Click on the dataset and then click on the "Open" button. You should now have the screen originally shown in Figure 1.1.

Most of the default settings for SPSS are fine and not worth changing. However, one minor change is worthwhile that will help you subsequently when you start exploring and analyzing the data. To make this change select **Edit → Options. . .** (or **SPSS → Preferences. . .** if you are using a Mac version). This will open the dialogue box shown in Figure 1.6. To help you find variables quickly and easily for analysis you should change the settings so that SPSS displays the shortened variable names. To do this, select "Display names" (or just "Names" for Mac versions) as shown and then click "OK." You will see what effect this has a little later. In addition, if you were dealing with a large dataset with a lot of variables then you may also find it useful to ask SPSS to display the variable names alphabetically. However, this is not necessary for the present book. Rather, we will stick to the default option of SPSS displaying variable names as they appear in the dataset.

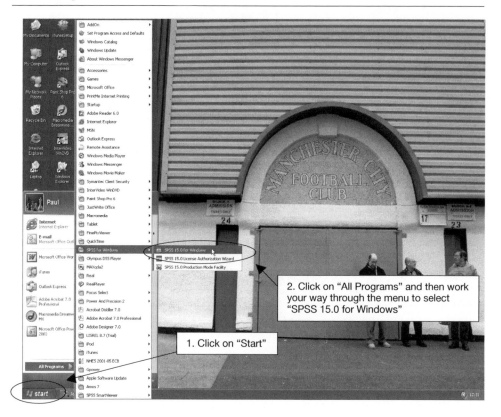

Figure 1.3 Opening SPSS in Windows XP

We can now begin to explore the dataset. You will see a number of short-cut icons running across the top of the SPSS window, immediately below the top menu. If you hover your cursor over any of the icons a short description will appear explaining what the icons represent. They are all pretty self-explanatory. There are just two that are worth pointing out here. The first is the **Value labels icon** second from the right, which looks like a luggage tag as indicated in Figure 1.7. Clicking on this icon will display the value labels rather than the numbers in the dataset itself. To see what this means try clicking on the icon. You should see that the numbers in the dataset are replaced by their labels as shown in Figure 1.7.

The other icon to note is the **Variables icon** as indicated in Figure 1.8. Clicking on this icon calls up the **Variables** window as also shown. This is a useful feature that helps you to explore the variables in the dataset. Clicking on any of the variables in the left-hand pane will automatically bring up its details, including how it is coded and labeled as shown in Figure 1.8. You can now also see what the effect was of changing the default setting in SPSS so that it displays the variable names in lists as here.

Another way to explore the variables is to click on the "Variable View" tab at the bottom left of the window. Doing this results in the view as shown in Figure 1.9. As can be seen, all the variables are now listed in rows with all of the relevant details, including the description of the variable ("Label") and how it is coded ("Values"). As can be seen

Figure 1.4
SPSS 15.0 for Windows
window in SPSS

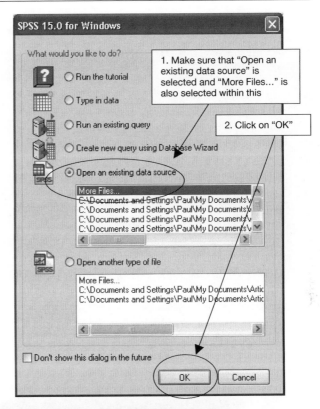

1. Make sure that "Open an existing data source" is selected and "More Files..." is also selected within this

2. Click on "OK"

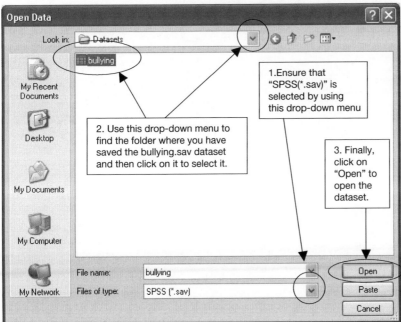

1.Ensure that "SPSS(*.sav)" is selected by using this drop-down menu

2. Use this drop-down menu to find the folder where you have saved the bullying.sav dataset and then click on it to select it.

3. Finally, click on "Open" to open the dataset.

Figure 1.5 Open Data window

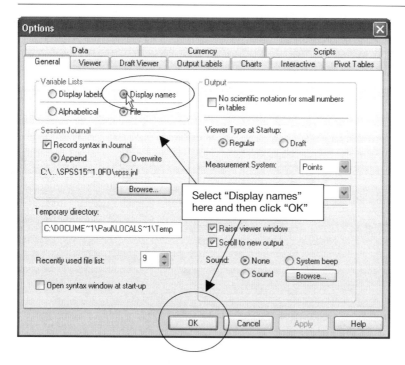

Figure 1.6 Options window in SPSS

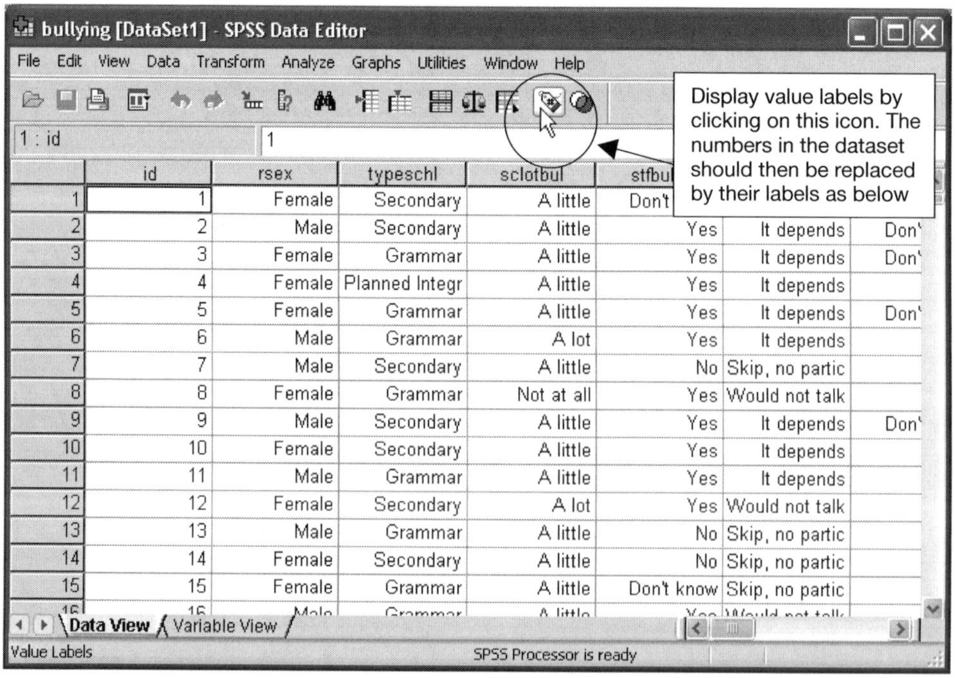

Figure 1.7 Value labels icon in SPSS

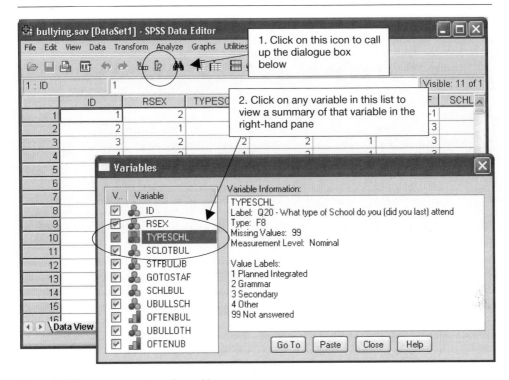

Figure 1.8 Viewing summaries of variables

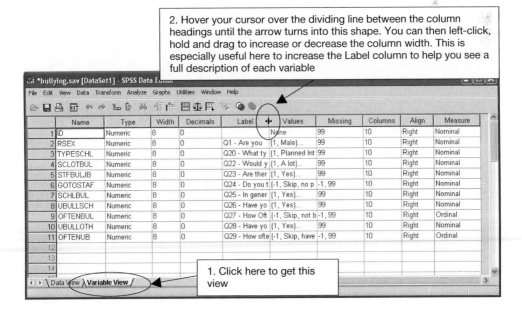

Figure 1.9 Variable View in SPSS

from Figure 1.9, only the first part of each of the variable labels is showing. This can be rectified by increasing the width of the Label column as explained in Figure 1.9.

If you want to view the list of values and how they have been coded for any of the variables then all you need to do is to click on the relevant cell in the Values column for the variable you are interested in. A small grey box then appears in the right-hand side of that cell. Clicking on this box calls up the **Value Labels** window shown in Figure 1.10. Also note in Figure 1.10 the effects of widening the Label column as suggested earlier.

We will examine more of the features of the Variable View in SPSS in the next section when we go through the procedure for creating your own dataset. For now, it would seem a shame having reached this stage if you were not given the chance just to have a little go at analyzing the data. With this in mind, let's just see what proportion of young people in the sample claimed to have been bullied in school. Suppose we want to calculate the actual numbers and percentages who answered "yes" and "no" to this question as well as display this with a bar chart. To do this we will examine the responses to Question 26 (see Box 1.1) which relates to the variable named "UBULLSCH."

To do this, select **Analyze** → **Descriptive Statistics** → **Frequencies. . .** from the top menu. This calls up the **Frequencies** window as shown in Figure 1.11. Select the variable you are interested in (i.e. "UBULLSCH") by clicking on it once. The variable should be highlighted and the arrow button in the middle of the window should become darkened. Click on the arrow button as shown to place that variable in the right-hand pane.

To generate a bar chart as well as a frequency table you need to click on the "Charts . . ." button as also shown in Figure 1.11. This calls up the additional **Frequencies: Charts** window. Select "Bar charts" and then "Percentages" as indicated. Once done, click the

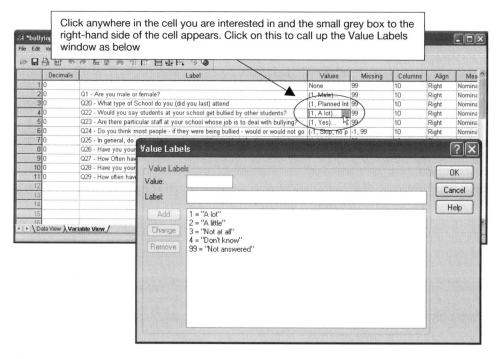

Figure 1.10 Value Labels window in SPSS

Continue button. Finally, click OK in the main **Frequencies** window. This will produce a new **Output** window with the results as shown in Figure 1.12.

As can be seen from the main frequency tables, 16 respondents (2.0 percent) did not answer the question. Of the rest, 30.4 percent claimed to have been bullied in school. While we have only done this to give you a bit of a taster of what SPSS can do, I cannot resist making two quick substantive points about this output. First, there is actually a problem of validity here in terms of what constitutes "being bullied" at school. Unfortunately, and as can be seen from the original questionnaire (Box 1.1), no definition of bullying was actually offered to respondents before being asked to answer this question. With no guidance, it is likely that different respondents will have different things in mind when they think of bullying. Therefore, we need to be careful in interpreting this statistic of 30.4 percent. The second point relates to the bar chart. I encouraged you to do this just so that you can see how easy it is with SPSS to generate charts like this. However, one of the points I will be making in Chapters 3 and 4 is that we need to think about the use of charts carefully. In cases where there are only two categories, as here, it is almost always unnecessary to include a bar chart to illustrate the findings. Simply stating the percentage figures of those who responded "yes" and "no" would be sufficient.

To continue analyzing the data all you need to do is to minimize this output window and continue working with the main dataset. Each time you do a further bit of analysis, the results are added to the ones already created in the output window. As you go on, therefore, this output window keeps a record of the results of all of your analysis.

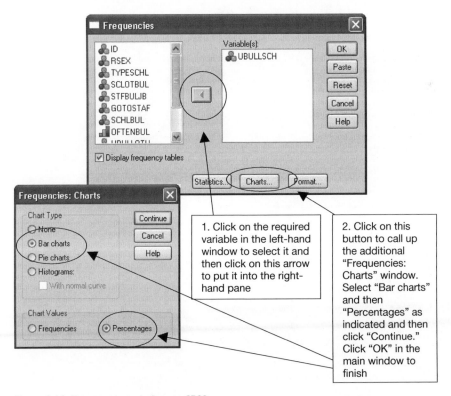

Figure 1.11 Frequencies window in SPSS

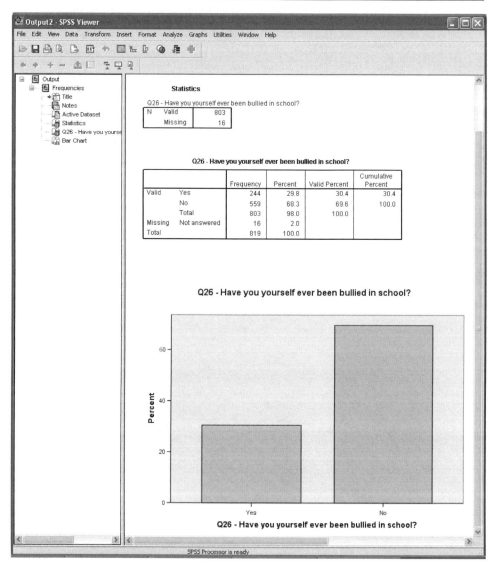

Figure 1.12 SPSS Output window

EXERCISE 1.1

Explore the data a little further. See if you can calculate the frequencies and percentage responses for the other questions asked. Try generating a few more bar charts. Also, have a go at creating a pie chart. You will learn a lot from SPSS by simply experimenting with data in this way.

When finished, you can save this output as a separate file. To do this, simply choose **File** → **Save As. . .** from the top menu of the **Output** window. You will need to give the file a name (give it something short but meaningful so that you will be able to distinguish between the many different output files you will tend to accumulate) and then choose a place to save it. The file will be saved with the suffix ".spo" that indicates that it is an output file.

Finally, whenever you come to analyze the data properly you are bound to want to make some changes to the dataset itself. You should always remember, therefore, to save the main dataset before closing it down. This can be done either by just clicking on the Save Icon contained within the list of icons towards the top of the main **Data View** window (resembling a floppy disc) or by selecting **File** → **Save As. . .** from the top menu.

Creating your own dataset

So far in this chapter you have been introduced to the SPSS environment and shown how to open, analyze and save an existing dataset. In this final section we will look at how you would create your own dataset from scratch. The dataset we will create this time involves basic educational and economic indicators for 20 countries as shown in Table 1.1. All of these data are freely available from the website of the United Nations Statistics Division— http://unstats.un.org—which provides an excellent example of how easy it is for you to collect quantitative data for secondary analysis. In fact, if you are a student there is no reason why you could not use data such as these as the basis for your dissertation.

EXERCISE 1.2

To start with, have a quick look at the website to see where these figures were taken from. See what other social, economic and educational indicators are available.

The 20 countries in Table 1.1 were chosen randomly from all those for whom information on illiteracy rates were available. As can be seen in Table 1.1, alongside male and female illiteracy rates, two further indicators have been included—school life expectancy (which is the total number of years of schooling that a child in that country can expect to receive on average) and per capita Gross Domestic Product (which is a measure of the value of the total output of economic goods and services produced in that country per head of population). Further details on each of these measures, together with an outline of their limitations, are provided on the UN Statistics Division website.

The dataset to be entered into SPSS will look just as it does in Table 1.1 but with an additional first column representing a unique "ID" number for each country. To begin creating the dataset we need to open SPSS as outlined earlier, selecting "Type in data" in the initial **SPSS 15.0 for Windows** window (see Figure 1.4) this time. Before typing in any numbers we begin by defining the variables. The following explanation is for SPSS Version 10.0 and above. For an outline of how to define variables for Version 9.0 and earlier see Appendix 1. To begin with, we click on the "Variable View" tab as shown in Figure 1.13. What we will do now is work our way across the columns to type in the information required.

Table 1.1 Educational and economic indicators for 20 countries

Country	Continent	Estimated adult (15+) illiteracy rates (%)		School life expectancy (years)	Per capita GDP (US$)
		Males	*Females*		
Argentina	Americas	3.0	3.0	16	3,375
Benin	Africa	45.2	74.5	7	521
Burundi	Africa	33.2	48.1	5	86
Chile	Americas	4.2	4.4	14	4,523
Dominican Republic	Americas	12.0	12.7	12	2,408
El Salvador	Americas	17.6	22.9	11	2,302
Ghana	Africa	37.1	54.3	7	354
Hungary	Europe	0.6	0.7	15	8,384
Iran	Asia	16.5	29.6	11	2,079
Laos	Asia	23.0	39.1	9	361
Malta	Europe	8.2	6.6	14	11,790
Mauritania	Africa	48.5	68.7	7	381
Morocco	Africa	36.7	61.7	9	1,463
Namibia	Africa	16.2	17.2	12	2,307
Senegal	Africa	43.9	71.5	6	641
Sierra Leone	Africa	60.2	79.5	7	197
Swaziland	Africa	19.6	21.9	10	1,653
Macedonia	Europe	1.8	5.9	12	2,225
United Arab Emirates	Asia	24.4	19.3	11	22,130
Uruguay	Americas	2.7	1.9	15	3,274

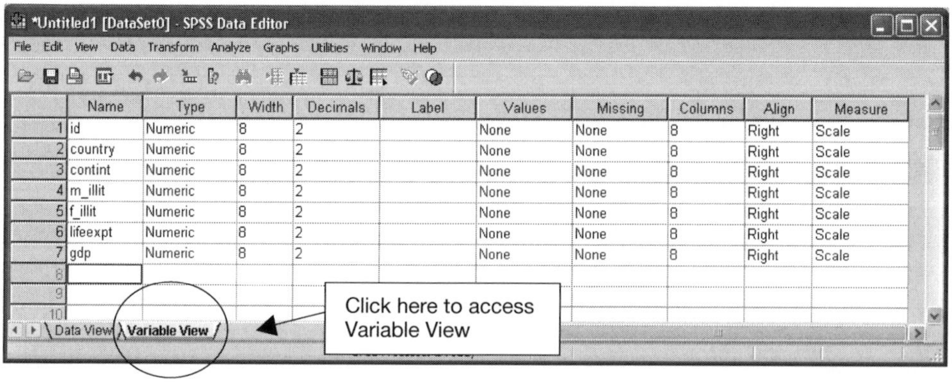

Figure 1.13 Defining variables in SPSS

The first column, headed "Name," is where you type in a shortened variable name for each of the variables. This has already been done in Figure 1.13 for all the variables that have simply been entered in the order they appear in Table 1.1 (but including the "id" variable first). To start entering the names simply click in the first cell (top left) and type in "id" and then click in the second cell below and type in the name of the second variable ("country") and so on. You will see I have used shortened names for each of the variables. From SPSS Version 14.0 onwards you can actually use names up to 64 characters.

However, as earlier versions restricted variable names to just eight characters I have just developed the habit of working to this and, because some of you may have earlier versions of SPSS, we will just stick to this practice. In terms of the names you use, you can choose any name you want but it is obviously useful to pick something that can help remind you of what that variable actually represents. All variable names have to begin with a letter and some characters are not allowed; SPSS will politely tell you if you try to use one of these!

As you type in each variable name and press return (or click in the next cell below) you will see that the remaining cells in that row are automatically filled with the default settings for variables. Once you have typed all the names in, you need to amend the information in these remaining cells as necessary for each variable, which is what we will do next.

The second column, headed "Type," simply defines what type of variable we are dealing with. In most cases this will be numeric (which is the default setting). As the name suggests, a **numeric variable** is one where all the values are represented by numbers. However, we can see in our dataset that there is at least one variable that is not numeric (i.e. "country") but actually consists of words. This is what is known within SPSS as a **string variable**. To amend numeric to string for the variable "country," click anywhere in the cell with the word "Numeric" in it and then click on the small grey square that will appear in the right-hand side of that cell, as shown in Figure 1.14. This opens the **Variable Type** window as also shown in Figure 1.14. Select "String" and enter the maximum number of characters for this variable. This should obviously be at least as much as the longest name included within this variable (in this case the "United Arab Emirates"). All the other variables will be numeric and so no other amendments are required in this column. (You may be thinking why do we not define the variable "Continent" as a string variable as well? This will become clear shortly.)

The next column, headed "Width," specifies the maximum number of digits or characters for each variable. As can be seen, for the variable "country" this has changed to 20 (characters) as we have just specified. For the other numeric variables, the default is 8 (digits) and this tends to be more than sufficient and therefore need not be changed.

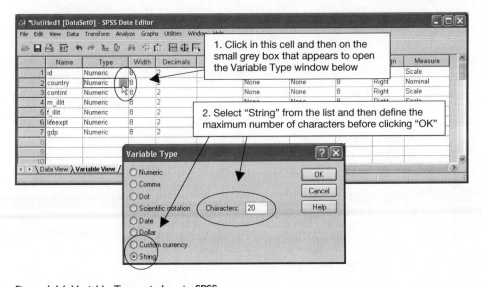

Figure 1.14 Variable Type window in SPSS

As the heading suggests, the next column—"Decimals"—specifies the number of decimal places that are displayed in SPSS for each variable. It is clearly no longer relevant to the string variable "country" and, hence, there is a "0" entered for that variable and this cannot be altered. For the remaining variables, to alter the number of decimal places simply click in the cell required and type in the required number. Alternatively you could use the "up" and "down" arrows that appear to the right-hand side of the cell when you click in it to increase or decrease the number as required. For the remaining variables, it can be seen from Table 1.1 that the male and female illiteracy rates are reported to just one decimal place while the remaining variables have no decimal places (including the variables "id" and "continent"). You should therefore alter the number of decimal places accordingly so that they appear as they do in Figure 1.17.

The next column, headed "Label," includes a proper description of each variable that will appear in any tables or charts you produce with SPSS. It is, therefore, worth naming these properly. To add in the variable names, simply click in the relevant cell and type in the name. You will find that the column width increases automatically as you type. The names you enter should be as shown in Figure 1.17.

The "Values" column is used to specify value labels where necessary. In this particular case this only needs to be done for the variable "continent." No labels are needed for the last four variables as the numbers actually represent real numbers (this will all be explained properly in the next chapter). Similarly, there is no need to add labels for "id" or for "country." As for "continent" it can be seen that there are four possible values, corresponding to the four continents. When typing in the data into SPSS, rather than making this a string variable, it is easier to give each continent a number and type that number in. Which number we assign to each continent is arbitrary. For now we can just code it as follows: Africa = 1; Americas = 2; Asia = 3; and Europe = 4.

What we need to do in this Values column is to set the labels for each of the four numbers. To do this we click in the cell corresponding to the variable "continent" and then click on the small grey box that appears to the right-hand side of the cell. This calls up the **Value Labels** window shown in Figure 1.15. For each value, type in the value and then its corresponding label in the fields indicated and click "Add." Repeat the process for the others and then click "OK" when finished.

The next column, headed Missing, is where you define any missing values for that variable. Missing values are simply used to indicate that data are missing for that variable. We saw an example of this when examining the bullying dataset earlier in this chapter (see Figure 1.9). In this case two missing values were actually defined. The first, as explained earlier was "-1" to indicate that the respondent had legitimately skipped that question because it did not apply to them. However, there was also a second missing value—"99"—that was used to indicate that the respondent did not answer a question they were expected to.

For missing values you can always just leave the cell empty, in which case SPSS will just insert a period—"."—to indicate nothing has been entered. However, the problem with just leaving it blank like this is that you will never know in the future whether it is blank because there are missing data or because of a mistake typing the data in. As such it is always better to choose a value that you can use to type in to indicate that data are missing. In choosing a value it is good practice to choose the same one for all variables and also one that is clearly different from the actual values used (i.e. "99" in this case) so that if it inadvertently gets included in any analysis it should stand out as peculiar. Some people specify a range of missing values (maybe "97," "98" and "99") to indicate different reasons for the data being missing.

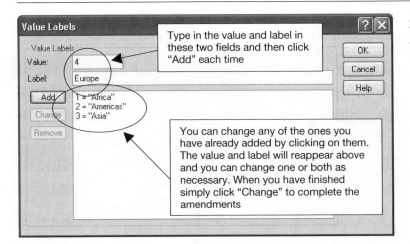

Figure 1.15
Value Labels
window in SPSS

The key thing you need to do is to define these values as missing in SPSS so that they are counted as missing and not then included in any subsequent analysis. In this present case there are no missing values and so this is not necessary. However, to do this simply click in the relevant cell within the column headed "Missing" and then click on the grey box that appears to the right-hand side. This would call up the **Missing Values** window shown in Figure 1.16. As an example, if we were creating the bullying dataset then we would select "Discrete missing values" and then type in "-1" and "99" as shown and then click "OK."

The next two columns, headed "Columns" and "Align," simply define the width of the columns as they appear in **Data View** as well as the alignment of the data in each cell. As a default setting, SPSS tends to align numeric data to the right and string variables to the left and you will notice that since you have defined "contint" as a string variable then it has automatically aligned it to the left. Generally, the only time you may want to amend these from the default settings is in relation to string variables such as "contint" where you may wish to widen the column width so that all of the names are visible in **Data View**. To do this you simply need to click in the relevant cell and change the value to 20.

Figure 1.16 Missing Values window in SPSS

The final column, headed "Measure," specifies the type of variable we are dealing with. This is something that will be covered in detail in the next chapter. For now, just trust me that "id," "country" and "contint" are all nominal variables and the rest are all scale variables. To set these simply click on each of the cells, in turn, and then use the drop-down menu that will appear to the right of that cell as shown in Figure 1.17. It is very important to define these properly so that you can use the Chart Builder function to be described in Chapter 4. Once you have done all of this you have finished defining the variables and your **Variable View** should look as it does in Figure 1.17.

You are now ready to enter the data in **Data View**. To do this click on the Data View tab (bottom left of the main SPSS window) and then simply type in the data as carefully as possible from Table 1.1. Once completed it should appear as it does in Figure 1.18. When you have got to this stage the first thing you should do is to save it as the dataset: "international.sav" in the same way as was explained earlier for the bullying.sav dataset.

This is a dataset we will return to in later chapters so keep it safe. A copy of it is also downloadable from the companion website (although I have waited until now to tell you this to make sure you get some experience of creating a dataset!). However, it would be wrong to come this far without at least having a little look at the data. We will do two quick bits of analysis here. First, let's explore the variable school life expectancy ("lifeexpt"). To do this select **Analyze → Descriptive Statistics → Explore. . .** from the top menu. This will open up the **Explore** window shown in Figure 1.19. Click on "lifeexpt" in the list on the left-hand field and then click on the arrow button as shown in Figure 1.19 to place it in the "Dependent List:" field. In this particular case we will just look at the statistics for this variable so select this as an option as shown. Click "OK" to finish.

The main output that appears from this is shown in Output 1.1. As can be seen, the average (mean) school life expectancy for the 20 countries is 10.5 years. It can also be seen that the minimum school life expectancy among the countries in the sample is 5 and the maximum is 16. You will also see a number of other statistics presented. Don't worry—we will cover what most of these mean in the next chapter. For now it is just worth checking whether you gained the same results as shown in Output 1.1. If not then this is probably because you made an error typing in the data.

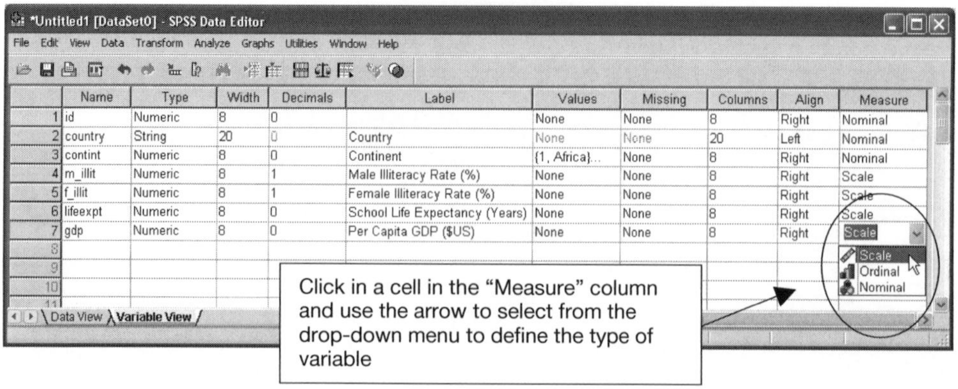
*Untitled1 [DataSet0] - SPSS Data Editor
File Edit View Data Transform Analyze Graphs Utilities Window Help
Name Type Width Decimals Label Values Missing Columns Align Measure
1 id Numeric 8 0 None None 8 Right Nominal
2 country String 20 0 Country None None 20 Left Nominal
3 contint Numeric 8 0 Continent {1, Africa}... None 8 Right Nominal
4 m_illit Numeric 8 1 Male Illiteracy Rate (%) None None 8 Right Scale
5 f_illit Numeric 8 1 Female Illiteracy Rate (%) None None 8 Right Scale
6 lifeexpt Numeric 8 0 School Life Expectancy (Years) None None 8 Right Scale
7 gdp Numeric 8 0 Per Capita GDP ($US) None None 8 Right Scale
Scale
Ordinal
Nominal
Data View
Variable View
Click in a cell in the "Measure" column and use the arrow to select from the drop-down menu to define the type of variable

Figure 1.17 Completed Variable View for the international.sav dataset

	id	country	contint	m_illit	f_illit	lifeexpt	gdp	
1	1	Argentina	Americas	3.0	3.0	16	3375	
2	2	Benin	Africa	45.2	74.5	7	521	
3	3	Burundi	Africa	33.2	48.1	5	86	
4	4	Chile	Americas	4.2	4.4	14	4523	
5	5	Dominican Republic	Americas	12.0	12.7	12	2408	
6	6	El Salvador	Americas	17.6	22.9	11	2302	
7	7	Ghana	Africa	37.1	54.3	7	354	
8	8	Hungary	Europe	.6	.7	15	8384	
9	9	Iran	Asia	16.5	29.6	11	2079	
10	10	Laos	Asia	23.0	39.1	9	361	
11	11	Malta	Europe	8.2	6.6	14	11790	
12	12	Mauritania	Africa	48.5	68.7	7	381	
13	13	Morocco	Africa	36.7	61.7	9	1463	
14	14	Namibia	Africa	16.2	17.2	12	2307	
15	15	Senegal	Africa	43.9	71.5	6	641	
16	16	Sierra Leone	Africa	60.2	79.5	7	197	
17	17	Swaziland	Africa	19.6	21.9	10	1653	
18	18	Macedonia	Europe	1.8	5.9	12	2225	
19	19	United Arab Emirates	Asia	24.4	19.3	11	22130	
20	20	Uruguay	Americas	2.7	1.9	15	3274	

Figure 1.18 Data View for international.sav dataset (with Value Labels showing)

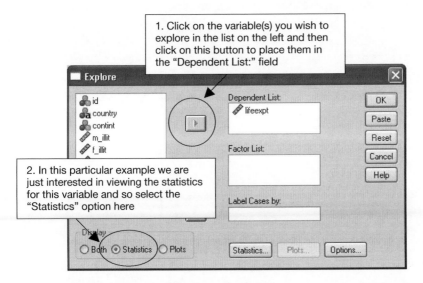

1. Click on the variable(s) you wish to explore in the list on the left and then click on this button to place them in the "Dependent List:" field

2. In this particular example we are just interested in viewing the statistics for this variable and so select the "Statistics" option here

Figure 1.19 Explore window in SPSS

Output 1.1

Descriptives

			Statistic	Std. Error
School Life Expectancy (Years)	Mean		10.50	.738
	95% Confidence Interval for Mean	Lower Bound	8.96	
		Upper Bound	12.04	
	5% Trimmed Mean		10.50	
	Median		11.00	
	Variance		10.895	
	Std. Deviation		3.301	
	Minimum		5	
	Maximum		16	
	Range		11	
	Interquartile Range		7	
	Skewness		.015	.512
	Kurtosis		−1.113	.992

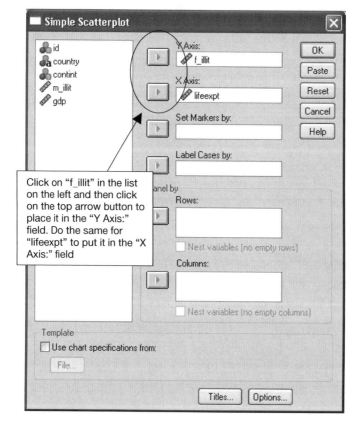

Click on "f_illit" in the list on the left and then click on the top arrow button to place it in the "Y Axis:" field. Do the same for "lifeexpt" to put it in the "X Axis:" field

Figure 1.20
Simple Scatterplot window in SPSS

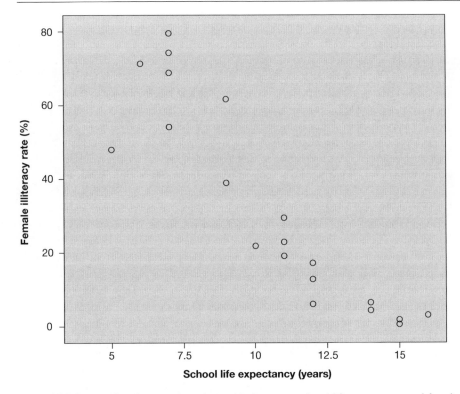

Figure 1.21 Scatterplot showing the relationship between school life expectancy and female adult illiteracy rates in 20 countries

Finally, let us have a look at what relationship exists between school life expectancy and levels of female illiteracy. What we would expect is that the higher the school life expectancy is for a country, the lower the levels of female illiteracy. We can see if this is the case using what is known as a scatterplot. To do this select **Graphs** → **Legacy Dialogues** → **Scatter/Dot...** from the main menu (for Version 14.0 and earlier you just need to select **Graphs** → **Scatter/Dot...**). This opens an initial Scatter/Dot window where you should select "Simple Scatter" and then click "Define." This opens the **Simple Scatterplot** window as shown in Figure 1.20. Click on the variable "f_illit" in the list on the left-hand side and then click on the top arrow button to place it into the "Y Axis:" field. Next, click on the variable "lifeexpt" in the list on the left-hand side and then click on the second arrow button to place it into the "X Axis:" field. Click "OK" to finish the procedure.

Figure 1.21 shows the resultant scatterplot that appears. As can be seen, there are 20 dots, each representing a specific country. There would certainly appear to be a relatively strong trend as was predicted with female illiteracy rates dropping as school life expectancy increases.

EXERCISE 1.3

Use the Explore function to generate summary statistics for male and female illiteracy rates (you should find that the mean rates are 22.73 and 32.175 respectively) and per capita GDP (mean is 3522.70). If you did not get these statistics go back and check whether you made an error in entering the data (and reflect on how easy it is to make mistakes doing this!). Try generating some more scatterplots between some of the other variables. For example, is there a relationship between male and female illiteracy rates? Also, is there a relationship between per capita GDP and male illiteracy? Check your methods and results on the companion website.

Conclusions

The main purpose of this chapter has been to give you an overview of the SPSS environment and the whole process that is involved in creating and analyzing datasets. I am hoping by this point that you have come to see that quantitative data analysis need not be difficult. If you have been following the exercises in this chapter you have, after all, calculated percentages as well as a range of summary statistics including: means, medians, standard deviations and interquartile ranges (even though you probably don't yet know what half of these mean—how clever is that?). In addition you have generated bar chartsand scatterplots. By the way, all of these charts can be adapted in terms of style (as we shall see in Chapter 4) and then copied and pasted directly into your research report or dissertation.

Having shown you that you can do quantitative data analysis and thus hopefully given you a little more confidence, it is now time to look in a little more detail at the meaning of some of the things you have just done.

Chapter 2

Exploring, displaying and summarizing data

Introduction

You will have seen from the last chapter just how powerful and user-friendly SPSS is. It is precisely because of this that routine quantitative data analysis need not be the preserve of a small number of professionally trained statisticians but is now within the reach of all of us. This is undoubtedly one of the key strengths of SPSS but also perhaps its main weakness. The thing is that SPSS cannot think for itself. If you ask it to do something, it will do it regardless of whether your request makes any statistical sense or not. There is a real danger therefore that people can begin using SPSS and producing statistical output that looks really impressive even though they haven't got a clue what they are doing and the output they are producing is utterly meaningless.

Therefore, while giving you the encouragement and confidence you need to do quantitative data analysis with SPSS, it is essential that this book also shows you how to do it meaningfully and appropriately. This is what the next five chapters are all about, starting in this chapter with a solid overview of the basics. By the end of this chapter you will:

- understand why it is important to distinguish between different types of variable and know what the main types of variable are and how to identify them;
- be able to explore data and present them graphically using SPSS in a number of different ways;
- understand what the most commonly used summary statistics actually mean and also how to calculate these using SPSS;
- be able to choose the most appropriate methods for summarizing data for the different types of variable that exist.

Different types of variable

The first thing you must understand before we go any further is that there are different types of variable. Being able to distinguish between the three main types of variable—**nominal, ordinal** and **scale** as they are named in SPSS—is crucial. Among other things it will help you determine which graphs and charts to use to display your data appropriately and also what types of statistics you should use to summarize those data. Moreover, and as we move onto significance testing and the calculation of effect sizes, you need to know precisely what type of variable you are dealing with in order to choose the correct test and measure of effect size.

To understand why it is important to distinguish between different types of variable look again at the international dataset you created in the last chapter and which is set out in Table 1.1. You will remember that one of the things we did was to calculate the average school life expectancy for the 20 countries listed. This only took a couple of clicks of the mouse in SPSS and the average (mean) was found to be 10.5 years. This is an example of a summary statistic. What it tells us is that, on average, a child will spend 10.5 years in school across these 20 countries.

Now, with just a few more clicks we can produce a summary statistic for the sample of countries in terms of which continents they are located in. By following the same procedure again we find that the average continent is 2.0. However, while SPSS has dutifully provided us with this summary statistic and while the output looks pretty convincing, this is clearly meaningless. The problem here, as explained previously, is that we are dealing with a different type of variable. While the numbers for school life expectancy actually represent real numbers (i.e. "7" means "7 years," "12" means "12 years" and so on), the numbers used to represent continents were assigned arbitrarily and simply for convenience. The numbers in this case do not actually represent real numbers at all but just categories. However, in calculating the average continent as "2" we have basically treated these numbers as if they are real numbers and then calculated the average for these.

You may think that this is an obvious point and such a silly mistake to make that nobody would do this in real life. However, almost every year I find students reporting the average gender for their sample being "1.43" or something similar; and this is not just first year undergraduates but mature students on Master's and taught doctorate programs. As before, such a statistic is meaningless but SPSS will dutifully provide it for you if you ask it to.

Even if you think this is obvious and is unlikely to be a mistake you will make yourself, there are slightly more subtle differences that exist (particularly between ordinal and scale variables) where mistakes are much more likely to occur and where, as a consequence, the findings you produce may either be equally meaningless as the examples above or certainly misleading. This is why we need to begin here with a discussion of the key differences between the three main types of variable.

Nominal variables

This is probably the simplest type of variable to understand. It is a variable that comprises a specific number of categories where each category simply describes a sub-group of cases. We have already used two examples of a nominal variable above in terms of continent and sex. The former variable, continent, comprises four categories (Africa, Americas, Asia, Europe) while the latter, sex, consists of just two categories (male and female). Other examples of a nominal variable are: a respondent's ethnic group; their religious background; the type of school they attend; or the county or state within which a school is located. In all of these examples, the assignment of numbers to categories for the purpose of creating a dataset is completely arbitrary. In other words, the actual numbers used have no meaning whatsoever. In relation to the continent variable, for example, the fact that Europe is coded "4" and the Americas "2" does not mean that Europe is two times that of the Americas. Similarly, the fact that Africa is coded "1" does not mean it is first in any sense. The numbers are no more than convenient labels and could easily have been assigned in a different way.

Ordinal variables

An ordinal variable is also one that comprises a certain number of categories. However, what makes an ordinal variable different from a nominal variable is that you can actually rank order the categories of an ordinal variable in some meaningful and relevant way. As an example, let's look back at the bullying dataset introduced in the previous chapter and the questionnaire shown in Box 1.1. The variable named "OFTENBUL" comprised young people's responses to the question "How often have you yourself been bullied at school in the last two months in school?" As was seen, there were three possible responses: "a lot," "a little" and "not at all." In this case these categories can actually be rank ordered in terms of how much a young person has been bullied. Thus we know that someone who has been bullied "a lot" will have been bullied more than someone who has been bullied "a little." Similarly, those who have been bullied "a little" have been bullied more than someone who has responded "not at all." Thus "a lot" is therefore greater than "a little" is greater than "not at all." In this case, the numbers we assign to the categories for the purpose of analysis do now actually have some meaning. More specifically they reflect the rank order of the categories involved. Thus the way this variable has actually been coded ("a lot" = 1; "a little" = 2; and "not at all" = 3) represents a meaningful order for these categories.

Box 2.1 provides some more examples of how ordinal variables can be coded. The coding for Variable 1 is very common and is often used to ascertain how much a person agrees or disagrees with a statement. As can be seen, it is an ordinal variable because the categories can be ranked, in that someone who selects "strongly agrees" clearly agrees more than someone who selects "agrees" who, in turn, agrees with the statement more than

---

Box 2.1 Examples of ordinal variables

Variable 1

"I really look forward to going to school each morning"

1 = Strongly agree
2 = Agree
3 = Undecided
4 = Disagree
5 = Strongly disagree

Variable 2

"How important is it to you to get good grades in school?"

1 = Very important
2 = Fairly important
3 = Not very important
4 = Unimportant

Variable 3

Socio-Economic Classification (ONS 2005)

1 = Higher managerial and professional occupations
2 = Lower managerial and professional occupations
3 = Intermediate occupations
4 = Small employers and own account workers
5 = Lower supervisory and technical occupations
6 = Semi-routine occupations
7 = Routine occupations

Variable 4

Age

1 = 0 to 10
2 = 11 to 20
3 = 21 to 30
4 = 31 to 40
5 = 41 and Over

someone who selects "undecided" and so on. Similarly, Variable 2 consists of categories that can be ordered in relation to the degree to which the respondent feels that getting good grades in school is important.

One key point to note with both of these first two variables, however, is that while the categories can be rank ordered it cannot be assumed that the differences between any two consecutive categories are the same. In other words, we cannot be more precise than this. All we know is that a person in one category is likely to agree more than a person in another category. Unfortunately we cannot tell exactly how much more they are likely to agree. This is because each category is likely to include a range of attitudes. Thus, for example, the "strongly agree" category will include those who strongly agree with an absolute passion as well as those who hovered between agree and strongly agree before finally putting themselves into the latter. Similarly, within the agree category there will be people who are bordering on agree/strongly agree and others who found it difficult to decide but, after some thought, ticked the category "agree" rather than that for "undecided."

Thus while the numbers do have meaning, they only have meaning in terms of representing rank orderings. We cannot therefore read anything into the actual numbers used as if they represent proper measures. For example, because of the variation within each category, it would be wrong to conclude that because "disagree" is coded as "4" this means that someone who disagrees feels exactly twice as negative as someone who agrees, simply because the latter is only coded as "2." Thus, while the ordering of these numbers is meaningful, the actual numbers themselves are not. Rather than coding the five categories for Variable 1 from "1" to "5," therefore, we could have easily coded them from "6" to "10" or even "96" to "100."

In both these cases therefore we can draw out three key features of an ordinal variable:

• it consists of a specific number of categories;
• these categories can be validly and meaningfully rank ordered in relation to some criterion;
• while the categories can be rank ordered, it is not possible to be any more precise in measurement terms than this.

While the first two variables listed in Box 2.1 are pretty straightforward, I have found from experience that the other two variables can tend to cause students some confusion. Variable 3, for example, represents the socio-economic background of a respondent (see ONS 2005). A common objection I have faced to this being regarded as an ordinal variable is that it is wrong to rank order the different categories. Students have sometimes argued, for example, that "just because someone is professional or managerial doesn't mean that they are better than someone who is skilled manual." Of course in one sense this is entirely true. However, the key point to understand here is the criterion by which the categories are being ranked. If it was just in terms of how "nice" the people in each category are then it would not be valid to rank them. However, this is not the reason we would typically want to rank order these categories. Rather, the main reason why these socio-economic categories are ranked is to reflect the relative income and social status that members of each group tend to have over the others. Thus, for example, those people in the categories "higher managerial and professional occupations" are likely to have higher incomes and status than those in "intermediate occupations" who, in turn, are likely to have higher incomes and status than those in semi-routine occupations and so on. As before, however, while we can rank order these seven categories in relation to their levels of income and status we cannot be any more precise than this. The income and status within each category is also likely to vary and thus the difference in income between people in any two consecutive categories cannot be assumed to be the same.

Finally, some people also tend to struggle a little with the fourth variable that is listed here as age but could represent any other variable where each respondent is assigned an actual numerical value, e.g. a pupil's average grade point score, a teacher's income and so on. The problem in this case relates to the fact that the categories do seem to represent real numbers and thus would seem to be more precise. However, it is fairly straightforward to understand why this is also an ordinal variable if we go back to the three characteristics of an ordinal variable listed above. In this sense we can see that Variable 4 comprises five categories and those five categories can be rank ordered in relation to age. Thus, we know that someone in the first category (labeled "0 to 10") is younger than someone in the second category (labeled "11 to 20") who, in turn, will be younger than someone in the third category (labeled "21 to 30") and so on.

However, and this is the third characteristic, we cannot be more precise than this. As with the other ordinal variables discussed, there will be a significant degree of variation in terms of the respondents' ages within each category. If we are comparing two people who happen to be in the first two categories respectively then while we know that the person in the first category (i.e. "0–10") is younger than the person in the second category (i.e. "11–20"), we do not know by how much. At one extreme there could be very little difference between them with one being aged 10 and the other aged 11. At the other extreme, however, there could be a large difference with one being less than one year old and the other aged 20.

The other thing to note about this variable is that the actual categories are coded "1" to "5." If we were to calculate the average age (mean) for a sample coded in this way then we would obviously get an answer somewhere between 1 and 5, even though people's ages range from 0 to over 40. This is clearly wrong and should act as a warning sign that you have done something wrong if you get an answer very different from what you expect.

Finally, and before conducting any analysis on an ordinal variable, it is very important that you check the precise way in which the categories are coded. As an example, let's go back to the bullying dataset and the questionnaire shown in Box 1.1. The young people were first asked in Question 23 if there are particular members of staff at their school whose job it is to deal with bullying. For those who answered "yes" to this question they were then asked: "Do you think that most people—if they were bullied—would or would not go and talk to one of these members of staff?" (Question 24). The response categories they could choose from and how they are coded is as follows:

"Would talk to them" = 1
"Would not talk to them" = 2
"It depends" = 3
"Don't know" = 4

As can be seen, this could be an ordinal variable as it has categories that can be ranked in order of how willing they think people would be to talk to the members of staff concerned. However, the problem is that it is not currently coded in that order and thus it would be wrong to perform any analysis on this variable as it currently stands. What we would need to do is to recode it so that the numbers do reflect the rank order of the categories as follows:

"Would talk to them" = 3
"It depends" = 2
"Would not talk to them" = 1
[Don't know = 0]—Define as "missing" in SPSS

We will look at how this can actually be done in SPSS in the next chapter. For now we should just concentrate on what has actually been done here. It can be seen that the first three categories do act as an ordinal variable and can be analyzed as such. However, there is the question of what to do with the fourth "Don't know" category. It cannot be just left in the analysis as it stands because it would invalidate the ordinal nature of the variable. In other words, to still treat the variable as ordinal would be to treat this last category (coded "0") as if it included people who were even less likely to think that people would talk to the members of staff concerned compared to those who felt they "Would not talk to them" (coded "1"). This is clearly wrong and would potentially lead to false results as those in this category have actually stated that they do not have an opinion.

One way of dealing with this problem is simply to define this "Don't know" category as "missing" in SPSS. This would have the effect of removing anyone in this category from the analysis and thus only focusing on the first three categories. As it happens, and in relation to the **bullying.sav** dataset this "don't know" category only accounts for 1.5 percent of the valid responses (i.e. the ones who were expected to answer this question rather than skip it because they answered "no" to the previous question). It would thus have little consequence to do this. However, for completeness it is always necessary in reporting your results to be clear about what you have done; in this case to explain clearly that the data you are analyzing relate only to those respondents who expressed an opinion.

Of course, alongside defining "don't know" as missing in SPSS it is also equally important to ensure that any missing data are clearly classified in SPSS as "missing" as well. For this particular variable it will be remembered that there were two types of missing categories that were coded: "-1" for those who legitimately skipped the question and then "99" for those who should have answered the question but did not. For the same reasons as above, it would cause equal problems if either or both of these categories were left in the analysis. Both therefore need to be removed by defining them as "missing" in Variable View as described in the previous chapter (see Figure 1.16).

Scale variables

The final main type of variable that you need to be aware of is known as a scale (or interval or continuous) variable. Variables of this type are clearly distinguishable because they are not organized into a particular number of categories but, rather, they take specific numerical values. Moreover, these numbers are usually meaningful in and of themselves. Thus, rather than "2" representing some category (i.e. "Females"), "2" actually represents two of something (e.g. "2 years of age" or "2 years of post-qualifying teaching experience" and so on). In this sense the numbers do not have any labels as they simply represent themselves. Moreover we can now be much more precise. We know, for example, that someone aged 30 is precisely 10 years older than someone aged 20. We can also calculate the average (mean) of these numerical values and this would still make sense. This was apparent, for example, in relation to the school life expectancy variable in the **international.sav** dataset (Table 1.1) where the average when calculated was 10.5 years.

There are three key things to note about scale variables. The first is the need for you to apply your own judgment at times in relation to the specific nature of the analysis you are undertaking and whether you should treat the variable as scale or ordinal. A good example of this is the variable age. If you are surveying teachers, for example, and you include a variable that consists of their age in years then this would constitute a scale variable. You would probably have a relatively wide range of ages for the teachers in your sample, possibly from 22 through to 65, and thus for the purposes of your particular analysis you could probably assume that if two people are of the same age in years (i.e. both are aged 34) then they are comparable (in terms of age). In other words, it would not particularly matter if one of these people had just turned 34 and the other was nearing her 35th birthday. For the type of analysis you intended to do this would probably be seen as being unnecessarily precise and thus "splitting hairs."

However, a variable consisting of age in years may not always be regarded as a scale variable. Take, for example, a study of young children in a preschool setting where you could be interested in examining their social, cognitive and emotional development. To simply work with age in years in this case would be far too crude. There is likely to be a huge difference between a child that has just reached his first birthday and another child that is only a few weeks off her second birthday; and yet they are both given the same value (i.e. 1 year old). Hopefully you can see that the measure of age in years here is too crude and imprecise for the type of analysis you would wish to undertake. What you would really need is a more precise measure, possibly age in months. What has in effect happened here then is that your variable of age in years has basically been reduced to an ordinal variable in that while we could rank order the children in terms of their age in years (i.e. into one of five categories: less than one, 1, 2, 3 and 4) we cannot really be more precise than this. The key point to draw from this example, therefore, is that your decision as to how to categorize a variable will depend upon your own judgment and the nature of the analysis you intend to conduct; it is not an exact science.

The second key thing to note is that there is a distinction to make between two types of scale variable; what some have called **ratio** and **interval** measures. The distinction is simply between those variables that have a true "0" value (i.e. ratio variables) and those that do not (i.e. interval variables). Having a true "0" value basically means that this is the lowest value that can be taken as there is none of whatever you are measuring. The variable school life expectancy is a ratio variable as it has a true "0" value in that "0" would mean that the people in that country are not expected to attend school at all. Moreover, this is clearly the lowest value that can be taken as having a school life expectancy of "-1" or "-2" does not make any sense. For very similar reasons, the male and female illiteracy rates in this international dataset are both ratio variables as is the per capita GDP.

In fact one of the few occasions when you are likely as an educational researcher to come across a scale variable that does not have a true "0" value (and is thus an interval variable rather than a ratio variable) is when a summative scale is used to measure a particular attitude, behavior or personality type. These are often called **likert scales** and an example is provided in Box 2.2 of a likert scale devised to measure the extent to which an elementary or primary school child likes school. As can be seen, a child would gain an

---

Box 2.2 Example of an interval variable: pupils' attitudes towards science education

Pell and Jarvis (2001) measured elementary or primary school children's attitudes towards science education. The attitudinal scales they developed were designed for use with 5-11 year olds and focused on measuring five different dimensions to their attitudes: their general liking of school; the extent to which they saw themselves as independent investigators; their enthusiasm for science; how important they felt science is to society; and the degree to which they regarded science as a difficult subject.

Each scale was based upon the pupils' responses to a series of statements. For the enthusiasm for science scale the eight statements were:

- "I should like to be a scientist"
- "I like science more than any other school work"
- "I often do science experiments at home"
- "I like to watch science programmes on TV"
- "School science clubs are a good idea"
- "I am always reading science stories"
- "I should like to be given a science kit as a present"
- "One day, I should like to go to the moon"

Their responses were rated into five categories with smiley faces used to depict a sliding scale from 1 (completely disagree) to 5 (completely agree). To create a score for each pupil on this scale, their responses to each statement were added together to create an overall rating scale ranging from 8 (where the pupil will have completely disagreed with all eight statements) to 40 (where the pupil will have completely agreed with all eight statements).

---

overall score ranging from 8 (indicating that they had very little enthusiasm for science) to 40 (indicating that they were very enthusiastic about science). These scores are themselves calculated by adding together the responses that the child gave to the eight statements.

Given everything that has just been said about ordinal variables and the need not to treat the values used as if they represented real numbers then it would be legitimate to question the validity of creating a summative measure by adding the scores from eight ordinal variables together like this. Unfortunately, a discussion of the validity and reliability of doing this is beyond the scope of this book. The key point to note here is simply that the summative measure produced now has 32 categories and this tends to justify it being seen as a more precise measure and one that can be treated as a scale measure for the purposes of analysis. However, in doing so it is important to note that it is an interval rather than a ratio variable as it does not have a true zero. As such, it is not possible to compare the scores of two children in exactly the same way as one would for a ratio variable. More specifically, it would be misleading to argue for example that a child with a score of 40 liked school "twice as much" as a child with a score of 20 (i.e. because $40 \div 20 = 2$). You can only make these types of ratio comparisons that involve dividing one score by another if you have a true zero and thus are dealing with a ratio variable.

Finally, the third key thing to note about a scale variable is that it is essential that any values you choose to signify missing data are selected well outside of the possible range for that variable (hence why people often use "999" or even "-999") and that these are then explicitly defined as missing in SPSS so that they are not included in the analysis. One reason for picking abnormally high values to represent missing data is to act as a warning in that if you should forget to define them as missing and thus they were inadvertently included in the analysis then the output you get will not look right.

By way of a summary and to help you distinguish between nominal, ordinal and scale variables a guide has been provided in Box 2.3 representing a simple decision-making tree that you can use to decide whether the particular variable you are interested in is nominal, ordinal or scale. Also, once you think you have identified what type of variable it is there is a checklist for you to run through just to ensure you have made the correct decision. Now we are able to clearly distinguish between the three different types of variable it is possible to look at how these might best be displayed graphically and what summary statistics would be most appropriate to use in each case.

EXERCISE 2.1

Open some of the other datasets being used for this book. Use the View Variables feature (see Figure 1.8) to examine some of the variables. Make sure you can understand why each variable is designated as nominal, ordinal or scale.

Displaying and summarizing scale variables

Before we even think about calculating summary statistics for a scale variable it is important to first look carefully at the data for that variable to see how they are distributed. There are basically three types of chart that you can do this with: the histogram; the stem and leaf display; and the box plot. We will look at the first two here using the variable school life expectancy from the international dataset. We will have to leave the boxplot until the next section as it relies upon a couple of concepts we have yet to encounter.

Histogram

Open the **international.sav** dataset you created in the last chapter. To create a histogram for the school life expectancy variable ("lifeexpt"), select **Graphs → Legacy Dialogs → Histogram. . .** (if you are using Version 14.0 or below or a Mac version then you just need to select **Graphs → Histogram. . .**). This opens the **Histogram** window shown in Figure 2.1. Click on "lifeexpt" from the list of variables shown in the left-hand field and click on the arrow button as shown to place it in the "Variable:" field. Click "OK" to complete the procedure.

Having done this you will get a histogram very similar to that shown in Figure 2.2. If you compare what you have just created with Figure 2.2 you will see that the only difference is the number of bars being displayed. I have changed this to make it simpler to read. However, don't worry about how to adapt charts now; we will cover this in the next chapter.

Box 2.3 Summary guide for distinguishing between different types of variable

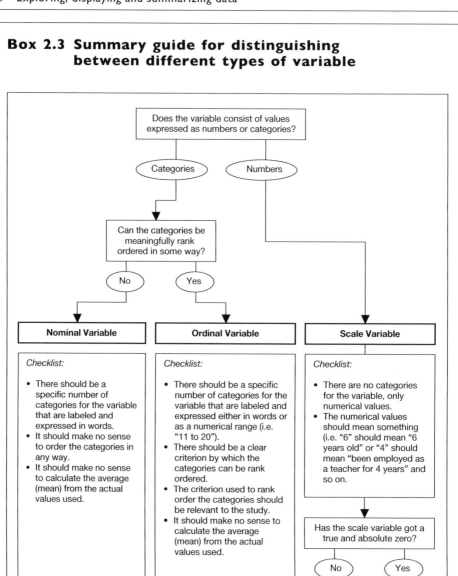

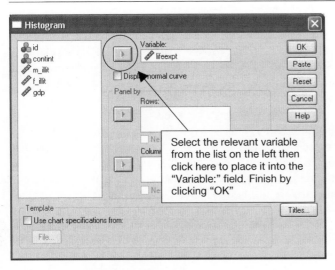

Figure 2.1 Histogram window in SPSS

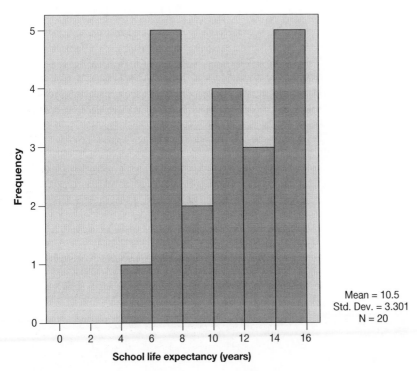

Figure 2.2 A histogram showing school life expectancy for 20 developing countries (international.sav dataset)

If you look at the histogram in Figure 2.2 you will see that it displays the number of countries within each given range. Thus there is: only one country with a school life expectancy within the range of 4.0 to 5.9; five countries with school life expectancies within the range 6.0 to 7.9 years; two schools in the range 8.0 to 9.9 years; and so on. Also, and by default, SPSS provides you with the mean, standard deviation and actual number of countries as part of the output (we will deal with means and standard deviations shortly).

The key characteristic of a histogram (and that which sets it apart from bar charts) is that all of the bars are touching one another. This is to represent the fact that this is a scale variable and thus the bars represent ranges of scores rather than clear and distinct categories. In reality, therefore, there are no actual gaps in the potential values that can be taken by a country. Overall the histogram is a good chart to use when displaying the characteristics of a single scale variable as it is simple to understand and is able to display the shape and distribution of the data very clearly and accessibly.

Stem and leaf display

Another way of displaying a scale variable is to use what is called a stem and leaf display. A stem and leaf display for the school life expectancy variable is shown in Output 2.1. You would produce this using SPSS by selecting **Analyze → Descriptive Statistics → Explore. . .** that would then call up the **Explore Window** that you have already been introduced to in the previous chapter (see Figure 1.19). Follow the same procedure as explained in the last chapter but select "Both" in the **Explore Window** in relation to "Display" rather than just "Statistics" as advised last time.

Before we go any further, have a look at the display and see if you can work out what it all means. Ask yourself: is it clear and simple? If you had something important to show teachers or educational policy makers about this variable, would this be the simplest and most effective way to do it? These are the types of questions you should always ask yourself when thinking about how best to present your findings. Exploring and presenting

Output 2.1

```
    School Life Expectancy (Years) Stem-and-Leaf Plot

    Frequency     Stem &  Leaf

          .00        0 .
         8.00        0 .  56777799
         9.00        1 .  011122244
         3.00        1 .  556

    Stem width:        10
    Each leaf:      1 case(s)
```

data is (or should be) seen as an art form rather than just a routine procedure. As the saying goes, a (good) picture does paint a thousand words. My point here is that while this is, in fact, a very useful chart and actually includes more information than the traditional histogram, we should always bear our eventual audience in mind. For the most part, unless you are writing a report solely for experienced statisticians then this is probably a chart you should avoid using. After all, if you are like any of my students then you probably struggled to make sense of the chart and what it is saying. While it may therefore be a useful chart information-wise, it is likely to just hinder the message you are trying to get across rather than help it. A well-designed histogram will, in most circumstances, do the job just as well as a stem and leaf display.

In terms of interpreting the stem and leaf display, it is useful to think of it as little more than a histogram on its side as illustrated in Figure 2.3. The rows of numbers under the heading "Leaf" can be viewed as the bars in the corresponding histogram. The column to the left of the stem and leaf display, headed "Frequency" tells you how many cases are in each of the bars. There are clearly none in the first bar, eight in the second, nine in the third and just three in the fourth bar.

The only real difference between a stem and leaf display and a histogram is that you have more information contained in the former. More specifically, you can actually see at a glance (when you know what you are looking for) what the values are for each of the individual cases. Each number in the rows under the heading "leaf" represents one case.

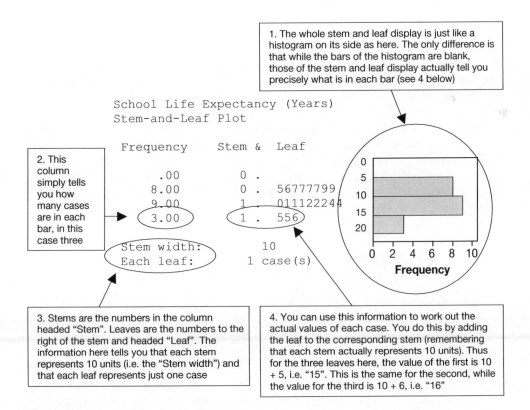

Figure 2.3 Interpreting a stem and leaf display

With larger samples, it may be necessary to have each leaf representing 10 or 100 cases. You are always told, however, how many cases each leaf represents at the bottom left of the stem and leaf display (in this instance: "Each leaf: 1 case(s)").

To work out the actual values for each leaf you need to:

- Put together the leaf with its corresponding stem, e.g. for the first figure in the top leaf this gives you "0" (from the stem) and "5" (from the leaf), i.e. "0.5". Similarly, for the first leaf in the bottom row this gives "1" (stem) and "5" (leaf), i.e. "1.5".
- Ascertain the size of each stem and then multiply the number you have got by this. In this instance the output tells us that the stem width is 10 and thus 0.5 becomes "5" and 1.5 becomes "15". These are the actual values that each leaf represents. Incidentally, if the stem width was "1" then the actual values would just be 0.5 and 1.5, respectively. Alternatively, if the stem width was "1,000" then the actual values would be 500 and 1,500, respectively.

When you do learn to read stem and leaf displays then you can see from this that they can actually be more useful than histograms. However, always remember your initial reaction when you looked at Output 2.1 for the first time. That should be enough to convince you not to bother using stem and leaf displays in your own reports (at least until they become fashionable!).

Mean and standard deviation

Having explored the nature and shape of a scale variable you are now in a position to decide what statistics to use to best summarize it. This brings us to what is known as the "normal distribution" (or sometimes termed the "Gaussian distribution"). The normal distribution plays an important role in statistics and was first discovered back in the 1730s. It emerged out of a discovery that if you plot many naturally occurring scale variables, the resultant histogram tends to take on a similar bell-shaped curve. Typical distributions that approximate to the normal distribution are shown Box 2.4. As can be seen, while some are thin and tall and others are shorter and more spread, they all tend to adopt the same characteristic bell-curve. The other thing to note is that each distribution is not entirely perfect in that the curves created by the bars are not smooth but tend to be a little jagged. This is to be expected however and simply reflects the fact that these are random samples. The basic idea is that as the sample size gets bigger and bigger it will more precisely come to adopt the shape of the normal distribution.

One of the great benefits of scale variables that tend to adopt a normal distribution is that they can be described fully with just two summary statistics:

- the **mean**, which tells us where the middle (and thus highest) point of the distribution is; and
- the **standard deviation**, which tells us how spread the bell-shaped curve is.

You should already be familiar with the idea of the mean. It is, after all, what most of us think of when we talk about "the average." It is therefore calculated simply by adding all the scores together for cases within a distribution and then dividing by the number of cases. Because it is so widely understood and used by the general public, when possible

Box 2.4 Examples of normal distributions

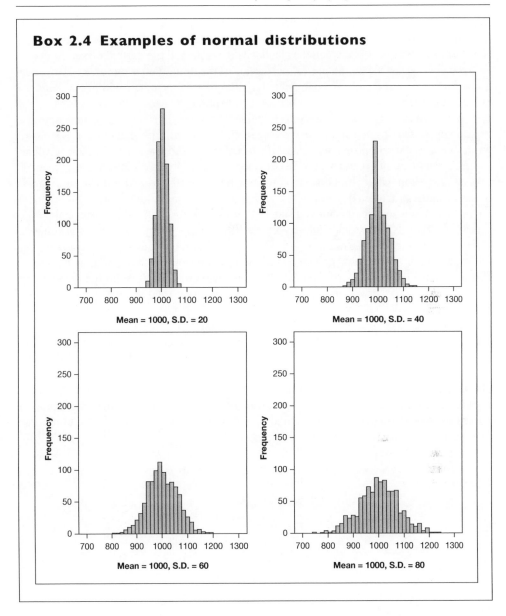

it is always preferable to use the mean when describing what the average is for a scale variable. Unfortunately, it is not always appropriate to use the mean and the reason for this will be explained shortly. In relation to the four distributions shown in Box 2.4 it can be seen that the mean is 1,000 in each case.

To give you some intuitive idea of what different standard deviations look like, the four distributions in Box 2.4 all have different standard deviations. What you can see is that the standard deviation tells us how spread out the distribution is: the larger the standard deviation the wider the distribution is spread. Fortunately, you don't need to know how to calculate standard deviations as SPSS does it for you. However, you do need to know how to interpret them practically. With this in mind, Figure 2.4 shows you how to make sense of the relationship between the standard deviation and the normal distribution.

In essence, from the mathematical properties of the normal distribution we know that around two thirds of cases (68.3 percent to be a little more precise) lie within one standard deviation of the mean. Similarly, we also know that nearly all cases (95.4 percent of cases) lie within two standard deviations of the mean. These last two statements may sound a little complicated but they are actually very straightforward. This can be seen if we take an example. Let us suppose that a class of students took a science test and their resultant scores had a mean of 60 and a standard deviation of 10. This is often stated as: "mean = 60, sd = 10". From what was said above, we can therefore take from this that roughly two-thirds of students achieved scores within one standard deviation of the mean. In practical terms this means that they achieved scores that were within either 10 marks below the mean (i.e. 50) or 10 marks above the mean (i.e. 70). In other words, two-thirds of students achieved a mark within the range 50–70. We also know that with a few exceptions, nearly all of the remaining students gained a mark within two standard deviations of the mean. If the standard deviation is 10 then two standard deviations is 20. With the mean being 60 then two standard deviations from the mean is within the range of 40 (i.e. 60—20) and 80 (i.e. 60 + 20).

Overall, therefore, once you know the mean and standard deviation for a scale variable you can map out its shape using Figure 2.4. Thus, in relation to the last example, you can write in "60" for the mean and then "70" for where it says "+1 SD" (i.e. one standard deviation above the mean) and "80" for where it says "+2 SD". Similarly, you can write "50" where it says "–1 SD" and "40" for where it says "–2 SD". For now, and as you get used to the concept, this might be a useful way for you to actually visualize the spread of the distribution. However, you will come to be able to interpret it directly with time.

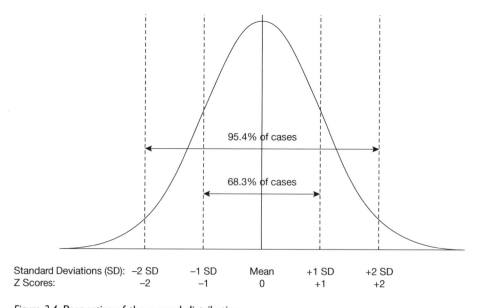

Figure 2.4 Properties of the normal distribution

Standardized scores (Z scores)

The last concept that we need to understand in relation to summarizing data that are normally distributed is the notion of the "standardized score," often referred to as the "Z score." A standardized score can be calculated for each case. What it does is give you some idea of where in a distribution that case sits. You can see how these scores relate to the standard deviation from Figure 2.4. As can be seen, if a case has a Z score of "0" this means that it is precisely in the middle of the distribution (i.e. its value is the same as the average or mean value). If the case has a Z score of "1" it means that it is situated precisely one standard deviation above the mean and, similarly, if it has a Z score of "–1" then it is situated exactly one standard deviation below the mean.

To take the example of the class of students taking a maths test discussed earlier, then if the Z score for a student is "0" that means they achieved a mark of 60 (i.e. the mean). However, if they achieved a Z score of +1.0 then they would have gained a mark of 70 (i.e. one standard deviation above the mean). Similarly, if their Z score is –0.5 then their mark is half a standard deviation below the mean; as half of 10 is 5 then this means they got a score of 55.

So long as the data are approximately normally distributed then a Z score can also be used to calculate what position a particular case occupies in that distribution. This is illustrated in Table 2.1 which lists a range of Z scores and then indicates where this would be positioned in terms of the percentage of cases that would be below and above it. As can be seen, a Z score of 0 would place it exactly in the middle of the distribution with 50 percent of the cases below it and 50 percent above it. This is clearly what we would expect given that if a case had a Z score of 0 then that would indicate that its actual score is the

Table 2.1 Calculating the position of a case within a normal distribution using Z scores

Z score of the case	% of distribution below the case	% of distribution above the case
−2.50	0.62	99.38
−2.25	1.22	98.78
−2.00	2.27	97.73
−1.75	4.01	95.99
−1.50	6.68	93.32
−1.25	10.56	89.44
−1.00	15.87	84.13
−0.75	22.66	77.34
−0.50	30.85	69.15
−0.25	40.13	59.87
0.00	50.00	50.00
+0.25	59.87	40.13
+0.50	69.15	30.85
+0.75	77.34	22.66
+1.00	84.13	15.87
+1.25	89.44	10.56
+1.50	93.32	6.68
+1.75	95.99	4.01
+2.00	97.73	2.27
+2.25	98.78	1.22
+2.50	99.38	0.62

same as the mean (and thus is in the middle). Alternatively, it can be seen from Table 2.1 that a Z score of +1 would put it towards the top of the distribution with 84 percent below it and 16 percent above it. Similarly, and given the symmetrical nature of the normal distribution, it can be seen that a Z score of –1 means that there are now 84 percent of cases above it and only 16 percent below it. If you do a search of the web with the key term "Z score" you will find a number of statistics websites that provide the facility for you to enter Z scores and calculate their position in a normal distribution. Links to some of these websites can be found on the companion website.

Let's now see how all this works together by looking at some real data. For this we will use a dataset from a national survey of early childhood care and education across America, involving a random final sample of 7,209 respondents. A brief summary of all the datasets used in this book can be found in the Introduction (Box 0.1) and further details can be found on the companion website. To begin with, therefore, you need to download and open the **earlychildhood.sav** dataset from the companion website in the same way as you did for the bullying dataset in the previous chapter. Once you have opened the dataset, and before you conduct any analysis of it, you need to do something known as weighting the cases. This is a procedure that is used in most large-scale surveys to help correct for any known biases in the final dataset due to non-response and also the particular sampling procedures used. In some cases, as in this present dataset, it also scales up the figures so that any output you produce from an analysis gives you the estimated figures for the American population as a whole. You need to be careful when using weights, especially when conducting tests for statistical significance. However, further discussion of this can wait until Chapter 6.

For now you just need to weight the dataset by selecting **Data → Weight Cases. . .** This brings up the **Weight Cases** window as shown in Figure 2.5. The main weighting

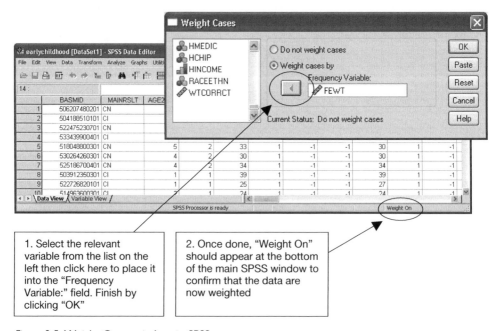

Figure 2.5 Weight Cases window in SPSS

variable—"FEWT"—can be found at the bottom of the variable list. Click on it and then transfer it to the "Frequency Variable:" field as shown. Once done, click "OK." As confirmation that the dataset is now weighted, you should see "Weight On" appear at the bottom of the main SPSS window as also shown in Figure 2.5.

You are now in a position to analyze the data. We will be exploring this dataset in much more detail in the next few chapters. Each case relates to one child. For now, let us just have a look at the age of the mothers of the children in the sample and how this is distributed. To do this, create a histogram as previously shown (see Figure 2.1) with the variable "MOMAGE1" (not to be confused with "MOMAGE2"). You should get the output shown in Figure 2.6. Note the effect of the weighting in terms of scaling up the sample size (i.e. providing the estimate that there are just over 20 million mothers of young children in America). As can be seen, the age distribution is approximately normal and so it makes sense to use the mean and standard deviation to describe it. Both statistics are actually provided in the histogram. As can be seen, the mean age of mothers in the sample is 31.37 with a standard deviation of 6.43. From before, we can use these two statistics to estimate that around two-thirds of mothers in the sample are within the age range of 24.94 (31.37 – 6.43) and 37.80 (31.37 + 6.43) i.e. within the range of plus or minus one standard deviation of the mean.

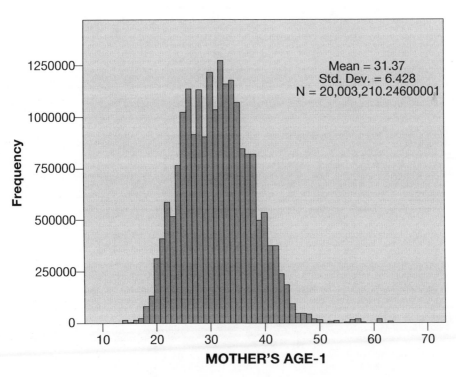

Cases weighted by FINAL ECPP INTV WEIGHT

Figure 2.6 Age distribution of mothers in the earlychildhood.sav dataset ("MOMAGE1")

EXERCISE 2.2

Try exploring the variable further using the procedure **Analyze → Descriptive Statistics → Explore...** Ensure you have "both" statistics and plots selected (refer back to Figure 1.18 if you need to). Confirm the mean and standard deviations shown in the histogram. Have a look at the stem and leaf display. Check what you have done on the companion website.

You can actually calculate the mean and standard deviation for any variable, along with the standardized scores for each case, using the **Analyze → Descriptive Statistics → Descriptives...** procedure. Try doing this for the "MOMAGE1" variable. The **Descriptives** window is shown in Figure 2.7. Select "MOMAGE1" and use the arrow button to place it into the "Variable(s):" field. Also select "Save standardized values as variables" before then clicking "OK" to complete the procedure. The output you should get from this is shown in Output 2.2. As can be seen, this verifies the mean age (31.37) and standard deviation (6.428) already shown in the histogram. Also, the output tells us that the youngest mother in the sample is 14 and the oldest is 66.

You are strongly advised, however, not to just calculate the mean and standard deviation for a variable in this way without first checking how the variable is distributed by using a histogram. As will be seen very shortly, you should only use the mean and standard deviation to summarize scale variables if they are normally distributed; otherwise, these statistics may well be misleading.

Finally, in Data View scroll across the dataset to the far right-hand side as shown in Figure 2.8. As can be seen, SPSS has created a new variable representing the standardized

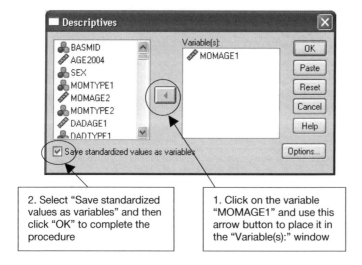

Figure 2.7 Descriptives window in SPSS

Output 2.2

Descriptive Statistics

	N	Minimum	Maximum	Mean	Std. Deviation
MOTHER'S AGE-1	20003210	14	66	31.37	6.428
Valid N (listwise)	20003210				

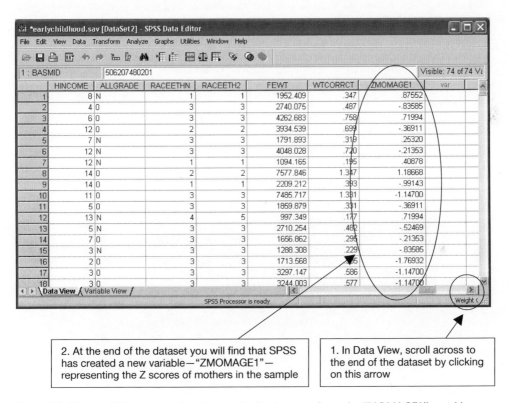

2. At the end of the dataset you will find that SPSS has created a new variable—"ZMOMAGE1"— representing the Z scores of mothers in the sample

1. In Data View, scroll across to the end of the dataset by clicking on this arrow

Figure 2.8 New variable representing the standardized scores from the "MOMAGE1" variable as seen in Data View in SPSS

scores (Z scores) for the "MOMAGE1" variable as requested. To take just the first case, it can be seen that this mother's Z score is 0.87552. In other words, her age is approximately 0.88 standard deviations above the mean. As we already know that the mean is 31.37 and the standard deviation is 6.428 then we can work out from this that her age will be 5.66 (i.e. 0.88 × 6.428) above the mean, i.e. 37 (31.37 + 5.66). If you now scroll back to the left in Data View to the variable "MOMAGE1" you can confirm that her age is, indeed, 37.

Medians and interquartile ranges

A good example of the problems of relying upon the mean to describe a scale variable can be seen if we go back to the **international.sav** dataset you created in the last chapter (and which can also be downloaded from the companion website). Let us take the scale variable per capita GDP ("GDP") and examine how it is distributed. Open the dataset and have a go at creating a histogram (you should know how to do this by now). You should get the chart shown in Figure 2.9. If you are wondering why the mean and standard deviation are shown at the top of my chart and yet seem to be to the bottom right of yours then it is because I moved it. You will be shown how to do this (and many other things) in Chapter 4.

As can be seen, the distribution is far from normal. In fact, it is what is known as "positively skewed" (i.e. rather than it being symmetrical there are a disproportionate number of values to the left). Incidentally, if it was the other way round (i.e. a disproportionate number of values bunching up on the right with a long tail stretching to the left) then it would be referred to as "negatively skewed." Unfortunately, there is no easy way to remember which is positive and which is negative—you will just learn to use the labels properly over time.

In relation to Figure 2.9, not only is it positively skewed but there are a few very large cases (what are termed "outliers") with the biggest being the United Arab Emirates with

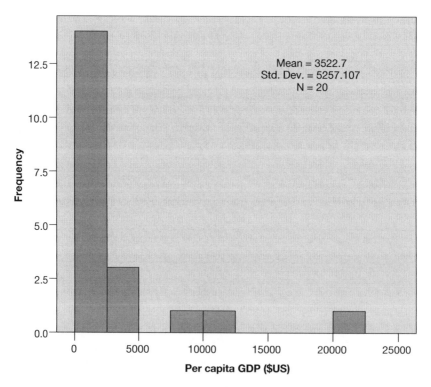

Figure 2.9 Distribution of per capita GDP among the 20 countries in the international.sav dataset ("GDP")

an extremely large per capita GDP (US$22,130) compared to the rest. The problem here is that this outlier is so large compared to the rest that it is likely to be having a disproportionate effect on the mean, making it larger than it should be. At present, it can be seen from Figure 2.9 that the mean per capita GDP for all 20 countries including the United Arab Emirates is $3,522.70. However, if you look at actual values in the dataset for per capita GDP for each country this does not seem to be a particularly representative measure as an average. In fact, the per capita GDP for a substantial majority of the countries (16 out of 20) is actually below this mean. Only the United Arab Emirates and three other countries are above the mean. This is clearly a problem. For the mean to be a good indicator of "the average" then it should be located in the middle of the distribution, with equal numbers of countries above and below it.

One way to deal with examples like this where there are a small number of extreme cases having a disproportionate effect on the mean is to use what is referred to as the **trimmed mean**. This is where a small and equal number of extreme cases at either end of the distribution are removed (i.e. trimmed off the ends) and then the mean is calculated on the rest. By default, SPSS calculates a "5% trimmed mean" which as the name suggests means that 5 percent of the cases (2.5 percent either end) are removed prior to the mean being calculated. In the present example, as there are only 20 cases then 5 percent equals just one case. Rather than removing only half of a case from either end of the distribution, SPSS removes two cases—the lowest and the highest.

To calculate the trimmed mean, you use the procedure **Analyze → Descriptive Statistics → Explore. . .** that you have already been introduced to (see Figure 1.19). Run the analysis using the "GDP" variable to get the output shown in Output 2.3. As can be seen, by removing the United Arab Emirates and its lowest counterpart (Burundi) the

Output 2.3

Descriptives

			Statistic	Std. Error
Per Capita GDP ($US)	Mean		3522.70	1175.525
	95% Confidence Interval for Mean	Lower Bound	1062.30	
		Upper Bound	5983.10	
	5% Trimmed Mean		2679.89	
	Median		2152.00	
	Variance		3E+007	
	Std. Deviation		5257.107	
	Minimum		86	
	Maximum		22130	
	Range		22044	
	Interquartile Range		2934	
	Skewness		2.767	.512
	Kurtosis		8.364	.992

mean has dramatically reduced from \$3,522.70 to \$2,679.89. This trimmed mean is certainly a better reflection of the average per capita GDP for these 20 countries. However, it is still not ideal as it is still not in the middle of the distribution. In fact, there are still 15 out of 20 countries with per capital GDP below this new trimmed mean. The reason for this is that it was not just the United Arab Emirates that was pulling the mean upwards but a couple of other countries with overly large per capita GDPs as well (most notably Malta, but also Hungary). The problem here then is not just with a few errant values but with the fact that the whole distribution is positively skewed.

In cases like this, where the distribution of a scale variable is clearly not symmetrical, there is a need to find another way of calculating the average; one that gives us a sense of what the middle point of a distribution is. This is precisely what an alternative measure of the average, the **median**, does. In essence, the median represents the mid-point of a distribution and, as such, it is the point whereby precisely half of the cases are below the median and half are above it. The median is calculated by placing all of the cases in order, from lowest to highest, and then simply picking the middle value. If there is an odd number of cases then there will be a case precisely in the middle and its value then becomes the median. If there are an even number of cases, as with our international dataset (i.e. n = 20) then you pick the middle two cases and calculate the mean for these two.

Fortunately, SPSS does all this for you. However, just to give you a sense of how this works go to the international dataset select **Data** → **Sort Cases. . .** This opens the **Sort Cases** window shown in Figure 2.10. What we want to do here is to sort the cases in order of their per capita GDP. Thus, select the "gdp" variable and place it into the "Sort by:" field. You can either do it so that the cases will be organized into ascending order (i.e. lowest first and then getting progressively higher) or descending order (i.e. highest first). It really does not matter in this case what you choose. Once you have transferred the "gdp" variable, click OK and your dataset should be re-arranged as also shown in Figure 2.10.

As can be seen, the two countries in the middle (i.e. those in places 10 and 11) are Iran and Macedonia, respectively. To calculate the median we simply work out the mean of these two values i.e. $(2,079 + 2,225)/2 = 2,152$. If we now look back at Output 2.3 from the **Explore. . .** procedure for per capita GDP we see that this is precisely what SPSS has calculated for us. Incidentally, if you want to return your dataset back to the original order then just do **Data** → **Sort Cases. . .** again but this time sort by "id" in ascending order.

What we have derived here, then, is a much more appropriate measure of the average for scale variables that are not normally distributed. However, what we still need alongside this sense of the mid-point is also a sense of the spread of the data; in other words a replacement for the standard deviation. SPSS gives us two measures of spread that can be used alongside the median. The first, as can be seen in Output 2.3 is the **range**. This is simply the distance between the lowest and highest values. In this case, SPSS actually tells us the minimum and maximum values and the difference between them is simply: $22,130 - 86 = 22,044$, i.e. the range.

However, this is not a particularly useful measure in itself as it is sensitive to extreme cases. For example, per capita GDP may have a range of \$22,044 for these 20 countries but that is only because we have the United Arab Emirates dragging the far end so high. If we removed the United Arab Emirates then the range for the remaining 19 countries would suddenly be reduced by almost half, i.e. $11,790 - 86 = 11,704$. A more useful measure of the spread of scores is what is called the "interquartile range." This basically tells us the range of the middle half of the cases. To understand this, consider Figure 2.11.

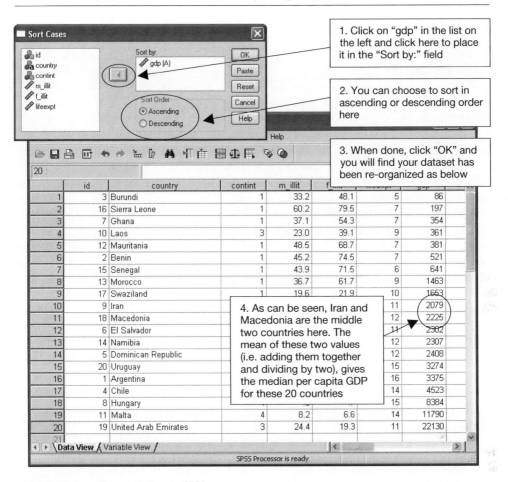

Figure 2.10 Sort Cases window in SPSS

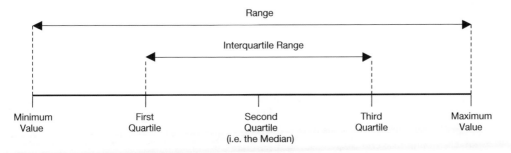

Figure 2.11 The median, interquartile range and range

The thick horizontal line represents a row of cases organized in ascending order. As can be seen, the minimum value is on the far end to the left and the maximum value is on the far end to the right. The range is, therefore, just the distance between these minimum and maximum values.

It has already been explained that the median is calculated by finding the middle value, as also shown in Figure 2.11. Therefore, the median basically splits the distribution in half. What we can also do is to split the two halves into two further halves thus effectively splitting the distribution into quarters. This is done by locating the **first quartile** (which is simply the mid-point between the minimum value and the median) and then the **third quartile** (which is the mid-point between the median and the maximum value).

What we know from all of this, then, is that precisely a quarter of cases will lie below the first quartile, and three-quarters will lie above it. Similarly, precisely half of all cases will lie below the second quartile (another term for the median) and half above it. Also, three-quarters of cases will lie below the third quartile and a quarter above it. With this in mind, we also know that precisely half of all cases lie between the first and third quartiles. Moreover, these cases are in the middle of the distribution. As indicated in Figure 2.11, the **interquartile range** is, therefore, simply the distance between the first and third quartiles. In other words, it is the range over which the middle half of cases lie when ranked in ascending order.

In general, it is the median and interquartile range (sometimes abbreviated to "IQR") that are used as alternatives to the mean and standard deviation to summarize scale variables that are skewed and/or otherwise not normally distributed. From the information in Output 2.3, therefore, we can appropriately summarize the variable per capita GDP as: "median = 2,152, IQR = 2,934".

The boxplot

Now we have covered the median and interquartile range it is time to introduce the final piece of the jigsaw in terms of displaying and summarizing scale variables—the boxplot. The boxplot is just a simple way of displaying the basic details of the distribution of a scale variable, whether it is normally distributed or not. As will be seen in the next chapter, it is a particularly useful method for comparing the distributions of two or more sub-groups. For now, we will simply look at how to generate a boxplot and understand its basic features.

To create a boxplot for the per capita GDP variable, select **Graphs → Legacy Dialogs → Box Plot. . .** (or just **Graphs → Boxplot. . .** for SPSS Version 14.0 and before and also Mac versions). This opens the **Boxplot** window shown in Figure 2.12. Select "Simple" and "Summaries of separate variables" as shown and then click "Define." This brings up the second window as also shown in Figure 2.12. As we are creating a boxplot of the per capita GDP variable, put "gdp" into the "Boxes Represent:" field. Also, put the string variable that includes the names of each country (i.e. "country") into the "Label Cases by:" field. Once you have clicked "OK" you will have the chart shown in Figure 2.13.

There are several points to make regarding the boxplot. The horizontal line in the middle of the box represents the median for the variable. The box itself represents the interquartile range or, in other words, the middle 50 percent of the distribution. As such, the lower edge of the box represents the first quartile and the upper edge the third quartile. The ends of the two whiskers protruding from the box represent the lowest and highest

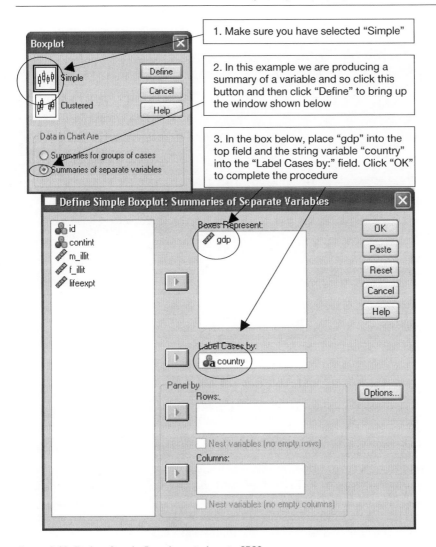

1. Make sure you have selected "Simple"

2. In this example we are producing a summary of a variable and so click this button and then click "Define" to bring up the window shown below

3. In the box below, place "gdp" into the top field and the string variable "country" into the "Label Cases by:" field. Click "OK" to complete the procedure

Figure 2.12 Define Simple Boxplot window in SPSS

values of the distribution (barring any outliers and extreme values). These whiskers, therefore, give a better sense of the range of the distribution without it being distorted by any extremes. Finally, any outliers and extreme values are indicated individually and, if you defined a label when generating the boxplot (as we did) then they will also be labeled as they are in Figure 2.14. There is no universally accepted way of defining outliers and extreme values. SPSS defines outliers (marked by circles) as any value over 1.5 times the box length beyond the lower or higher edges of the box and within 3.0 box lengths. As the length of the box is the interquartile range, and the edges of the box represent the first and third quartiles, an outlier can be defined alternatively as any case that is over one and a half times the interquartile range beyond the first or third quartile and within three times the interquartile range of these.

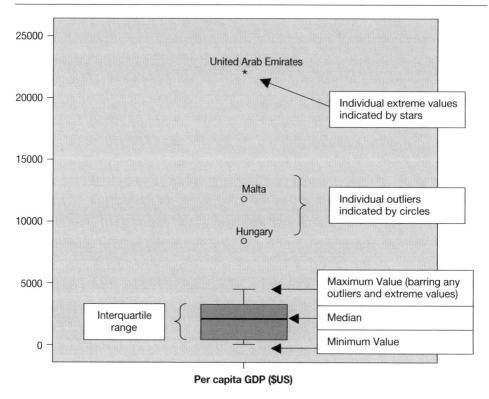

Figure 2.13 Boxplot showing the distribution of per capita GDP for the 20 countries in the international.sav dataset

Not surprisingly, an extreme value is defined by SPSS as any value beyond three box lengths (or interquartile ranges) of either edge of the box (or either the first or third quartile). As can be seen from Figure 2.13, the boxplot certainly illustrates the extreme position of the United Arab Emirates relative to the rest of the sample and thus some sense of why it was so influential in dragging the mean upwards.

EXERCISE 2.3

Try creating histograms, stem and leaf displays and boxplots for some of the other scale variables in the international.sav dataset. Check what you have done on the companion website. Which do you feel best displays each variable?

Displaying and summarizing nominal and ordinal variables

This final section looks at how we might best display and summarize nominal and ordinal variables. These two types of variable are being covered together because they are both categorical variables; in other words they consist of a specific number of distinct categories. As such we need ways of displaying both ordinal and nominal variables that can clearly show how any given sample of cases is distributed across the categories that comprise one of these variables. Probably the two simplest and most effective ways of displaying either of these types of categorical variable is with either a simple **frequency table** or with a **bar chart**.

To illustrate this, we shall go back to the **earlychildhood.sav** dataset and examine parents' and/or guardians' responses to the question: "How many times have you or someone in your family read to [your child] in the past week?" The variable in this case is "FOREADTO" and the response categories are: "Not at all"; "Once or twice"; "3 or more times"; and "Every day." To create a frequency table and bar chart for this ordinal variable you need to begin by opening the earlychildhood dataset and then ensure that the dataset is weighted with the variable "FEWT." You have already been shown how to generate a frequency table and bar chart in one go using the **Analyze → Descriptive Statistics → Frequencies. . .** procedure in the last chapter (see Figure 1.11). Do this again now with the "FOREADTO" variable. This will produce the frequency table and bar chart shown in Figure 2.14.

While the bar chart is fairly self-explanatory, there are three points to note about the frequency table. First, the percentages you should actually use are those listed in the "Valid Percent" column. These percentages have been calculated once any cases with missing data have been removed. It is good practice to include a note explaining what proportion of the data is missing (in this case none) and then to explain that the percentages listed relate to those who actually answered the question.

Second, it would be appropriate to use the "Cumulative Percent" column for an ordinal variable but not a nominal variable. The reason for this is that because the categories for an ordinal variable can be rank ordered, it does make sense to cumulatively add categories together. For example, and looking at the frequency table, it can be seen that cumulative percentages might be useful on this occasion as they allow us to note that while 5.5 percent of children in America were not read to at all, 19.7 percent have at best only been read to once or twice during the last week. However, and as for nominal variables, as there is no meaningful way of ordering categories it would not make sense to progressively add the categories together to produce a cumulative percent column.

Third, when a sample is weighted like this so that the frequencies are purposely increased to the size of the population, it is important to include a separate column, headed "Base Frequencies," to show exactly what size the actual sample is that these estimated frequencies and percentages are based upon. This is important as you could have a situation where some of the categories are actually only based upon a handful of actual respondents and yet because they are weighted and scaled up to the size of the population as a whole the reader is given a false sense of the findings. To calculate the actual frequencies, you simply re-run the **Analyze → Descriptive Statistics → Frequencies . . .** procedure but this time without the weighting variable being applied. Try doing this (you obviously need to select **Data → Weight Cases. . .** first to "Reset" weight cases). The base frequencies you should get, and how you can display them are shown in Table 2.2.

In relation to nominal variables, there is also the option of using a pie chart. To illustrate this we will stay with the earlychildhood dataset and generate a pie chart to illustrate the racial and ethnic breakdown of the sample. A pie chart can be produced either through

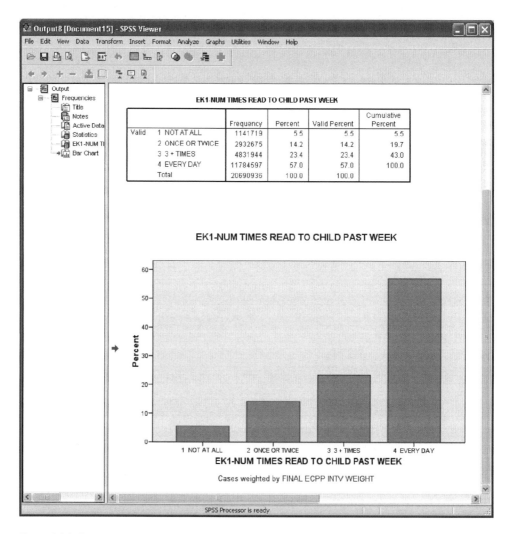

Figure 2.14 Output window in SPSS

Table 2.2 The extent to which parents in America stated that they read to their young children (aged 0–6) in the past week

Variable I	Base frequencies	Estimated frequencies[1]	Percent[2]	Cumulative percent[2]
Not at all	388	1,141,719	5.5	5.5
Once or twice	987	2,932,675	14.2	19.7
Three or more times	1,675	4,831,944	23.4	43.0
Every day	4,159	11,784,597	57.0	100.0
Total	7,209	20,690,936	100.0	

Notes:
1 Weighted estimates for the population as a whole
2 Based on weighted estimates

the **Analyze** → **Descriptive Statistics** → **Frequencies. . .** procedure where you would select "pie chart" rather than "bar chart" as you did last time, or through the **Graphs** → **Legacy Dialogs** → **Pie. . .** procedure. Following this last procedure would produce the **Pie Charts** window shown in Figure 2.15. Choose "Summaries for groups of cases" and then click "Define." This produces the **Define Pie Chart** window also shown in Figure 2.15. Place the "RACEETHN" variable (third from the end of the variable list) in the "Define Slices by:" field, click "% of cases" and then "OK." This produces the pie chart in Figure 2.16 (with a few slight amendments—to be covered in the next chapter).

As can be seen, the pie chart has been placed side-by-side with a bar chart illustrating the same data. There are two points to draw out from this. The first is that while a pie chart is appropriate for a nominal variable it is not really appropriate for an ordinal variable.

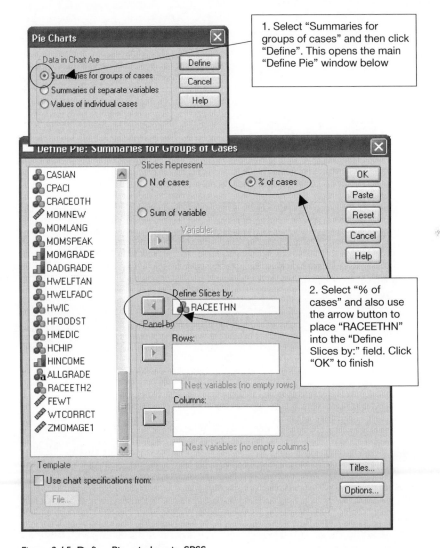

Figure 2.15 Define Pie window in SPSS

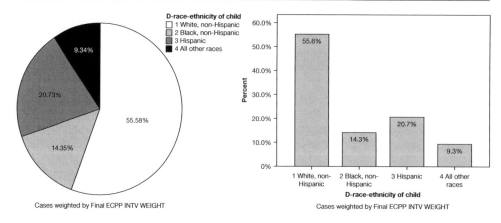

Cases weighted by Final ECPP INTV WEIGHT

Cases weighted by Final ECPP INTV WEIGHT

Figure 2.16 Pie chart and bar chart showing ethnic breakdown of the earlychildhood.sav sample

This is because you lose a sense of the ordered nature of the categories when they are placed in a pie chart. The second key point to make is that a pie chart tends to be less useful than a bar chart in terms of displaying data. This should be clear from Figure 2.16. In relation to the bar chart, it is very easy to see at a glance how the different categories compare in terms of their relative sizes. This, however, is not so easy to do with the pie chart where it takes a little more time to gain an appreciation of how the various categories compare to one another. It is for this reason that my own personal preference is to stick with bar charts when displaying nominal data. One exception to this is where, for example, you may wish to illustrate how a school's budget is spent over a year. In this case you would be attempting to show what share of the budget went on staffing, what share went on building repairs, what share was spent on books and other equipment and so on. In this case, as you would be attempting to show how the budget had been shared out, the use of a pie chart would seem appropriate.

EXERCISE 2.4

Explore some of the ordinal and nominal variables in the **earlychildhood.sav** dataset. Try different techniques to display them graphically. Which ones do you think best summarize these variables?

Conclusions

This chapter has covered the key issues involved in displaying and summarizing data. You should now have a good sense of the main ways in which data can be displayed in charts and tables and the most appropriate ways to use these. You should also have a sound understanding of the key types of summary statistics available and when each should be used. A key theme running through the whole chapter has been the need to distinguish between the three main types of variable—scale, ordinal and nominal. Having a clear understanding of the distinctions between each of these three types of variable will take you a long way in terms of developing an ability to use charts and summary statistics appropriately. As a reminder, Box 2.5 provides a recap of the most appropriate ways to display and summarize these three types of variable.

Box 2.5 Summary guide as to the appropriate way to display and summarize a variable

Scale Variable	Ordinal Variable	Nominal Variable
Appropriate Ways to Display the Data		
• Histogram • Stem and Leaf Display • Boxplot	• Bar Chart • Frequency Table	• Bar Chart • Pie Chart • Frequency Table
Appropriate Ways to Summarize the Data		
If normally distributed: • Mean and Standard Deviation *If not normally distributed:* • Median and Interquartile Range	• Percentages • Cumulative Percentages	• Percentages

Chapter 3

Analyzing relationships between variables

Introduction

Now that you have gained a sound understanding of the different types of variable that exist and the most appropriate ways of displaying and summarizing them, we are in a position to begin analyzing the data and, in particular, examining relationships between variables. This is really the core of routine quantitative data analysis. It allows you to use the data to answer questions such as: are there differences in educational attainment between girls and boys? Does a relationship exist between a young child's socio-economic background and their emergent literacy skills? And are there different reasons for adults enrolling on basic adult education programs depending upon their racial and ethnic background?

The purpose of this chapter is to give you the skills needed to analyze quantitative data in order to answer questions just like these. By the end of this chapter you will therefore:

- be able to handle and manipulate quantitative data to get it in the form required for your analysis;
- know what the most appropriate ways of examining and summarizing relationships between different types of variable are and will be able to do this using SPSS;
- have the knowledge and skills to be able to display and report findings from quantitative data analysis in an effective and appropriate manner.

Preparing variables and the dataset for analysis

Before we can begin to analyze the data there are a few important procedures you need to learn about with SPSS to help you handle the data. The first three are: recoding variables; selecting cases; and splitting files. We will look at each of these in turn in this section. A fourth procedure, computing new variables, will be introduced a little later in the chapter. With these four techniques at your disposal you should be able to undertake most forms of routine quantitative data analysis.

Recoding variables

There will be times when you need to recode a categorical variable (i.e. a nominal or ordinal variable) prior to analysis. One of the reasons you would wish to do this is so that you can reduce the number of categories in a particular variable to make it manageable.

This may be because there are only a few categories that you are actually interested in and so you could recode the rest under a generic category of "other." It may also be the case that the number of cases in some categories is very small and/or they naturally group together in some way.

In order to explain the general procedure for recoding variables we will take the **afterschools.sav** dataset and recode the variable "RACEETHN2." Open up the dataset and have a look at the variable. You will see that it consists of five categories coded as follows:

1 = White, Non-Hispanic
2 = Black, Non-Hispanic
3 = Hispanic
4 = Asian or Pacific Islander
5 = All Other Races

It is important to note from the outset that such categories are not objective in any sense but are highly contested and political in nature, especially in relation to the use of the term "Hispanic" (see, for example, Delgardo and Stefancic, 1998). Unfortunately, and as with most forms of secondary analysis, we are forced to work with the categories that are given. However, while we have little option but to do this, it is important to reflect upon the problems and limitations of these in relation to the analysis you wish to undertake. This is something we will consider further in Chapter 5.

For now, we will simply use this variable to show you how you can reduce it down to just two categories: "White, Non Hispanic" and "All Other Races." To do this start by selecting **Transform → Recode into Different Variables. . .** (for SPSS Version 14.0 and earlier and Mac versions, there is an extra level to this selection process, i.e. **Transform → Recode → Into Different Variables. . .**). As a general rule (and certainly until you really know what you are doing) you should always keep the original variable by choosing this option to recode into a different variable. Should you choose the other option (i.e. "Recode into Same Variables. . .") you will be permanently altering the original variables and this leaves you no room for maneuver should you make a mistake. Selecting these options results in the **Recode into Different Variables** window appearing as shown in Figure 3.1.

First of all you need to select the variable you wish to re-code and then place it into the middle "Numeric Variable → Output Variable:" field as shown. You then need to name the new variable you wish to create and also place this into the field as shown. With this done the final task is to actually specify what you wish to recode. To do this you should click on the "Old and New Values. . ." button to bring up the second window also shown in Figure 3.1. To help clarify what you want to do it is sometimes a good idea to create two lists side-by-side: one with the categories and their values for the original variable and then one for the categories and values you wish to create for the new variable. You can then see clearly what each original value has to be changed to, and even draw line arrows to show this clearly and thus to check you have not missed any out. This is a particularly useful thing to do when you are dealing with variables with a large number of categories. In this case it is fairly simple. If the categories in our new variable are: 1 = "White, Non-Hispanic" and 2 = "All Other Racial Groups" then the changes we need to make are:

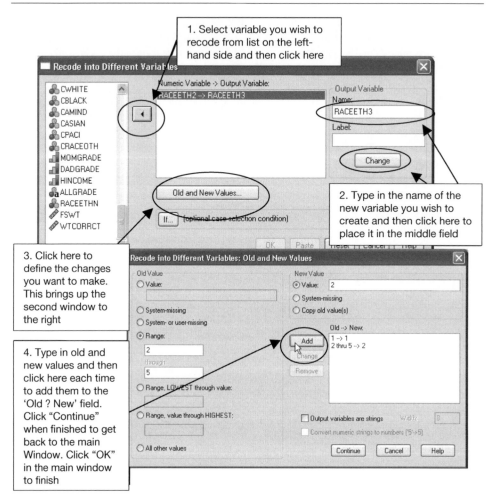

Figure 3.1 Recoding variables in SPSS

- "1" should be kept as it is in the new variable;
- "2," "3," "4" and "5" should all be coded as "2" in the new variable.

To define this in the window, first of all look at the list of options under the heading "Old Value:" and click on "Value:". The field underneath will become activated and you should just type in "1". Now look at the list of options under the heading "New Value:" and make sure "Value:" is selected there. Type "1" into the field associated with this option. Once you have done this click on the button "Add" as shown. You should see "1 → 1" appear in the "Old → New" field. For the remaining four categories in the original variable, these are all to be recoded as "2". You could do this individually for each category (i.e. change: "2" to "2"; "3" to "2"; "4" to "2"; and finally "5" to "2"). This is a little laborious and unnecessary however. Instead, under the list of options for "Old Value:" select "Range" and then type in "2" and "5" as shown. After this just type "2" in the

"Value:" field on the right-hand side as also shown in Figure 3.1. Once you have done this click "Add" and you should see "2 thru 5 → 2" appear in the "Old → New" field. To complete the procedure, click on the "Continue" button and then the "OK" button in the main **Recode into Different Variables** window.

What this procedure does is to create a new variable "RACEETH3" at the end of the dataset. Click on "Variable View" and scroll down to see it. While there you can give the variable a name, add labels for the two categories and then remove the decimal places and define the variable as "nominal"—all of which you were shown how to do in Chapter 1. Finally, it is a good idea to compare the old and new variables to check that you have not made any mistakes in the recoding. To do this select **Analyze → Descriptive Statistics → Crosstabs. . . .** We will be exploring this procedure in more detail shortly (see Figure 3.5). For now, simply select the original variable ("RACEETH2") and place it in the "Row(s):" field and similarly place the newly created variable ("RACEETH3") into the "Column(s):" field and click "OK." This will produce the output shown in Output 3.1.

As can be seen, all the categories of the original variable are listed down the left-hand side and then the new categories across the top. For each category within the original variable you can look across to see where the cases in that category have now been placed in relation to the new variable. As can be seen, in this case everything is fine. The "White, Non-Hispanic" group in the original variable (a total of 6,742) has now been re-assigned to the "White, Non-Hispanic" group in the new variable. Similarly, all of the other groups in the original variable have been assigned to the "All Other Races" category in the new variable. This is actually a simple example. However, with more complex variables, especially those involving missing categories, checking what you have done with a frequency table in this way is essential. Before you finish, make sure you save the amended dataset as we will be using this new variable for analysis in Chapter 5.

Output 3.1

D-DETAILED RACE-ETHNICITY OF CHILD * RACE-ETHNICITY OF CHILD (REDUCED)
Crosstabulation

Count

		RACE-ETHNICITY OF CHILD (REDUCED)		
		WHITE, NON-HISPANIC	ALL OTHER RACES	Total
D-DETAILED RACE-ETHNICITY OF CHILD	1 WHITE, NON-HISPANIC	6742	0	6742
	2 BLACK, NON-HISPANIC	0	1430	1430
	3 HISPANIC	0	2559	2559
	4 ASIAN OR PACIFIC ISLANDER	0	322	322
	5 ALL OTHER RACES	0	631	631
Total		6742	4942	11684

EXERCISE 3.1

Create a new variable, "HINCOME2" by recoding the variable "HINCOME" from the **afterschools.sav** dataset. This variable represents the household income earned by each child's family. Recode it into just three categories: $0–$30,000; $30,001–$60,000; and $60,001 and over. Run a simple frequency analysis to calculate what percentage of the sample fits into each of these three categories. Check your method and findings on the companion website. Save the dataset and thus this new variable as we will use it in a later exercise.

Selecting cases

The purpose of using the select cases procedure is simply to identify particular sub-samples within the dataset for analysis. For example, you may just want to analyze women in the sample or women aged 40 and over or, in fact, any sub-group you wish to define. What this procedure does is to ensure that, once you have defined your sub-sample, any further analysis you conduct is only run on that sub-sample. To illustrate this, let us continue with the **afterschools.sav** dataset and focus our analysis simply on Hispanic boys. To do this, choose **Data** → **Select Cases. . . .** This brings up the **Select Cases** window shown in Figure 3.2.

Select "If condition is satisfied" as shown and then click the "If" button. This brings up a second window where you need to specify which cases to select. Here we want to select only Hispanic boys and so we need to select only those cases where the variable "RACEETHN" = 3 (i.e. the value for the "Hispanic" category) and "SEX" = 1 (the value for the category "boys"). To do this we need to create the following expression in the right-hand top field: "RACEETHN = 3 & SEX = 1." To do this, you begin by selecting the "RACEETHN" variable from the list to the left and then click on the arrow button to place it into the top, right-hand field. You then use the buttons below this field, as shown in Figure 3.2, to add in the next parts of the expression. Next, you select "SEX" from the list and place this in the top, right-hand field before completing the expression using the buttons below. Click "Continue" when finished and this will take you back to the main **Select Cases** window. You should now see the expression you have created appear next to the "If" button.

In the main window, under the heading "Output," make sure that the "Filter out unselected cases" option is selected (this is the default setting in SPSS). If it is not, then you run the risk of losing all of the cases that you have not selected. Once done, click "OK" to finish the procedure. The main dataset should now appear as in Figure 3.3. You can tell that the Select Cases procedure is currently being used because the "Filter On" label has now appeared bottom right as indicated and also, the cases that do not fall into the sub-sample chosen are all scored out to the left. An important piece of advice is for you to always "reset" Select Cases when you have finished your analysis. You do this by calling up the **Select Cases** window again and simply clicking on "Reset" and then "OK." It is very easy to forget to do this with the consequence that any subsequent analysis will actually only be of the sub-sample rather than the sample as a whole.

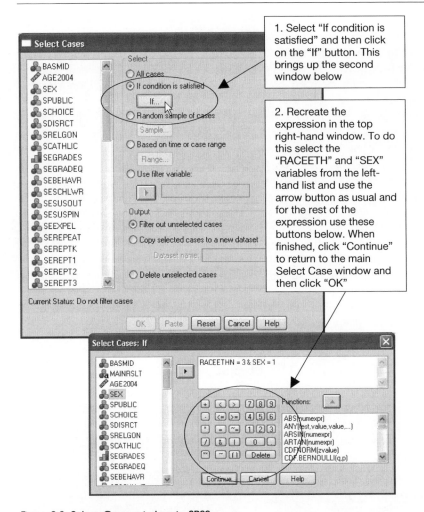

Figure 3.2 Select Cases window in SPSS

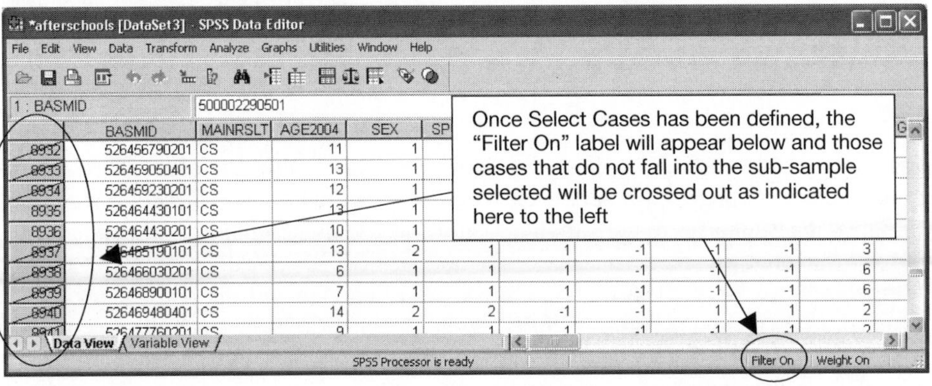

Figure 3.3 Main SPSS window indicating that the "Select Cases" procedure is being used

With the Select Cases procedure being used, any analysis you now do on the dataset will only be run for Hispanic boys. To check this, try running the **Analyze → Descriptive Statistics → Frequencies. . .** procedure (as covered in Chapter 1—see Figure 1.11) but this time select the two variables RACEETHN and SEX and click "OK." This will produce two frequency tables, one for each variable. However, because Select Cases is on, you will only see "3 Hispanic" in the first table and "1 Male" in the second table. You should also only have a total sample size of 588 children. This is with the sample weighted by the variable "WTCORRCT"—if you did not get the figure of 588, apply this weighting variable (see Figure 2.5) and try again.

This example was fairly straightforward. However, you can identify quite complex sub-samples using the array of buttons shown in Figure 3.2. If you do not understand the meaning of any of them, simply right-click on the button you are interested in and a dialog box will appear explaining it to you. Most of the buttons are relatively straightforward, however. Perhaps the two that may need to be explained are the "|" button that represents "or" and also the "~=" button that represents "not equal to." To illustrate the use of these two buttons, Box 3.1 provides a few examples of expressions that could be used to select cases, and their meaning. Note the use of parentheses in the last two examples in the table. It is always advisable to use parentheses with more complex expressions. Parentheses provide an order for SPSS to follow, with commands inside parentheses always being dealt with first. The effects of parentheses can be seen in relation to the final two expressions. This should also alert you to the dangers of not using parentheses. In this particular case, if you just typed in the expression without any parentheses then you could not be certain which of the two interpretations listed at the bottom of Box 3.1 SPSS would take.

EXERCISE 3.2

Use select cases to select a sub-sample from the **afterschools.sav** dataset that consists of white, non-Hispanic boys aged six. Using this sub-sample, run a simple frequency analysis to estimate what percentage of these boys in America is likely to have a speech impairment ("HDSPEEC"). Also estimate what percentage is likely to be autistic ("HDAUTISM"). Check your method and findings on the companion website.

Split File

The final procedure to show you for the moment is the Split File procedure. The Split File command is a simple and yet very useful tool. Once set, it basically organizes all of your output by the categories of the variable(s) you specify. In the following example we will ask SPSS to split the file by the sex of the child ("SEX"). As will be seen, the effect of doing this is that for any analysis run, SPSS will provide the results for boys and girls in turn. To do this, choose **Data → Split File. . . .** This brings up the **Split File** window shown in Figure 3.4. Select the option: "Organize output by groups." This will activate the field below the window. Choose the variable "SEX" from the list on the left and place it in the field using the arrow button before clicking "OK" to finish.

Box 3.1 Examples of expressions to select cases and their meanings

Example	Meaning: Selects cases if:
AGE2004 >= 6	the age of the child is greater than or equal to six
RACEETHN ~= 1	the race/ethnicity of the child is not White, Non Hispanic (i.e. selects all children that are not White, Non-Hispanic)
AGE2004 = 4 | AGE2004 = 6	the age of the child is either four or six (i.e. selects all four and six year olds)
AGE2004 = 4 & AGE2004 = 6	the age of the child is four and six (a mistake as a child cannot be both. This would result in all cases being deselected!).
SEX = 1 & (AGE2004 = 4 | AGE2004 = 6)	the child is male and also either four or six years of age (i.e. selects all boys aged four and six).
(SEX = 1 & AGE2004 = 4) | AGE2004 = 6	The child is either male and aged four or is aged six (i.e. selects all four year old boys and all six year old children whether they are boys or girls).

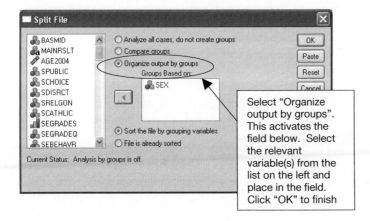

Figure 3.4 Split File window in SPSS

To see the effects of this use the **Analyze → Descriptive Statistics → Explore...** procedure to calculate the mean age ("AGE2004") for the children in the sample. Once you have done this you will see that the output is split into two; giving you the results for the males and females in the sample separately. If you have done it properly you should have a mean of 9.51 years (SD = 2.67) for the males in the sample and a mean of 9.40 (SD = 2.68) for the females. If you have not got this, check that: (1) you have the **afterschools.sav** dataset open; (2) you have the weight cases on (weighted by the variable "WTCORRCT"); and (3) you remembered to reset Select Cases after the last exercise.

The only other point to note about the Split File procedure is that you can split a file by more than one variable if you wish. Try splitting the file by the variables "SEX" and "RACEETHN" and then run the **Analyze → Descriptive Statistics → Explore...** procedure again to see what happens. What you will see this time is that the output is split into ten groups defined by the sex and race/ethnicity of the child. Thus you will see that the first output is for white, non-Hispanic males, the next will be for black, non-Hispanic males, and so on.

EXERCISE 3.3

Use the split file procedure to see whether a child's racial/ethnic background ("RACEETHN") and family income (use your newly created variable "HINCOME2") are associated with whether they have ever had to repeat a grade or not ("SEREPEAT"). Check your method and findings on the companion website.

Analyzing relationships between two variables

Having covered some of the basic procedures you will need in order to work with quantitative data, we can now move onto analyzing relationships between two variables (called bivariate analysis). As you may be able to guess, the type of analysis you conduct depends on the types of variable you are dealing with. With three types of variable (nominal, ordinal and scale), there are six possible pairings that we will look at in turn. In each case we will start with a real-life research question relating to one of the datasets and look at how you would most appropriately handle and analyze the data and display the findings.

Analyzing the relationship between two nominal variables

In this first example we will look at how you would analyze the relationship between two nominal variables. We will use the **afterschools.sav** dataset and address the following research question:

> *Is there a relationship in the United States between a child's racial/ethnic background and their likelihood of being suspended from school?*

The first thing you need to do when faced with a research question like this is to determine what variables are involved. In this case there are two: a child's racial/ethnic background and also whether they have been suspended from school or not. There are two variables from the **afterschools.sav** dataset we can use for this analysis. The first is "RACEETHN2" which consists of five basic categories as you will remember from earlier in the chapter. The second is "SESUSOUT" which relates to the question: "During this school year, has your child had an out-of-school suspension?" Responses to this question are coded as simply "yes" or "no." In both cases, therefore, we are dealing with nominal variables. This should be obvious by now in relation to "RACEETHN2." However, you may ask why cannot "SESUSOUT" be regarded as an ordinal variable as the two categories can be ordered in the sense of whether a child has been suspended or not (in this case the category "yes" is therefore more than the category "no"). This is a grey area and some people would define this second variable as ordinal for the purpose of analysis. However, this can cause problems later when undertaking some of the tests for statistical significance (Chapter 6). As a general rule, therefore, I would recommend that any variable with just two categories is treated as a nominal variable.

In choosing these two categories to answer the question posed, we are making a decision that these are valid as measures for the two variables we are interested in. However, there are problems in both bases. For "RACEETHN2," while five categories are being used, each one still encompasses children from a very broad range of back-grounds. While the findings from this analysis may provide some useful pointers in terms of a possible relationship between race/ethnicity and suspension from school, we need to be mindful that there may well be sub-groups within each category where any relationship found could either be much stronger or much weaker/non-existent. Thus, we always need to be cautious when reporting the findings. For the second variable, there is also a question over its validity in the sense that it only covers out-of-school suspensions. What it does not cover, for example, is in-school suspensions and also instances where a child is actually expelled from school. Again, this is not a fundamental problem as such but it does mean that we need to be careful in explaining precisely what our analysis focuses on and to reflect upon whether that may produce a distorted picture. Fortunately, for this dataset the other two instances mentioned are also included as variables ("SESUSPIN" and "SEEXPEL") and so we can also have a look at these a little later.

For now we will focus on the relationship between the two variables "RACEETHN2" and "SESUSOUT." When dealing with two nominal variables like this, the only real option is to examine the data through what is called a **contingency table**. This is a table that displays the frequencies and percentages of children from each category of one variable across the categories of another variable. Before we start the analysis, ensure you have weighted the dataset by the weighting variable "WTCORRCT." Once you have done this, you create a contingency table by choosing **Analyze → Descriptive Statistics → Crosstabs. . . .** This opens the window shown in Figure 3.5.

In this example we will place "RACEETH2" into the "Row(s):" field and "SESUSOUT" into the "Columns(s):" field as shown. Putting a variable in rows means that its categories will be displayed down the left-hand side of a contingency table whereas putting a variable in columns means that its categories will be displayed across the top of the table. There is a general principle governing which variable goes where. Basically, the variable that includes the categories you wish to compare should be put in rows. In this case, we are primarily interested in making comparisons between the different racial/ethnic groups and, hence, we have placed "RACEETH2" in the "Rows(s):" field. However, this principle is not a hard-and-fast one and there will be occasions where it is

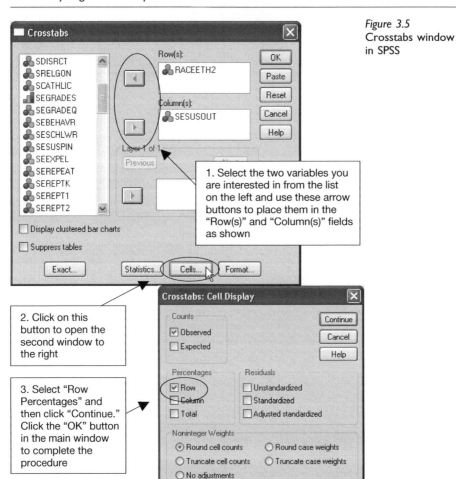

Figure 3.5
Crosstabs window
in SPSS

not practical to do this (especially in cases where there are a large number of categories comprising the other variable and just in terms of fitting the table on a page it is better to place that variable in rows).

Once you have done this you then need to ensure that percentages are calculated and included in the table. When you want to compare two or more categories of a variable in this way it is essential that you compare them using percentages rather than simple frequencies. The reason for this will be explained in a moment when we look at the output. Click on the "Cells. . ." button to bring up the second window as also shown in Figure 3.5. You are now faced with whether to calculate percentages by rows or columns. The difference between these two options will be explained a little later. For now, the basic rule of thumb is that you choose the option that relates to the variable you are interested in making comparisons with. In other words, we are interested in comparing children from different racial/ethnic backgrounds. As we have placed the associated variable "RACEETH2" into rows, we now need to select "Row Percentages" here. Similarly, if we had placed "RACEETH2" into columns, then we would have selected "Column

Percentages". Once you have selected "Row Percentages", click "Continue" and then "OK" in the main window to complete the procedure. The output produced from the analysis is shown in Output 3.2.

As can be seen, the percentages have been calculated in rows as requested. This is evident because the percentages sum to 100.0 percent across each row. What can be seen from this table is that there does appear to be a relationship between the racial/ethnic background of a child and whether they have received an out-of-school suspension over the last year. More specifically, the most noticeable finding is the relatively high rate of suspensions experienced by black, non-Hispanic children with the figures suggesting they are around five times more likely to be suspended than their white, non-Hispanic peers. This figure of "five times" was gained by dividing the percentage of black, non-Hispanic children by the percentage of white, non-Hispanic (i.e. 10.4/2.1 = 4.95). In addition, Hispanic children seem to be marginally more likely to be suspended than their white, non-Hispanic peers.

There are three points to draw out regarding the analysis of this table. The first relates to the importance of using percentages to compare groups. This is particularly important when the sizes of each group are different. Imagine, for example, if we only compared

Output 3.2

D-DETAILED RACE-ETHNICITY OF CHILD * SE5-OUT-OF-SCHOOL SUSPENSION Crosstabulation

| | | | SE5-OUT-OF-SCHOOL SUSPENSION | | |
			1 YES	2 NO	Total
D-DETAILED RACE-ETHNICITY OF CHILD	1 WHITE, NON-HISPANIC	Count	69	3268	3337
		% within D-DETAILED RACE-ETHNICITY OF CHILD	2.1%	97.9%	100.0%
	2 BLACK, NON-HISPANIC	Count	94	806	900
		% within D-DETAILED RACE-ETHNICITY OF CHILD	10.4%	89.6%	100.0%
	3 HISPANIC	Count	29	1057	1086
		% within D-DETAILED RACE-ETHNICITY OF CHILD	2.7%	97.3%	100.0%
	4 ASIAN OR PACIFIC ISLANDER	Count	3	155	158
		% within D-DETAILED RACE-ETHNICITY OF CHILD	1.9%	98.1%	100.0%
	5 ALL OTHER RACES	Count	21	324	345
		% within D-DETAILED RACE-ETHNICITY OF CHILD	6.1%	93.9%	100.0%
Total		Count	216	5610	5826
		% within D-DETAILED RACE-ETHNICITY OF CHILD	3.7%	96.3%	100.0%

the actual frequency counts for each group. By just comparing the raw numbers we would reach completely incorrect conclusions. See, for example, what we would get if we compared the raw numbers (frequency counts) for white, non-Hispanic and Hispanic children. In this case we would get the misleading finding that white, non-Hispanic children are over twice as likely to be suspended than Hispanic children (i.e. 69/29 = 2.38).

Second, while these figures raise important questions about the experiences of racial and ethnic minority children in American schools, we need to be mindful that we are dealing with very broad categories. There may, for example, be particular sub-groups within the "Black, Non-Hispanic" category that may actually be under-represented among those suspended from school compared to their white, non-Hispanic peers. Similarly, there may be some sub-groups within the Hispanic category who are much more likely to be suspended from school than their white, non-Hispanic counterparts. One of the interesting findings from this table is the percentage of "All Other Races" who are suspended from school. Those in this category are three times more likely to be suspended than their white, non-Hispanic peers. However, because this is a "catch-all" category, it is difficult to know which particular racial/ethnic groups contribute to this figure.

Perhaps the main point to draw out from this analysis is that quantitative research rarely provides definitive answers to anything. As in this case, it has played an important role in highlighting key trends but these trends need to be explored much further. Moreover, the figures tell us nothing about why certain groups are more likely to be suspended than others. To answer this we need to do further research to begin understanding some of the processes within and beyond school that lead to trends like this. This, in turn, requires us to study interactions between pupils, and also pupils and teachers, and to understand their experiences and perspectives. This is where qualitative research becomes important as an additional tool to help us develop a more comprehensive picture overall.

The third point relates to the calculation of percentages. In this case, the percentages sum to 100.0 percent in rows. If we take the first category—"White, Non-Hispanic"—then what this means is that 2.1 percent of white, non-Hispanic pupils have been suspended from school. Now, run the analysis again but this time select "Column Percentages" rather than row percentages. If you do this you should get the output shown in Output 3.3. Have a look at the results this time and spend some time comparing the percentages in this table with those in Output 3.2. As you will be able to see, the percentages now sum to 100.0 percent downwards in columns. The important point to make here is that, as a consequence, the percentages this time relate to the two "SESUSOUT" categories. Thus, the 31.9 percent you should get for white, non-Hispanic pupils in the "Yes" column now relates to the proportion of pupils who were suspended over the last year. In other words, we would interpret this as showing that 31.9 percent of all pupils receiving out-of-school suspensions over the last year were white, non-Hispanic (similarly, 43.5 percent were black, non-Hispanic and 13.4 percent were Hispanic). As you can see, these percentage figures are very different to those shown in Output 3.2. It is crucial, therefore, that you think very carefully about how you wish to calculate percentages.

A simple table like this contains all the information you need while also being simple to read and interpret. As such, it is debatable in this case as to whether there is a need to display the findings graphically. If you wanted to do so then the most appropriate method would be the use of a **clustered bar chart**. This is something you will be introduced to in the next section.

Output 3.3

D-DETAILED RACE-ETHNICITY OF CHILD * SE5-OUT-OF-SCHOOL SUSPENSION Crosstabulation

			SE5-OUT-OF-SCHOOL SUSPENSION		
			1 YES	2 NO	Total
D-DETAILED RACE-ETHNICITY OF CHILD	1 WHITE, NON-HISPANIC	Count	69	3268	3337
		% within SE5-OUT-OF-SCHOOL SUSPENSION	31.9%	58.3%	57.3%
	2 BLACK, NON-HISPANIC	Count	94	806	900
		% within SE5-OUT-OF-SCHOOL SUSPENSION	43.5%	14.4%	15.4%
	3 HISPANIC	Count	29	1057	1086
		% within SE5-OUT-OF-SCHOOL SUSPENSION	13.4%	18.8%	18.6%
	4 ASIAN OR PACIFIC ISLANDER	Count	3	155	158
		% within SE5-OUT-OF-SCHOOL SUSPENSION	1.4%	2.8%	2.7%
	5 ALL OTHER RACES	Count	21	324	345
		% within SE5-OUT-OF-SCHOOL SUSPENSION	9.7%	5.8%	5.9%
Total		Count	216	5610	5826
		% within SE5-OUT-OF-SCHOOL SUSPENSION	100.0%	100.0%	100.0%

EXERCISE 3.4

Use the **Crosstabs...** procedure to see whether there is a difference between boys and girls ("SEX") in relation to whether they have been suspended from school or not ("SESUSOUT"). Next, split the file by "RACEETHN" and run the analysis again. Check your method and findings on the companion website.

Analyzing the relationship between a nominal and an ordinal variable

For this second example, we will look at how to analyze the relationship between a nominal and an ordinal variable. To do this we will address the question:

Is there a difference in the school grades achieved by boys and girls in America?

To address this question we will stick with the **afterschools.sav** dataset. As before, we need to begin by identifying what the two variables are in this instance. Clearly, the sex of a child is one and their average school grades achieved is the other. From the dataset the two variables we could use would be "SEX" and "SEGRADES." The first is very straightforward and is a nominal variable coded into just two categories: "Male" and "Female." The second variable relates to the following question asked of parents/ guardians: "Now, I would like to ask you about [your child's] grades during this school year. Overall, across all subjects he/she takes at school, does he/she get mostly . . .". The respondent then has the choice of seven categories: "A's"; "B's"; "C's"; "D's"; "E's"; "F's"; and "The school does not give grades." This second variable is ordinal in the sense that while one can rank responses in order of grades achieved (i.e. gaining A's is better than B's, is better than C's and so on), we cannot be more precise than that. However, to make it ordinal we need to define the last category as missing ("6 NO LTR GRADES"). Do this before going any further. The comparisons we are then going to make are only for those pupils in schools that give grades.

Also, and as before, we need to consider the validity and reliability of these two measures. While "SEX" is straightforward, there are problems with the second variable, "SEGRADES." The problem is mainly to do with the fact that it relies upon the perceptions of parents/guardians. As such there are problems of reliability and validity here. In terms of reliability, a parent's perceptions of what grades their child is achieving may be different from the reality. Without being asked to provide specific information on each subject taken and the respective grades achieved, the answers here rely upon the ability of parents to accurately recall their child's grades and then to determine whether they were mostly A's or B's and so on. There is thus room for error here, especially as grade profiles may be fairly complex. In this latter case, there is more room for error as the parent/guardian is expected to translate a complex range of grades into a simple category.

Beyond this there is also the potential for bias as parents/guardians may either wish to over-emphasize the achievements of their own children or have a genuinely mistaken perception of their achievements. As regards the latter, consider the example of a child that took ten subjects and received four A's and six B's. In this case the parent may have been so taken by the four A's that this is what they recall during the interview and therefore choose "mostly A's" whereas strictly it should have been "mostly B's."

Finally, and beyond all of these questions concerning the reliability (or accuracy) of the measure used, there is the question of validity and whether this variable is a particularly useful measure of educational attainment. At best it is likely to give a rough sense of a child's level of attainment (reliability issues notwithstanding). However, it tells us nothing about how he or she has fared in relation to different subjects and thus lacks any detail as to their actual profile. Overall, however, "SEGRADES" is likely to provide us with some sense of any general tendencies regarding differential attainment between boys and girls. This in itself is fine so long as these limitations are recognized explicitly and thus any interpretations of the findings are made with suitable caution.

As these are both categorical variables, the most appropriate way to analyze the data is, again, by the use of a contingency table. As in the last example, because we are interested in comparing categories within the "SEX" variable (i.e. males and females), wherever we place this variable in the contingency table we need to ensure that percentages are calculated that way as well. While in principle we should put "SEX" in rows, this is an example where it would not be practical given that there are five categories for the other variable, which is too many to run across the top of a contingency table. Thus, when creating the contingency table, follow the same procedure as in the last example but put "SEX" in columns and "SEGRADES" in rows and ensure you ask SPSS to calculate column percentages. The output you should get from this is shown in Output 3.4.

As can be seen, girls would appear to be more likely to achieve mostly A's than boys (54.8 percent compared to 43.0 percent). Beyond this top grade, this is an example where cumulative percentages may be useful to compare achievement across the remaining categories. To gain cumulative frequencies you need to split the file by "SEX" as shown earlier in the chapter and then run a simple **Analyze → Descriptive Statistics → Frequencies...** analysis for the variable "SEGRADES." Try this and you should get the output shown in Output 3.5. As can be seen, the cumulative percentages allow us to now compare the achievements of boys and girls at any threshold we would like to set. For example, if we want to consider those achieving mostly B's or above, then we can see that while 79.3 percent of boys have achieved this, 87.7 percent of girls have.

These two frequency tables also illustrate more clearly the difference between the "Percent" and "Valid Percent" columns. As can be seen, the former is based upon percentages calculated on the whole sample, including any cases where data are defined as missing. While we should report the proportion of missing cases (32.3 percent for boys and 32.2 percent for girls), it is the percentages from the next column that we should generally use. These are the percentages calculated on cases for which there are data (i.e. excluding any missing data). They are also the percentages, as can be seen, upon which the cumulative percentages are calculated.

In terms of displaying the data, because we are dealing with two categorical variables, the most appropriate method to use, as with the last example, is the clustered bar chart. Moreover, in this present example it may be beneficial to use a chart to illustrate the key trends. To generate a clustered bar chart, choose **Graphs → Legacy Dialogs → Bar...**

Output 3.4

SE1–CHILD'S GRADES ACROSS ALL SUBJECTS * CHILD'S SEX Crosstabulation

			CHILD'S SEX		Total
			1 MALE	2 FEMALE	
SE1–CHILD'S GRADES ACROSS ALL SUBJECTS	1 MOSTLY A'S	Count	902	1064	1966
		% within CHILD'S SEX	43.0%	54.8%	48.7%
	2 MOSTLY B'S	Count	762	638	1400
		% within CHILD'S SEX	36.3%	32.9%	34.7%
	3 MOSTLY C'S	Count	344	193	537
		% within CHILD'S SEX	16.4%	9.9%	13.3%
	4 MOSTLY D'S	Count	63	28	91
		% within CHILD'S SEX	3.0%	1.4%	2.3%
	5 MOSTLY F'S	Count	29	17	46
		% within CHILD'S SEX	1.4%	.9%	1.1%
Total		Count	2100	1940	4040
		% within CHILD'S SEX	100.0%	100.0%	100.0%

Output 3.5

CHILD'S SEX = 1 MALE

SE1-CHILD'S GRADES ACROSS ALL SUBJECTS[a]

		Frequency	Percent	Valid Percent	Cumulative Percent
Valid	1 MOSTLY A'S	902	29.1	42.9	42.9
	2 MOSTLY B'S	762	24.6	36.3	79.3
	3 MOSTLY C'S	344	11.1	16.4	95.6
	4 MOSTLY D'S	63	2.0	3.0	98.6
	5 MOSTLY F'S	29	.9	1.4	100.0
	Total	2100	67.7	100.0	
Missing	-1 INAPPLICABLE	64	2.1		
	6 NO LTR GRADES	937	30.2		
	Total	1001	32.3		
Total		3101	100.0		

a. CHILD'S SEX = 1 MALE

CHILD'S SEX = 2 FEMALE

SE1-CHILD'S GRADES ACROSS ALL SUBJECTS[a]

		Frequency	Percent	Valid Percent	Cumulative Percent
Valid	1 MOSTLY A'S	1064	37.2	54.8	54.8
	2 MOSTLY B'S	638	22.3	32.9	87.7
	3 MOSTLY C'S	193	6.7	9.9	97.7
	4 MOSTLY D'S	28	1.0	1.5	99.1
	5 MOSTLY F'S	17	.6	.9	100.0
	Total	1940	67.8	100.0	
Missing	-1 INAPPLICABLE	73	2.6		
	6 NO LTR GRADES	847	29.6		
	Total	920	32.2		
Total		2860	100.0		

a. CHILD'S SEX = 2 FEMALE

(or just **Graphs → Bar. . .** in SPSS Version 14.0 and earlier and in Mac versions). This opens up an initial **Bar Charts** window, from which you should select "Clustered" and then click "Define." This will open up the **Define Clustered Bar Chart** window shown in Figure 3.6. Place "SEGRADES" in the "Category Axis:" field and "SEX" into the "Define Clusters by:" field as shown. In addition, and for reasons explained in relation to the last example, you must ensure that you are comparing percentages rather than actual frequency counts. As such, make sure you select one of the two options as shown. In this case we will run the procedure twice, to compare the results of both options.

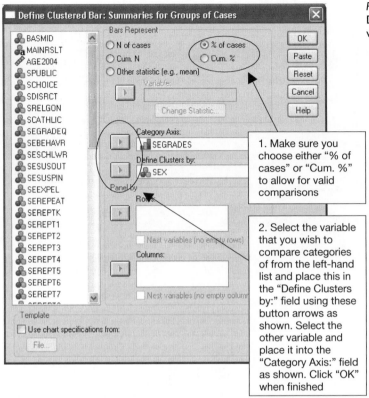

Figure 3.6
Define Clustered Bar
window in SPSS

1. Make sure you choose either "% of cases" or "Cum. %" to allow for valid comparisons

2. Select the variable that you wish to compare categories of from the left-hand list and place this in the "Define Clusters by:" field using these button arrows as shown. Select the other variable and place it into the "Category Axis:" field as shown. Click "OK" when finished

What you should get are the two clustered bar charts shown in Figure 3.7. You will notice that the layout of these two charts is slightly different to what you have obtained. There are ways of amending your charts in SPSS into the style you need. Explanations relating to how to do this are provided in the next chapter. For now if you look at the top chart you can see it is a basic clustered bar chart in that it compares the percentages of boys and girls in each category of "SEGRADES." This is probably the most common way of presenting data like these. However, another equally useful way when considering ordinal data can be seen in the bottom chart which displays cumulative percentages. This has the added value of being able to show gender differences at each threshold (i.e. those that achieved mostly B's or higher; those that achieved mostly C's or higher; and so on). What we can see at a glance using this chart is that gender differences are more pronounced at the highest thresholds and almost disappear at the threshold of mostly D's and below.

As before, in interpreting these findings we need to be cautious. While we can say that they demonstrate a general trend for girls to achieve higher grades than boys we need to acknowledge the limitations of the data in terms of its reliability and validity. In particular, we need to stress that these findings focus simply on overall grades across subjects and possibly mask important differences within subjects. Moreover, we must restrict ourselves to reporting the trends found. We should resist any temptation to hypothesize why these differences exist as we simply do not have the evidence to tell us. Again, we need to interview boys and girls directly to begin to find out their own experiences of, and perspectives on, schooling and what motivates them.

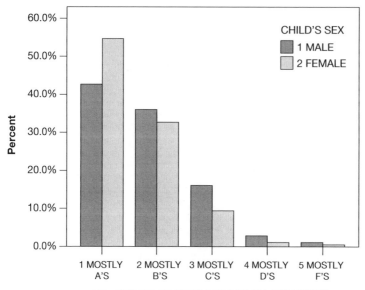

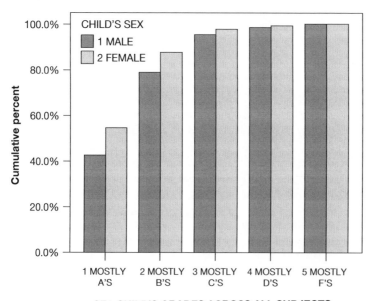

Figure 3.7 Two different ways of presenting gender differences in school grades achieved using a clustered bar chart

Analyzing the relationship between a nominal and a scale variable

For this third example, we will look at how to analyze the relationship between a nominal and a scale variable. To do this we will address the question:

> *Is there a difference in levels of attainment between school leavers from differing racial/ethnic backgrounds in England?*

There are two variables in this case—the race/ethnicity of the young person and their school-leaving attainment. To answer this question we will use the **youthcohort.sav** dataset which is based upon a survey of a large, random sample of school leavers in England (n = 13,201). This dataset is very unusual in that it includes detailed individual data on each pupil's performance in public examinations (GCSEs and their equivalents) at age 16 as well as background variables such as their racial/ethnic background, social class background and sex. Before doing anything else, open the dataset and weight the cases by the variable "s1weight."

Within this dataset there are two variables that we can use to address this question. The first is "ethsfr" that is a nominal variable and corresponds to the young person's racial/ethnic background and consists of seven substantive categories. Use the variable view short-cut button to have a look at this variable. The second variable is "gcsepts" that is a scale variable representing each young person's GCSE point score. These scores were calculated by giving points to each GCSE subject examination passed. The grades a person can achieve ranged from an A* (= 8 points), A (= 7 points), B (= 6 points) through to an F (= 2 points) and finally a G (= 1 point). While all of these grades are considered "passes", it is usual for colleges and employers to require grade C's or above. To create the final GCSE score for each young person, the points are all simply added together for all of the examinations they have passed in their final year of compulsory schooling. In addition, points are also calculated and added to the overall score for other qualifications achieved that are considered equivalent to GCSEs (such as vocational GNVQ qualifications).

When dealing with scale variables it is always important to begin by examining their nature and distribution. To do this run the **Analyze → Descriptive Statistics → Explore ...** procedure. If you use the "Options" button to select "histogram" then you will find the histogram shown in Figure 3.8 as part of your output. As can be seen, the distribution ranges from 0 and 117 points and broadly resembles a normal distribution, although one should note the disproportionate number of cases achieving "0"—a product of the "floor effect" (i.e. the fact that young people cannot get less than "0" and so there is likely to be some bunching right at the bottom).

Because of this, and to be on the cautious side, it is better to use the median and interquartile range as a summary of the distribution (although it would not be a real problem to use the mean and standard deviation given the overall shape of the distribution). In this case, and from the statistics produced through the explore procedure, we find that the average (median) is 44 points (IQR = 29). To examine and summarize the differences between racial/ethnic groups, you can use the Split File function to organize output by the variable "ethsfr" and then run the **Analyze → Descriptive Statistics → Explore...** function again. Having done this you can then take the relevant details and summarize them in a table similar to Table 3.1. As you can see, for each group we have provided the

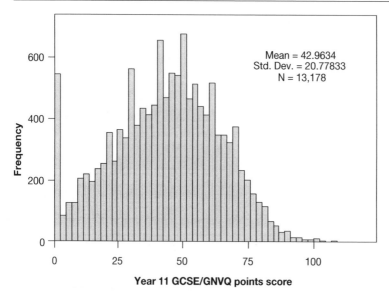

Figure 3.8 Histogram showing the distribution of GCSE point scores for the youthcohort.sav dataset

Table 3.1 Average GCSE point scores by racial/ethnic group for school leavers in England, 2003

Racial/ethnic group	Average (median)	Interquartile range	Minimum score	Maximum score
Other Asian (inc. Chinese)	53.2	36.3	0	107.0
Indian	52.0	23.0	0	105.0
White	44.5	29.0	0	117.0
Bangladeshi	40.0	34.2	0	91.5
Pakistani	35.0	30.5	0	94.5
Black	33.0	28.4	0	94.0

Source: Secondary analysis of data from the Youth Cohort Study of England and Wales, Cohort 12 (Sweep 1)

basic details in relation to their average (median), spread (IQR) and overall range (minimum and maximum scores). You should note that the categories have been placed in order (highest-achieving first) to help read the data and also that details of the source of the data are also included. This is all good practice in relation to setting out tabular data as will be covered in the next chapter.

Finally, this is definitely a case where the graphical display of the data would be useful. More specifically, even though we have included information on the spread of scores within each group, many readers will simply focus on the average (median) scores and compare groups in relation to this. While there is actually a substantial overlap between the scores in each group, this tends to be lost when we just provide summary statistics (see Connolly, 2006c). As a result we will often find crude generalizations being made from data like these such as "Chinese and Indian pupils achieve better than White pupils" and so forth. This may be true *on average* when looking at group-level data; however, stating it crudely in this way tends to give the impression that *all* Chinese and Indian pupils are performing better than *all* white pupils and so on.

To avoid this, therefore, it is always useful to display the differences with a chart. In this case as we are dealing with scale data and a number of different categories, the most appropriate way to display the data is with boxplots. To do this you should, first of all, reset **Split File**. You should then choose **Graphs** → **Legacy Dialogs** → **Boxplot. . .** (or just **Graphs** → **Boxplot. . .** in SPSS Version 14.0 and earlier and in Mac versions). An initial **Boxplot** window will open and you should select "Simple" and then click on the "Define" button. This opens the **Define Simple Boxplot** window shown in Figure 3.9. Select "gcsepts" from the list on the left and place in the "Variable:" field using the arrow button as shown. Also, select "ethsfr" and place in the "Category Axis:" field as shown before clicking "OK" to finish. This will produce the output shown in Figure 3.10.

As you will see, the chart shown in Figure 3.10 will be different to the one you initially obtain from SPSS. Again, all I have done is edit the chart to get it into this format. How to do this will be covered in the next chapter. Overall, this is a good example of the need to display data. There are differences in the average attainment between racial/ ethnic groups as evident when comparing the median lines for each boxplot. Therefore, it is clearly something of concern and in need of further investigation. However, the overlapping of the distributions for each group should help us to avoid type-casting whole groups by the use of terms such as "black underachievement" (Troyna, 1984; Connolly, 2006c). As can be seen, while the average attainment of black pupils is a cause for concern, there is a wide range of scores within that group with some black pupils achieving at a high level. Displaying data in this way, therefore, helps us to identify underlying patterns and trends in the data clearly without having to paint crude and simplistic pictures.

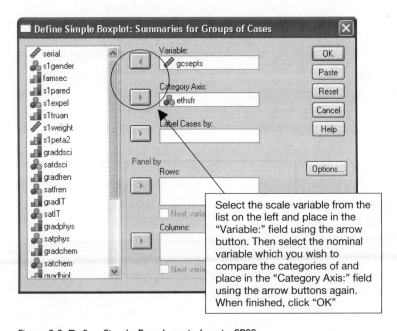

Figure 3.9 Define Simple Boxplot window in SPSS

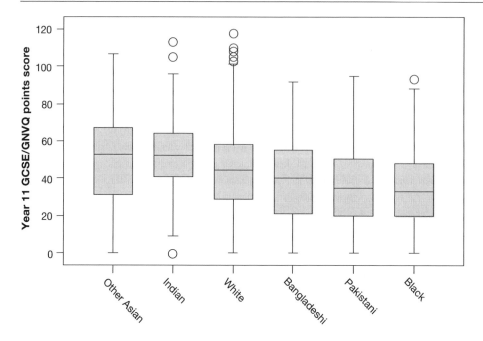

Figure 3.10 Racial/ethnic differences in the GCSE scores obtained by Year 11 pupils in England in 2002

The final issue to note, once again, is the issue of validity; not just in terms of the use of GCSE point scores as a measure of attainment, but also in terms of the racial/ethnic categories used. In this particular case, a significant degree of caution should be noted in relation to the category "Black" as this encompasses Black African and Black Caribbean pupils even though the evidence suggests that there are clear differences between these two groups (Gillborn and Mirza, 2000).

EXERCISE 3.5

Use the split file procedure (split by "s1gender") and then calculate the mean GCSE scores ("gcsepts") for boys and girls. Is there a difference? Have a look at the standard deviations for both mean scores. What does this tell you? Finally, have a go at creating a population pyramid (**Graphs → Legacy Dialogs → Population Pyramid. . .**) showing the distribution of GCSE scores between boys and girls (put "gcsepts" into the "Show Distribution Over:" field and "s1gender" into the "Split by:" field). What does the chart tell you? Check your method and findings on the companion website.

Analyzing the relationship between two ordinal variables

This fourth example focuses on how to analyze relationships between two ordinal variables. An example of a question we might ask involving two ordinal variables is:

Is there a relationship between the school grades achieved by a child and the highest level of educational qualifications gained by their mothers in America?

This question involves two variables: the child's school grades and also the highest educational qualifications achieved by the mother. To answer this question we will return to the **afterschools.sav** dataset. We have already come across one of the variables we will use for this—"SEGRADES"—which is an ordinal measure and provides some indication of the child's school grades. For the other variable we will use "MOMGRADE" which is also ordinal and records the highest level of educational qualifications achieved by the mother. Both variables and how they are coded are shown in Box 3.2.

As both variables are categorical, the main ways in which we can present the data appropriately are through a contingency table and/or a clustered bar chart. One immediate

---

Box 3.2 Details of the variables "SEGRADES" and "MOMGRADE" from the afterschools.sav dataset

Variable Name:	'SEGRADES'	'MOMGRADE'
Variable Label:	School grades that the child achieved during the current school year	Highest grade or year of school that the child's mother completed

Categories:	1 = Mostly A's
	2 = Mostly B's
	3 = Mostly C's
	4 = Mostly D's
	5 = Mostly F's
	6 = School does not give grades
	------------- 	
	-9 = Not ascertained
	-8 = Don't know
	-7 = Refused to answer
	-1 = Inapplicable
		1 = Up to 8th grade
		2 = 9th to 11th grade
		3 = 12th grade but no diploma
		4 = High school diploma/equivalent
		5 = Voc/tech program after high school
		     but no voc/tech diploma
		6 = Voc/tech dipoma after high school
		7 = Some college but no degree
		8 = Associate's degree (AA, AS)
		9 = Bachelor's degree (BA, BS)
		10 = Graduate or professional school but
		     no degree
		11 = Master's degree (MA, MS)
		12 = Doctorate degree (PhD, EdD)
		13 = Professional degree beyond
		     bachelor's degree (medicine/MD;
		     dentistry/DDS; law/JD/LLB; etc.)
		---------------- 	
		-9 = Not ascertained
		-8 = Don't know
		-7 = Refused to answer
		-1 = Inapplicable

problem here, however, is simply the number of categories involved. In order to make either of these options meaningful in terms of displaying the data in a report it is therefore necessary to conflate the categories for both variables in order to illustrate any key trends that may be apparent. In this case, therefore, we need to create two new variables by using the **Transform → Recode → Into Different Variables. . .** procedure introduced earlier. We will conflate both variables into just three categories. For "SEGRADES" the categories for the new variable (call it "SEGRD2") will be:

- Mostly A's (i.e. recode 1 → 1)
- Mostly B's (i.e. recode 2 → 2)
- Mostly C's or below (i.e. recode 3 thru 5 → 3)
- Recode "6" as "missing" so it is not included in the analysis
- Recode "All other values" → "Copy old value(s)"

We need to remove "6" from the analysis as this category is for children whose schools do not give grades. If we left it in the analysis and coded as "6" then this would imply that any pupil in this category achieved less well than those gaining "Mostly F's" which is not true. The problem is we do not know how children in this category performed and so we need to exclude them from the analysis.

For "MOMGRADE" the categories for the new variable (call it "MOMGRD2") will be:

- "Up to and including high school diploma" (i.e. recode 1 thru 4 → 1)
- "Post-school programs up to and including Bachelor's degree" (i.e. recode 5 thru 9 → 2)
- "Master's degree or higher" (i.e. recode 10 thru 13 → 3)
- Recode "All other values" → "Copy old value(s)"

Have a go at recoding these two variables and do not forget to add the labels to each of the new categories you created. Once you have done this you can create a contingency table. In this case we are interested in looking at whether the children's grades differed for mothers who reached different grades. As such we will be comparing different categories within the new "MOMGRD2" variable. With this in mind place "MOMGRD2" into rows and "SEGRD2" into columns and select "Row Percentages." You should get the contingency table shown in Output 3.6. The findings certainly suggest that there is a relationship between the level of education reached by mothers and their children's school grades. As can be seen, for mothers whose highest level of achievement was a high school diploma the proportion of their children achieving mainly A grades at school was 37.2 percent; this compares with 69.0 percent for those mothers who achieved a Master's degree or higher.

Fortunately, when analyzing two ordinal variables like this there is a procedure for gaining a more precise measure of the strength of the relationship between them. This measure is called a correlation coefficient. A correlation coefficient will always take a value between 0 and 1 (or –1). If the value is 0 this means there is no relationship at all between the two ordinal variables. If it is 1 (or –1) then it means there is a perfect relationship (or correlation) between the two variables. The only other thing to note beyond this is that if the correlation coefficient is positive then this indicates that a "positive

Output 3.6

Mother's Highest Grade Achieved * Child's School Grades Crosstabulation

			Child's School Grades			
			Mostly A's	Mostly B's	Mostly C's or Below	Total
Mother's Highest Grade Achieved	Up to and including high school diploma	Count	600	635	379	1614
		% within Mother's Highest Grade Achieved	37.2%	39.3%	23.5%	100.0%
	Post-school programs up to and including bachelor's degree	Count	1023	607	235	1865
		% within Mother's Highest Grade Achieved	54.9%	32.5%	12.6%	100.0%
	Master's degree or higher	Count	265	96	23	384
		% within Mother's Highest Grade Achieved	69.0%	25.0%	6.0%	100.0%
Total		Count	1888	1338	637	3863
		% within Mother's Highest Grade Achieved	48.9%	34.6%	16.5%	100.0%

correlation" exists such that increases in the values of one ordinal variable are associated with increases in the values of the other ordinal variable. In contrast, if the value of the correlation coefficient is negative then this means that a "negative correlation" exists. In this later case this would mean a tendency exists such that an increase in the values of one ordinal variable are actually associated with a decrease in the values of the other ordinal variable.

Do not worry if this sounds a little confusing—it will all make sense now as we look at some examples. To start with, let us calculate the correlation coefficient between the two original variables "MOMGRADE" and "SEGRADES." Before you do this you need to re-define "6" as a missing value in Variable View for "SEGRADES" to ensure it is removed from the analysis for reasons explained earlier. Once done, choose **Analyze →** **Correlate → Bivariate. . . .** This opens the **Bivariate Correlations** window shown in Figure 3.11. All you need to do is to select both variables in turn and place them into the "Variables:" field as shown before, clicking "OK" to finish. This will produce the output shown in Output 3.7.

As can be seen, a negative correlation exists (reported as $r_s = -0.240$) between the highest grade completed by mothers and their children's school grades. This may seem contradictory at first but it is not once you look again at Box 3.2 and how the two variables have been coded. It will be remembered that a negative correlation means that increases in values for one ordinal variable are associated with decreases in values for another (or, to put it as plainly as possible, as one variable goes up the other goes down). With this in mind look at how the two variables have been coded. For "MOMGRADE" higher values represent higher levels of education completed (ranging from 1 for "up to 8th grade" up to 13 for "professional degree"). By contrast, higher values for "SEGRADES" are actually associated with lower school grades (ranging from 1 for mostly A's up to 5 for mostly F's). As such, a negative correlation makes absolute sense—as the values for "MOMGRADE"

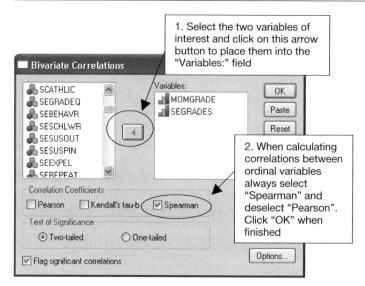

1. Select the two variables of interest and click on this arrow button to place them into the "Variables:" field

2. When calculating correlations between ordinal variables always select "Spearman" and deselect "Pearson". Click "OK" when finished

Figure 3.11
Bivariate Correlations window in SPSS

Output 3.7

Correlations

			SE1-CHILD'S GRADES ACROSS ALL SUBJECTS	PU6-HIGHEST GRADE/YR MOM COMPLETED
Spearman's rho	SE1-CHILD'S GRADES ACROSS ALL SUBJECTS	Correlation Coefficient	1.000	−.240**
		Sig. (2-tailed)	.	.000
		N	3029	2893
	PU6-HIGHEST GRADE/YR MOM COMPLETED	Correlation Coefficient	−.240**	1.000
		Sig. (2-tailed)	.000	.
		N	2893	4418

**Correlation is significant at the 0.01 level (2-tailed).

go up (i.e. as the level of education completed goes up for the mother) the values for "SEGRADES" goes down (i.e. the school grades achieved by children goes up).

This will take a little time for you to get used to. However, it shows you the importance of coding ordinal variables properly in the first place. It is actually always better to give higher values to those categories considered to be "most of" whatever you are interested in. In this case, "MOMGRADE" is correctly coded because increases in values represent increases in levels of education completed. However, it would have been better to have coded "SEGRADES" the other way around (i.e. 1 = "Mostly F's"; 2 = "Mostly D's"; 3 = "Mostly C's"; and so on). This would then mean that increases in the values for this variable would reflect increases in the school grades attained. Doing this would then give us a positive correlation that would make more intuitive sense.

There are four points to draw out from this example. The first follows on from the above discussion and relates to the importance of checking how variables are coded before running a correlational analysis. This is important, not only to remove any categories that are not part of the rank order for that variable but also to help you interpret the correlation coefficient to be produced. In this present case, while we obtained a negative correlation this was only because of the way the ordinal variables were coded. When reporting the result it would make more sense to turn it into, and report it as, a positive correlation, as most people will interpret a negative correlation as implying that higher educational levels completed by the mother are associated with lower school grades among their children.

The second point relates to how you should actually interpret the values of the correlation coefficient (i.e. 0.240). Many textbooks provide a rule of thumb along the lines of:

- A correlation coefficient between 0 and 0.3 = "weak"
- A correlation coefficient higher than 0.3 and up to 0.6 = "moderate"
- A correlation coefficient above 0.6 = "strong"

Of course, the same would be true if the coefficients were all negative as well. In this present example, therefore, we would describe the relationship between the educational level completed by the mother and her child's school grades achieved as being "weak." Personally, I find this to be a little too formulaic, however. A better way to interpret a correlation coefficient is to multiply it by itself and then by 100. This gives you the percentage of variation that the two variables share in common. In this present example we would therefore multiply 0.240 by itself (i.e. $0.240 \times 0.240 = 0.0576$) and then multiply this by 100 (i.e. $0.0576 \times 100 = 5.76$). This would tell us that the two variables only share 5.76 percent of their variation in common. As such there is a relationship there but it is very weak and leaves just over 94 percent of the variation found in the two variables unexplained. Overall, while it is fine to use the rule of thumb outlined above it is always good practice to convert the correlation coefficient into the actual percentage of variation explained. If nothing else, it will help to prevent you from over-claiming the strength of a correlation between two variables.

The third point is that while you have found a correlation between these two variables (albeit a pretty weak one), this does not tell you anything about the nature of that relationship. You cannot interpret this, for example, as implying that a mother's level of education completed is the cause of a child's school grades. For one thing, even if this was the case then the correlation coefficient would suggest that the mother's level of education completed could actually only explain less than 6 percent of the variation in children's school grades—hardly an important factor. However, without any further information we simply do not know what the nature of this relationship is. It may be a simple causal relationship (i.e. mother's education having a direct influence on the child's school grades). However, it could be that these two variables are not actually directly related at all. For example, there could be a third variable—such as the level of poverty within the local community—that influences both. Thus, increasing levels of poverty could result in lower levels of education completed by mothers and could also result in lower school grades achieved by children. In this sense mother's level of education completed will be correlated with children's school grades, however, this is not because there is a direct relationship between the two. Rather, it is that they are both influenced by a third variable (in this case the level of poverty within the local community). Of course, life is often much more complex than this, which is why we should never interpret any correlations we find as evidence of a causal relationship.

The fourth and final point to stress from this example is that the strength of the correlation found between the two variables is partly a result of the quality of the two variables used. For example, because both measures are fairly crude indicators of the levels of educational attainment achieved by mothers and children, this will have an effect on the strength of the correlation found. As such, it may be that there is a much stronger correlation between a mother's educational attainment and her child's. However, we have simply been unable to measure it properly given the crude variables at our disposal. To illustrate this, calculate the correlation coefficient between the two new variables you created for the last example ("MOMGRD2" and "SEGRD2"). You will remember that these variables are conflated versions of the "MOMGRADE" and "SEGRADES" and thus are likely to be even poorer measures of the mother's and child's educational attainment. If you do this you will see that the correlation coefficient has now gone down slightly (from 0.240 to 0.234). To be honest this is a little surprising as I would have expected it to fall more than this. However, it possibly demonstrates just how poor the original measures were. Either way, the general point still holds— that any effects found between variables are partly the result of the quality of the measures used. This is an important point to remember and will be returned to in later chapters.

EXERCISE 3.6

Run another correlational analysis to see what the relationship is between a child's school grades ("SEGRADES") and their father's highest educational qualifications achieved ("DADGRADE"). Is this relationship stronger or weaker than the one between the child's grades and the mother's educational qualifications? Also, is there a correlation between the highest qualifications achieved by mothers and fathers? Check your method and findings on the companion website.

Analyzing the relationship between an ordinal and a scale variable

This penultimate example focuses on analyzing the relationship between an ordinal and scale variable. To illustrate how to do this we will use the following example:

Is there a relationship between levels of truancy from school and educational attainment in England?

To answer this question we will turn back to the **youthcohort.sav** dataset. There are two variables relating to this question: levels of truancy from school and educational attainment. For the latter we will use the scale variable "gcsepts" that we met earlier in the chapter and which provides the GCSE score each young person attained in public examinations at the end of compulsory schooling. For the other variable we will use "s1truan" which is an ordinal measure of levels of truancy from school by those in the sample during their last year at school. It comprises three categories: "Persistent truancy"; "Occasional truancy"; and "No truancy." To examine and illustrate the nature of the relationship we can generate a boxplot just as done previously with the **Graphs → Legacy Dialogs → Boxplot. . .** procedure (or **Graphs → Boxplot. . .** in SPSS Version 14.0 and earlier and in Mac versions). Before you begin make sure you weight the data with "s1weight." Once you have done this follow the procedure to create boxplots as before (see Figure 3.9) but this time place the scale variable "gcsepts" into the "Variable:" field and the categorical variable "s1truan" into the "Category Axis:" field. With a little bit of tidying up you should get the boxplot shown in Figure 3.12. As can be seen, there would appear to be a definite relationship with higher rates of truancy being associated with lower GCSE point scores.

To obtain a more detailed appreciation of the strength of this relationship we can just calculate a correlation coefficient as before. Because one of our variables is ordinal we need to calculate the Spearman correlation coefficient. Try doing this—you should get a correlation coefficient of $r_s = 0.312$. As before, with a little calculation this can be interpreted as showing that the two variables only share 9.7 percent of their variation in common ($0.312 \times 0.312 \times 100 = 9.7$). This is not too surprising given the boxplot shown in Figure 3.12. As can be seen, for each level of truancy there remains a relatively large range of GCSE point scores attained by respondents.

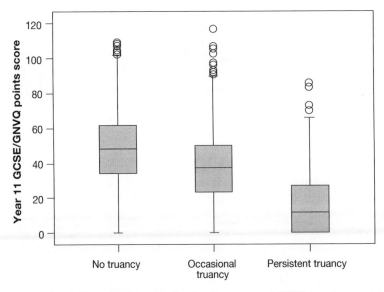

Figure 3.12 Relationship between levels of truancy and GCSE scores among Year 11 pupils in England in 2002

Analyzing the relationship between two scale variables

The only combination of variables we have yet to consider how to analyze is the relationship between two scale variables. To illustrate how to do this we will use a few examples, beginning with the **international.sav** dataset you created in Chapter 1. In relation to this dataset we will ask two questions:

> Is there a relationship between school life expectancy (i.e. the expected number of years a child is expected to attend school on average) and levels of male illiteracy for the 20 developing countries?

> Is there a relationship between male and female illiteracy rates for the 20 developing countries?

There are three variables arising from these three questions: school life expectancy ("lifeexpt"), male illiteracy ("m_illit") and female illiteracy ("f_illit"). The validity and reliability of these measures is discussed in detail on the UN Statistics Division website (see: http://unstats.un.org). To answer these two questions we need to start by examining the data with a scatterplot. You have already been shown this procedure in Chapter 1 (see Figure 1.20). When choosing which variable to put onto which axis, the general rule is that if there is reason to think that one variable is likely to have an influence on the other then you put that variable on the "x-axis" (i.e. the horizontal axis) and the variable it is thought to influence on the "y-axis" (i.e. the vertical axis). In relation to the first question above, the relationship is clearly one whereby school life expectancy is likely to influence male illiteracy (rather than the other way round). As such "lifeexpt" goes onto the "x-axis" and "m_illit" on the "y-axis." For the second question, however, there is no obvious direction of influence between male and female illiteracy and so it does not matter which axis each variable is placed on.

Following the procedures shown previously (Figure 1.20), generate these first two scatterplots. You should get those shown in Figure 3.13. As can be seen there appears to be a strong relationship with both. More specifically, there is a negative correlation for the first chart (i.e. increases in school life expectancy are associated with reductions in male illiteracy rates) as we would expect. Similarly, there is a strong positive correlation for the second chart such that increases in male illiteracy rates are strongly associated with increases in female illiteracy rates.

To calculate the strength of the correlation we simply run the **Analyze → Correlate → Bivariate. . .** procedure you are already familiar with. However, this time as both pairs of variables are scale you should calculate the Pearson correlation coefficient rather than Spearman. However, to gain a valid measure of the relationship between the two variables it is important that the relationship is linear (i.e. that the dots tend to form a straight line). In both of these first two cases the scatterplot confirms this and so it is appropriate to proceed and calculate the Pearson correlation coefficient for each; try doing this. You should find that the correlation coefficient between school life expectancy and male illiteracy is –0.893 (i.e. the two variables share 79.7 percent of their variation in common) and the correlation between male and female illiteracy rates is 0.974 (i.e. the two variables share 94.9 percent of their variation in common).

For another example open the **valueadded.sav** dataset. This is a dataset that Gorard (2006a) has recently used to raise questions about the efficacy of using value added

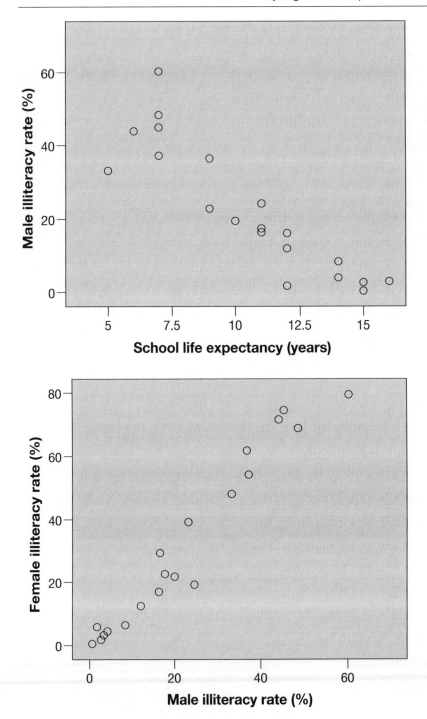

Figure 3.13 Relationships between male and female illiteracy rates and between male illiteracy rates and school life expectancy in 20 countries

measures for school performance. The data are taken from the Department for Education and Skills website (DfES, 2005a) which holds performance data for most schools in England. It certainly provides an example of how easy it can be to access secondary quantitative data for analysis (Gorard, 2001). The data included in **valueadded.sav** simply reflect the data Gorard used originally for his analysis and consist of two school performance measures for 124 schools selected from four local education authority areas in the north of England. The first of the two measures (see the variable "gcse") consists simply of the percentage of pupils at that school that gained five or more GCSEs Grades A*–C. GCSEs in the UK are the main public examinations that pupils take when they reach the end of compulsory education. This particular measure (sometimes called the "GCSE Benchmark") has become a very popular measure of school performance and for some years has provided the main method for compiling school league tables.

The second measure ("score") is a "value added" measure of school performance that has been calculated by the DfES in order to take into account pupils' prior attainment. One of the problems of using the GCSE Benchmark measure is that it simply focuses on the end-of-school achievements of pupils. It is therefore not possible to determine whether a high score on this measure is due to the efforts of the school in increasing achievement levels or is simply due to the nature of the school intake (i.e. comprising pupils with already high levels of prior attainment). The idea of the value added score is, therefore, to provide a measure of the relative progress made by pupils in relation to educational achievement at any particular school, taking into account their prior attainment. In theory, therefore, it should provide a more valid measure of the effects of the school itself in raising performance, once the nature of the school's intake is controlled for.

The actual details regarding how the value added measure is calculated are provided elsewhere (see DfES, 2005b) and need not concern us here. Rather, the point of interest is Gorard's (2006a) use of a scatterplot to examine the relationship between the two measures of educational performance. Try generating a simple scatterplot yourself using the **valueadded.sav** dataset. If you place the GCSE Benchmark ("gcse") on the x-axis and the value added measure ("score") on the y-axis then you should obtain the scatterplot shown in Figure 3.14 which replicates the one Gorard (2006a: 53) produced.

It can be seen that the two measures are actually highly correlated with $r_p = 0.907$. In fact, SPSS tends to report the R^2 ("r squared") value for the correlation by default. As can be seen, $R^2 = 0.822$ which, if multiplied by 100 gives us the percentage of variance shared between the two measures (i.e. 82.2 percent). The key point Gorard makes from this is that the two variables are actually measuring the same thing and that any unexplained variation is simply due to measurement errors as well as weaknesses in the two measures used. As he argues:

> Given that the assessment system in England is not wholly reliable, and that no data collection, transcription, aggregation or analysis process is wholly accurate, this strong relationship between the DfES value-added figures and the raw-scores of absolute attainment suggests that they are both actually measuring the same thing.
>
> (Gorard, 2006a: 53)

For Gorard, this shows that the value added measure is "largely meaningless" (p. 50) and has no more credibility as a measure of school performance than the crude, and widely discredited, GCSE Benchmark. While this is certainly an interesting and fairly persuasive

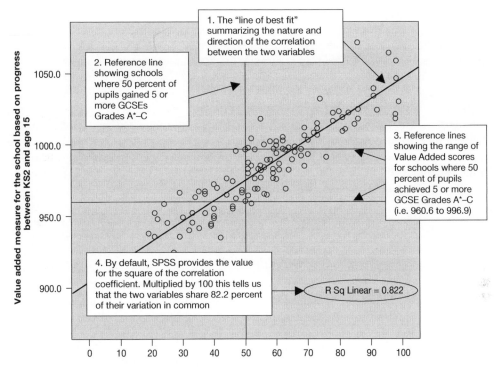

Figure 3.14 The relationship between the simple measure of school performance taken by the percentage of pupils gaining five or more GCSE grades A*–C and the more complex value added measure of school performance

argument it is worth reflecting a little more on the strength of the correlation between the two variables and asking whether they do actually measure the same thing. As explained, while they are strongly related there remains a little under a fifth of the variation between the two measures that is unaccounted for. This variation can be illustrated by Figure 3.14. As can be seen, a vertical reference line has been added along which schools where 50 percent of pupils achieved the GCSE Benchmark are located. If we now look along that line we see two schools that actually lie on it. If we now use the horizontal reference lines we can read off their value added scores. As can be seen, while they both have the same score for the GCSE Benchmark their value added scores vary from 960.6 to 996.9. In fact, we would get similar results in terms of this level of variation wherever we drew the vertical reference line.

This is actually the 17.8 percent of "unexplained variation" that exists. Thus while the GCSE Benchmark is a good predictor of the value added scores (being able to account for 82.2 percent of its variation) there is still a small but significant level of variation in value added scores that does not relate to the GCSE Benchmark. Whether this can all be explained by measurement errors is debatable given that we are dealing here with composite scores for schools, and thus much of this measurement error will be cancelled out when you calculate averages for the school as a whole. Either way, it is certainly an interesting debate and one that illustrates very well the use of scatterplots and correlations to assess the relationship between two scale variables.

More generally, one final point to note about the Pearson correlation coefficient is that it only gives a valid measure of the strength of the association between two variables if the relationship between them is linear. This has been the case in all three examples discussed above. It can be confirmed through the use of scatterplots which, as we have seen, all suggest a linear (i.e. straight-line) relationship between the different pairs of variables concerned. As shown in Figure 3.14 it is actually possible to ask SPSS to add in what is called a "line of best fit" to see how well the data conforms to a linear relationship. The position of this line of best fit is actually calculated mathematically so that it is as close as possible to the cases plotted.

However, the problem is that we will not always find that the relationship between two scale variables is linear. We can see this in relation to the final example we will consider from the **international.sav** dataset. In this case the question is:

> *Is there a relationship between per capita GDP and female illiteracy rates for the 20 developing countries?*

As before, we should start by exploring the nature of the relationship between the two variables by way of a scatterplot. This gives us the scatterplot shown in Figure 3.15. As can be seen, while there would appear to be a strong relationship it is clearly not a linear one. In this case the "line of best fit" would be likely to be curvilinear. Now, it is still quite possible to calculate a Pearson correlation coefficient for these two variables. Try it yourself, you should get $r_p = -0.448$. At one level this feels intuitively right in that it is a negative correlation suggesting that as the wealth of a country increases (i.e. its per capita

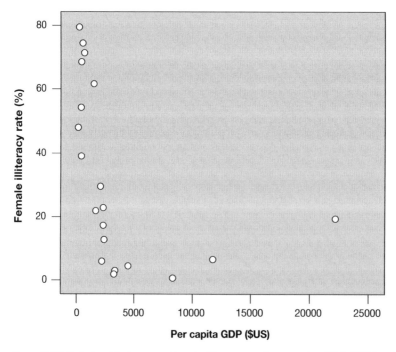

Figure 3.15 Relationship between female illiteracy and per capita GDP (US$) in 20 countries

GDP), the rates of female illiteracy decrease. However, the correlation coefficient this time suggests that there is only a moderate relationship; indicating, in fact, that the two variables only share 20 percent of their variation in common. Looking again at the scatterplot in Figure 3.15 this seems to be underestimating the strength of the relationship.

The problem here is that the Pearson correlation coefficient is calculated on the assumption that the relationship between the two variables is linear. What is happening here is that if we try to add a straight "line of best fit" then however it is placed it will not fit the data well. As such, the correlation coefficient will underestimate the strength of the association between the two variables. Rather, what we would actually need to fit is a curved line. Unfortunately, this does start to get complicated and is beyond the scope of this book. For our purposes it is also unnecessary because there is a simpler solution— when the relationship is not linear we simply calculate the Spearman correlation coefficient instead. Try doing this for the present data. What you should find is that you now obtain a much stronger correlation coefficient, $r_s = -0.818$. While confirming the fact that it is a negative correlation it also gives a better estimate of the strength of the association between the two variables (in this case the coefficient suggests that the two variables share 66.9 percent of their variation in common).

EXERCISE 3.7

Visit the United Nations Statistics Division website (www.unstats.un.org) that you first encountered in Chapter 1 (see Exercise 1.2). Have a look at other country indicators and select one or two to add to the **international.sav** dataset for the 20 countries listed. Examine the relationships between these new variables and the existing ones. Can you find a variable that is more strongly associated with female illiteracy rates than per capita GDP? Check out the answer to this question on the companion website.

Analyzing trends over time

Finally, one common form of analysis in education that is worth briefly covering in this chapter is that associated with examining statistical trends over time. Perhaps the most obvious example of this, which has attracted significant media and political interest in the UK over recent years, has been that associated with gender differences in achievement in public examinations at the end of compulsory schooling (Year 11). The tendency within this has been to report and compare the proportions of boys and girls gaining five or more good passes (grades A*–C) in GCSE examinations or their equivalent. In this section we will use the **timeseries.sav** dataset which includes data on the percentages of boys and girls in England gaining five or more good GCSE passes (or their equivalents)—in other words the GCSE Benchmark discussed earlier—over a 30-year period from 1974/5 through to 2004/5.

With this dataset we will first look at how we can effectively display trends over time using line graphs in SPSS, and then we will examine the more thorny problem of how precisely we can measure and compare the size of any differences between boys and girls over time.

Displaying trends over time

First of all, open the **timeseries.sav** dataset and have a look at it. You will see that each row represents a year and the dataset consists of four variables: the year; the percentage of girls gaining five or more good passes; the percentage of boys gaining the same; and then the total percentage of pupils gaining five or more good passes. We will first of all take this last variable—the total percentage of pupils gaining five or more good passes— to create a diagram to look at how overall performance in public examinations has progressed over the last 30 years. To do this, choose **Graphs → Legacy Dialogs → Line** ... (or just **Graphs → Line. . .** in SPSS Version 14.0 and earlier and in Mac versions). This opens an initial **Line Charts** window and you should select "Simple" and ensure that "Summaries for groups of cases" is also selected and then click "Define." This brings up the window shown in Figure 3.16. Here we wish our trend line to represent the total proportion of pupils gaining five or more good passes and so you need to select "Other statistic" for "Line Represents:" as shown and then click on the variable "total" and place it into the "Variable:" field with the arrow button as shown. You should then select the variable "year" and place this in the "Category Axis:" field before completing the procedure by clicking "OK." This produces the line chart shown in Figure 3.17.

As can be seen, there has been a steady, year-on-year rise in the proportions of pupils gaining five good examination passes since the mid-1970s. The next question is whether there are any differences in relation to this overall trend between boys and girls. To

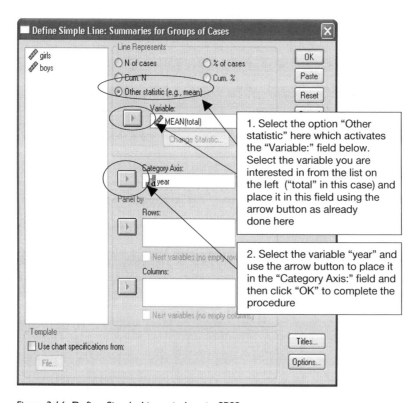

Figure 3.16 Define Simple Line window in SPSS

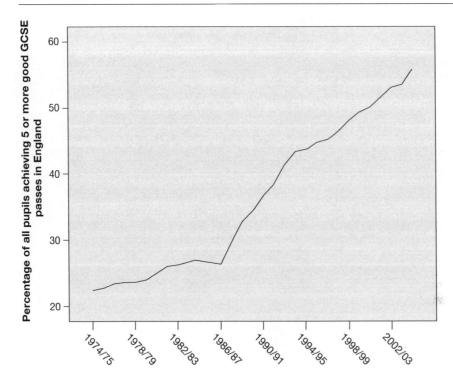

Figure 3.17 Percentage of Year 11 pupils in England achieving five or more GCSE grades A*–C
(or their equivalent) between 1974/5 and 2003/4

ascertain this we can generate a new line chart but this time with separate lines for boys
and girls. To do this we begin with the same procedure as before: **Graphs** → **Legacy
Dialogs** → **Line. . .** but this time in the initial **Line Charts** window that appears we select
"Multiple" and also, because we are comparing two variables this time, "Summaries of
separate variables." When you click the "Define" button the **Define Multiple Line**
window opens as shown in Figure 3.18. This time, place the variables "boys" and "girls"
into the "Lines Represent:" field and then place "years" into the "Category Axis:" field
as shown. Once you click "OK" you will obtain the line diagram shown in Figure 3.19.

Calculating and comparing differences between groups over time

From Figure 3.19 there would certainly seem to be an increasing "gender gap" in
educational achievement opening up; one that appears to have begun in the mid-1980s and
has grown larger year by year. This conclusion is drawn simply by analyzing the size of
the vertical gap between the two lines. What we are doing here, in effect, is using the
percentage point difference between the percentages of boys and girls gaining five or
more GCSE Grades A*–C in any one year as the measure of difference. Thus in1984/85,
27.4 percent of girls and 26.3 percent of boys achieved the relevant standard, representing
a percentage point difference of 1.1 (i.e. 27.4 – 26.3). However, just ten years later in

Figure 3.18
Define Multiple Line
window in SPSS

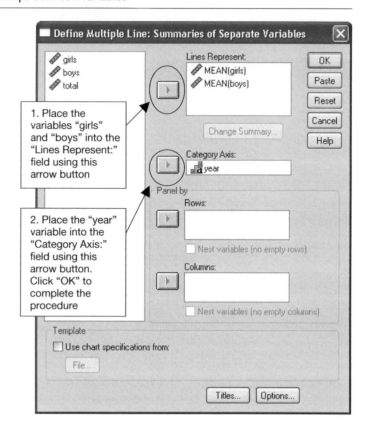

1994/95, 48.1 percent of girls and 39 percent of boys were reaching the same standard, a percentage point difference now of 9.1.

Such calculations, based on percentage point differences, tend to be those used by politicians and the media when reporting and comparing gender differences (and indeed any other differences that may be considered between two groups) over time. The problem is that such comparisons can be misleading as they take no account of the actual proportions of boys and girls involved at any one point. This has been a point argued strongly by Gorard. As he explains:

> A percentage point difference of 10 would represent an enormous gap in a year in which five per cent of boys and 15 per cent of girls reached the benchmark, but it would be much less in a year where 85 per cent of boys and 95 per cent of girls did so. To consider the 10 percentage point difference to be constant over time . . . is to commit the politician's error.

(Gorard, 1999: 239–240)

To understand why there is apparently a difference between the two scenarios Gorard refers to, he suggests that one needs to examine the data proportionately; in this case by comparing the ratios of the proportions of boys to girls in the two cases. In the former case it can be seen that girls are three times as likely to reach the benchmark than boys (i.e. $15 \div 5 = 3$) whereas, in the latter case, girls are only marginally more likely (i.e. $95 \div 85 = 1.118$ times more likely). It is precisely for this reason that Gorard argues that one cannot

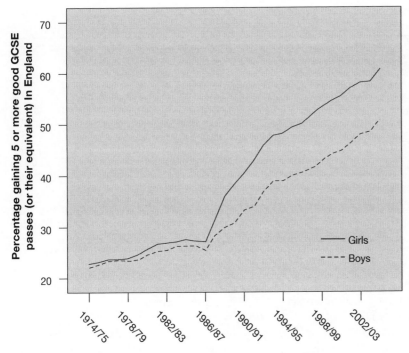

Figure 3.19 Percentage of Year 11 pupils in England achieving five or more GCSE grades A*–C (or their equivalent) between 1974/5 and 2003/4 by sex

simply compare the percentage point gap between years as if it is constant over time but, rather, one needs to analyze the data proportionately.

There are many ways in which data such as these in the current **timeseries.sav** dataset can be analyzed proportionately (i.e. deriving measures of the difference between boys and girls that take account of the actual size of the proportions of the two groups involved). Unfortunately, there is some disagreement over the reliability of some of these methods (see Connolly, 2006a, 2006b; Gorard, 2006b). One method that is generally agreed, however, and that will be explained here involves calculating the cross-product ratio (also known as the odds ratio).

Unfortunately, SPSS does not calculate the cross-product ratio directly and so we need to do it using the **Transform → Compute Variable. . .** facility. Before we do this, however, it is worth looking briefly at how the cross-product ratio is calculated to help you understand what is to follow. Table 3.2 shows the data derived from the **timeseries.sav** dataset for the year 2004/5. As can be seen it simply shows the percentages of boys and girls gaining five or more higher grade GCSE passes in that year and then the corresponding percentages that did not. When we have any table like this with just four main cells (labeled in Table 3.2 as "a" to "d") we can calculate the cross-product ratio very simply using the following formula: $(a \times d)/(b \times c)$. Putting the figures in this formula from Table 3.2 we get: $(60.8 \times 49.2)/(39.2 \times 50.8) = 1.502$. What this figure actually tells us is that the odds of a girl getting five or more GCSE higher passes is 1.502 times higher than the odds of a boy doing so (hence, why it is also referred to as an odds ratio).

For us to develop a reliable measure of how differences between boys and girls have changed over time in relation to the current data, all we need to do, therefore, is to calculate

Table 3.2 Percentage of boys and girls gaining 5 or more GCSE higher grade passes in England in 2004/05

	% gaining 5 or more GCSE higher passes	% gaining fewer than 5 GCSE higher passes	Total
Girls	60.8 (a)	39.2 (b)	100
Boys	50.8 (c)	49.2 (d)	100

the cross-product ratio for each year. To do this we need four figures for each year: the percentages of boys and girls gaining five or more higher grade passes (as is already in the dataset) and also the percentages of boys and girls not achieving this. To create these additional two variables we need to select **Transform** → **Compute Variable. . .** which brings up the **Compute Variable** window shown in Figure 3.20. To create the first new variable—the percentage of girls who did not achieve at least five GCSE higher grade passes—we need to give the new variable a name and type it into the "Target Variable:" field as shown (we can call it "girls_no") and then in the "Numeric Expression:" field we need to tell SPSS how to calculate this new variable. In this case it is very simple. Because we already have a variable ("girls") representing the percentage who gained five or more GCSE higher grade passes, the percentage who did not is simple "100 – girls." You can add this into the "Numeric Expression:" field by using the buttons as shown. When you have done this, click "OK" to finish the procedure. What you should notice is that a new variable has been created ("girls_no") and can be seen in the main **Data View** window.

Once you have done this, do the same for boys so that you have another variable "boys_no." With all four variables now in place the last task is to compute a final variable

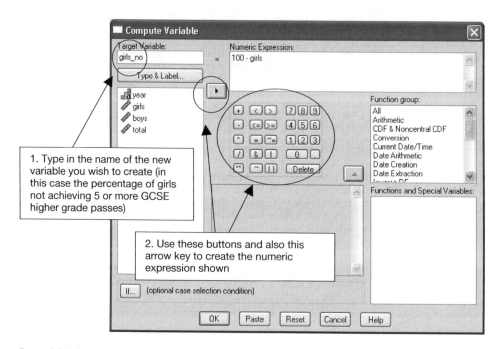

Figure 3.20 Compute Variable window in SPSS

representing the cross-product ratio. You can call this "cp_ratio" and from earlier the formula you need to type into the "Numeric Expression:" field should be:

(girls*boys_no)/(boys*girls_no)

Once the cross-product ratio has been calculated the final dataset should appear as it does in Figure 3.21. Do not forget to go to Variable View to define each of the variables properly (i.e. give them a full label, amend the number of decimal places and so on). As can be seen, the cross-product ratio for 2004/5 is 1.502 just as we calculated earlier. With

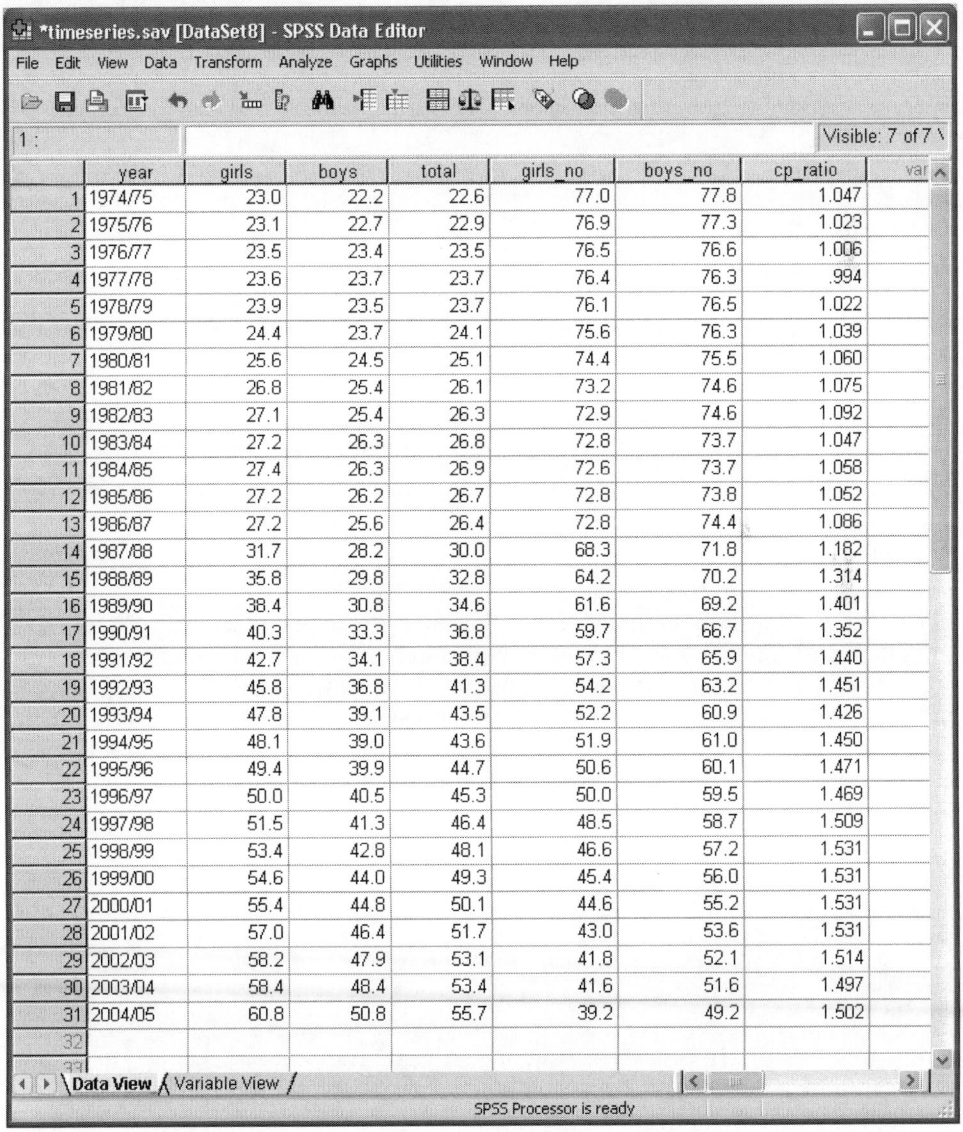

	year	girls	boys	total	girls_no	boys_no	cp_ratio	var
1	1974/75	23.0	22.2	22.6	77.0	77.8	1.047	
2	1975/76	23.1	22.7	22.9	76.9	77.3	1.023	
3	1976/77	23.5	23.4	23.5	76.5	76.6	1.006	
4	1977/78	23.6	23.7	23.7	76.4	76.3	.994	
5	1978/79	23.9	23.5	23.7	76.1	76.5	1.022	
6	1979/80	24.4	23.7	24.1	75.6	76.3	1.039	
7	1980/81	25.6	24.5	25.1	74.4	75.5	1.060	
8	1981/82	26.8	25.4	26.1	73.2	74.6	1.075	
9	1982/83	27.1	25.4	26.3	72.9	74.6	1.092	
10	1983/84	27.2	26.3	26.8	72.8	73.7	1.047	
11	1984/85	27.4	26.3	26.9	72.6	73.7	1.058	
12	1985/86	27.2	26.2	26.7	72.8	73.8	1.052	
13	1986/87	27.2	25.6	26.4	72.8	74.4	1.086	
14	1987/88	31.7	28.2	30.0	68.3	71.8	1.182	
15	1988/89	35.8	29.8	32.8	64.2	70.2	1.314	
16	1989/90	38.4	30.8	34.6	61.6	69.2	1.401	
17	1990/91	40.3	33.3	36.8	59.7	66.7	1.352	
18	1991/92	42.7	34.1	38.4	57.3	65.9	1.440	
19	1992/93	45.8	36.8	41.3	54.2	63.2	1.451	
20	1993/94	47.8	39.1	43.5	52.2	60.9	1.426	
21	1994/95	48.1	39.0	43.6	51.9	61.0	1.450	
22	1995/96	49.4	39.9	44.7	50.6	60.1	1.471	
23	1996/97	50.0	40.5	45.3	50.0	59.5	1.469	
24	1997/98	51.5	41.3	46.4	48.5	58.7	1.509	
25	1998/99	53.4	42.8	48.1	46.6	57.2	1.531	
26	1999/00	54.6	44.0	49.3	45.4	56.0	1.531	
27	2000/01	55.4	44.8	50.1	44.6	55.2	1.531	
28	2001/02	57.0	46.4	51.7	43.0	53.6	1.531	
29	2002/03	58.2	47.9	53.1	41.8	52.1	1.514	
30	2003/04	58.4	48.4	53.4	41.6	51.6	1.497	
31	2004/05	60.8	50.8	55.7	39.2	49.2	1.502	

Figure 3.21 Data View showing timeseries.sav dataset with new computed variables added

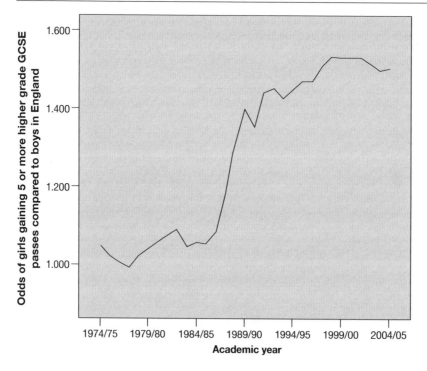

Figure 3.22 Sex differences in the percentage of Year 11 pupils in England achieving five or more GCSE grades A*–C (or their equivalent) between 1974/5 and 2003/4

this new variable we can now create a simple line chart showing how the cross-product ratio changes over time. This is shown in Figure 3.22.

In relation to the line chart, notice how the cross-product ratio has been given a more meaningful title that the general reader is more likely to understand. More substantively, it can be seen that the gap between boys and girls did increase quite substantially between the mid-1980s and the early 1990s. Since then it seems to have leveled off and has been relatively constant for the last five or so years. While the percentage point difference measure can be misleading, the main picture to emerge from it (and as illustrated in Figure 3.19) is not actually that dissimilar to this.

EXERCISE 3.8

Use the compute facility to create a new variable that is simply the percentage point difference between the percentage of boys and girls achieving the GCSE Benchmark (i.e. "girls – boys"). Examine this new variable with a simple line chart. How does it compare to the line chart created for the cross-product ratio? Check your method and findings on the companion website.

Conclusions

Having worked your way through this chapter you now have the core knowledge and skills to be able to undertake routine quantitative data analysis to a high level. You have learnt how to manipulate your dataset into the form required for analysis (via the Recode Variables, Select Cases, Split File and Compute procedures) and you have also learnt how to analyze relationships between variables in the most appropriate and effective manner. By way of a summary, Box 3.3 lists the most appropriate ways to display and statistically analyze relationships between the various combinations of variable types that exist.

Box 3.3 Summary guide as to the appropriate way to analyze the relationship between two variables

Types of variable being analyzed	Ways of displaying the relationship between the variables	Appropriate method for analyzing the relationship
Nominal – Nominal	• Contingency tables • Clustered bar charts	• Percentage comparisons between categories of one of the variables
Nominal – Ordinal	• Contingency tables • Clustered bar charts (Standard or cumulative)	• Percentage comparisons between categories of the nominal variable
Nominal – Scale	• Boxplots	• Comparisons of means or medians between categories of the nominal variable
Ordinal – Ordinal	• Contingency tables • Clustered bar charts	• Spearman correlation
Ordinal – Scale	• Boxplots	• Spearman correlation
Scale – Scale	• Scatterplots	• Pearson correlation (if linear) • Spearman correlation (if non-linear)

Chapter 4

Good practice in presenting findings

Introduction

One of the things that tends to frustrate me at times when I read research reports is the lack of time that appears to have been taken to think about the most effective way to present findings. It is frustrating because invariably the authors have done all of the hard work in analyzing the data, and may actually have some very interesting findings, and yet this can sometimes get lost because of the way that these findings have been poorly presented. If you have gone to all the trouble to collect data and to analyze them, it is important that you spend time thinking carefully about how best to display those findings through tables and charts. As the old saying goes, "a picture paints a thousand words" and this is so true of quantitative research. It is possible to greatly increase people's understanding of your findings and also their impact simply through the use of a few well-designed tables and charts.

The purpose of this chapter, therefore, is to provide you with a sound understanding of good practice in relation to the presentation of findings. Fortunately, SPSS has some really impressive features that allow you to adapt and manipulate the tables and charts you produce so that they are in precisely the format and style in which you want them. As you will see, the effective presentation of findings is ultimately an art form and requires you to explore and experiment with the differing ways in which you can present data through tables and diagrams. By the end of this chapter therefore you will:

- be able to generate tables in SPSS and to adapt them into the format and style you need;
- be able to generate the most commonly used charts in SPSS and know how to amend them into the format and style necessary;
- know how to cut and paste the tables and charts you have created directly into your reports;
- have gained a sound understanding of good practice in relation to the presentation of tables and charts.

Generating and editing tables in SPSS

One of the most common things that students do is simply to cut and paste unedited SPSS tables into their reports. To understand the problem in doing this let's take a simple example from the **youthcohort.sav** dataset. Open the dataset and make sure you weight the dataset using the variable "s1weight" (see Figure 2.5 for a reminder of how to do this). Once you have done this use **Analyze → Descriptive Statistics → Frequencies. . .** to create a simple frequency table for the grades that school leavers in England gained in the GCSE English examination ("gradeng"). The table you should obtain is shown in Output 4.1.

There are three general principles that you should follow in relation to designing tables and charts so that they can be included in reports:

- They should be **self-contained** in that they should make sense in and of themselves without the reader having to refer to any of the accompanying text in the report.
- They should be as **efficient** as possible so that they only include data that are necessary to illustrate the findings to which you wish to draw attention.
- They should be as **effective** as possible in terms of choosing a style and format that clearly draws attention to the key findings you wish to highlight.

EXERCISE 4.1

With these three general principles in mind, have a look at the table in SPSS Output 4.1 for a moment and list some of the reasons why it may not be appropriate simply to cut and paste this directly into a report.

Output 4.1

English Grade

		Frequency	Percent	Valid Percent	Cumulative Percent
Valid	A*	473	3.6	3.8	3.8
	A	1619	12.3	12.9	16.6
	B	2549	19.3	20.3	36.9
	C	2989	22.7	23.8	60.7
	D	2465	18.7	19.6	80.3
	E	1481	11.2	11.8	92.1
	F	654	5.0	5.2	97.3
	G	223	1.7	1.8	99.1
	Fail	119	.9	.9	100.0
	Total	12573	95.4	100.0	
Missing	Didn't take	605	4.6		
Total		13178	100.0		

Hopefully, and with these three principles in mind, you should have identified at least some of the following problems with the table as it stands:

- The title of the table fails to provide basic information regarding the examination taken (i.e. GCSE English), when it was taken (i.e. 2003) and by whom (i.e. Year 11 pupils in England).
- There is no information about the source of the data (i.e. taken from a secondary analysis of the Youth Cohort Study of England and Wales, Cohort 12, Sweep 1).
- It is unnecessary to include a separate category for "missing" responses. Rather, the table could be just concerned with the grades obtained by those who took the examination.
- The table is potentially confusing for the reader given that it includes three different percentage columns.

What we will do now is to show you how to edit the table in SPSS so that it is self-contained and as efficient as possible. Also, depending upon the nature of your report it may also be necessary to change the style of the table and you will also be shown how to do this. To keep things as simple as possible let's address each of the above four points above in turn.

Editing the title of a table

To start with we need to give the table a more meaningful title. To do this we need to put the table into edit mode and this is done by double-clicking anywhere on the table itself. You will know that it is in edit mode when a box appears surrounding the table with little dashed lines all around it as shown in Figure 4.1. To edit any text in the table you need to double-click on the text itself. Doing this on the title "English Grade" transforms it into the text box as also shown in Figure 4.1. You can then delete the existing text and type a new title directly into this box. Here we will call it "Table 1. Grades achieved by Year 11 pupils in England who took GCSE English in 2003." Notice that we have numbered the table (i.e. "Table 1"); this is always a good thing to do in order to make it as simple as possible when referring to specific tables in the main text of your report. Once you have done this just click anywhere outside of the table to return to the original view.

Adding a footnote to a table

Next we need to provide information on the source of the data, which we can do by adding a footnote to the title. To do this double-click on the table again to ensure it is in edit mode and then select the title by clicking on it once. A dark border should appear around the title as shown in Figure 4.2. With the title selected, choose **Insert** → **Footnote** from the main menu. Having done this you will see that a superscript "a" has appeared at the end of the title and also a footnote has appeared at the bottom of the table. At present the default text for the footnote is just "Footnote." You can now edit this to add the text you want by double-clicking on it in just the same way as you edited the title. For the footnote add the following text: "Source: Secondary analysis of the Youth Cohort Study of England and Wales (Cohort 12, Sweep 1)."

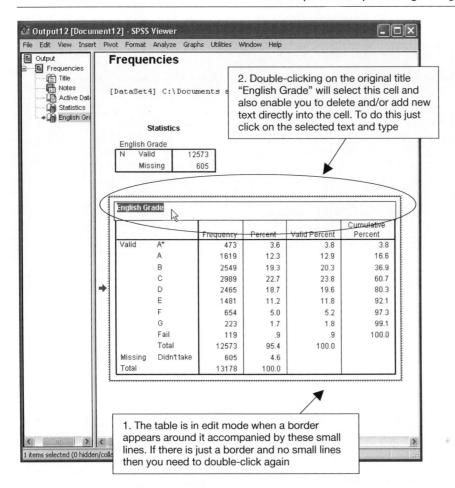

Figure 4.1 Changing the title of a table in SPSS

Removing columns and rows from a table

Next we need to remove the "Missing" values from the table. Whenever you want to edit a row or column of figures you need to select them by first clicking once on the main heading for that row or column (which in this case is the term "Missing"). This adds a dark border around the heading as shown in Figure 4.3. Second, you need to choose **Edit →** **Select → Data and Label Cells**. This selects the whole row which should now appear as it does in Figure 4.3. Once selected, just press the "Delete" key on your keyboard to remove the row (or you can select **Edit → Clear** if you like doing things the long way round!).

In the same way, you need to remove the bottom row "Total" as this is the total calculated with missing values (which you have just removed from the table). The fourth and final point to address is the confusing number of percentage columns. As we have removed the row of missing values, the first "Percent" column is no longer required (as the percentages in this column were calculated with missing values included). By exactly

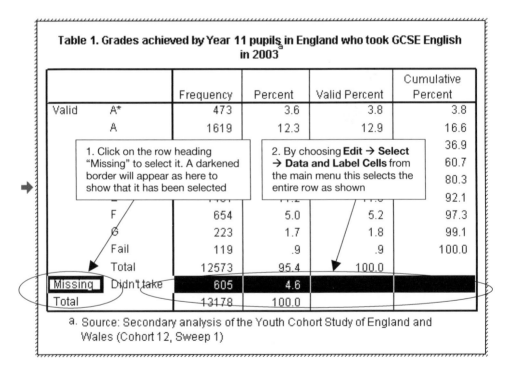

Table 1. Grades achieved by Year 11 pupils in England who took GCSE English in 2003

		Frequency	Percent	Valid Percent	Cumulative Percent
Valid	A*	473	3.6	3.8	3.8
	A	1619	12.3	12.9	16.6
	B	2549	19.3	20.3	36.9
	C	2989			60.7
	D	2465			80.3
	E	1481			92.1
	F	654	5.0	5.2	97.3
	G	223	1.7	1.8	99.1
	Fail	119	.9	.9	100.0
	Total	12573	95.4	100.0	
Missing	Didn't take	605	4.6		
Total		13178	100.0		

Click on the title once to select it. A darkened boarder will appear to indicate that the cell is selected

Figure 4.2 Selecting a cell in a table in SPSS

Table 1. Grades achieved by Year 11 pupils in England who took GCSE English in 2003

		Frequency	Percent	Valid Percent	Cumulative Percent
Valid	A*	473	3.6	3.8	3.8
	A	1619	12.3	12.9	16.6
					36.9
					60.7
					80.3
					92.1
	F	654	5.0	5.2	97.3
	G	223	1.7	1.8	99.1
	Fail	119	.9	.9	100.0
	Total	12573	95.4	100.0	
Missing	Didn't take	605	4.6		
Total		13178	100.0		

1. Click on the row heading "Missing" to select it. A darkened border will appear as here to show that it has been selected

2. By choosing **Edit → Select → Data and Label Cells** from the main menu this selects the entire row as shown

a. Source: Secondary analysis of the Youth Cohort Study of England and Wales (Cohort 12, Sweep 1)

Figure 4.3 Selecting a row in a table in SPSS

the same procedure as shown above, click on the column heading "Percent" and then choose **Edit** → **Select** → **Data and Label Cells**. You can then delete this column in exactly the same way by pressing the "Delete" key.

The table is now nearly ready for cutting and pasting into your report. Before doing this, however, we need to change the title of the column "Valid Percent" so that it just reads "Percent." You do this by double-clicking on the column heading and then amending the text just as you did for the main title and the footnote previously. Second, as we have removed the missing values we no longer need the word "Valid" situated to the left of the grades that are listed. To remove this, just click on the word "Valid" to select it and then press the "Delete" key. However, this does leave a rather big gap to the left of the grades listed. To change this, click once on the area to the left of the grades to select it. A box will appear around it as shown in Figure 4.4. If you now hover your cursor over the right-hand side of the box it will change into a double headed arrow as also shown in Figure 4.4. You can now click and drag this border to the left to reduce the gap.

Changing the style of a table

The final thing you may wish to do is to change the style of the table. As an example, let us assume that you wish to publish your final report. This being the case you are likely to find that your intended publisher has a "house style" requiring you to only use horizontal lines when setting out tables. To change the overall style of the table to conform to this style you need to double-click on it to ensure it is in edit mode and then choose **Format** → **TableLooks. . .** from the top menu. This brings up the **TableLooks** window shown in

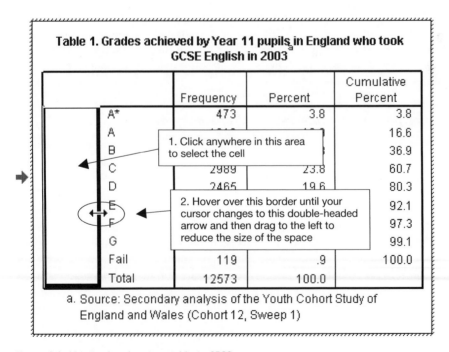

Figure 4.4 Altering borders in a table in SPSS

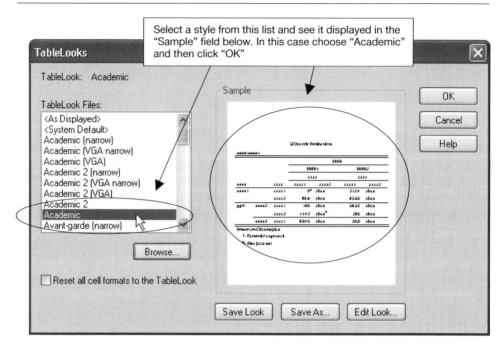

Figure 4.5 TableLooks window in SPSS

Figure 4.5. You will find a wide range of potential styles in the "TableLook Files:" field to the left. Try browsing through some of these. For each one you click on you will see the style displayed in the "Sample" field to the right. In this instance we will choose "Academic." Once selected, click "OK." You should now find the table in the new "Academic" style.

Cutting and pasting a table into a Word document

Once you have modified your table exactly as you would like it, you can cut and paste it directly into your report. To do this, click on the table once to select it. You will know it has been selected as a single line box will appear around it. If the box has little lines around its edges then you have clicked too many times as it is now back in edit mode. Click anywhere outside the table and then try clicking on it again. Once you have selected the table choose **Edit → Copy** from the main menu (or press the "Ctrl" and "C" keys together). Open up the document you wish to paste the table into. In this case we will assume it is a Microsoft Word document. Click at the place in the text where you want the chart to appear. You should now have a blinking cursor at that point as shown in the left-hand image in Figure 4.6. In the Word document choose **Edit → Paste Special. . . .** This gives you three options:

•   Paste the table as **Formatted Text (RTF)**. This creates a table in Word in the place chosen. You may, however, need to edit the table in terms of re-sizing columns and also amending the borders to get it back to the style you had specifically chosen.

- Paste the table as **Unformatted Text**. This just pastes the labels and data from the table with no formatting at all and thus with only spaces added to separate the labels and columns.
- Paste the table as **Pictures (Windows Metafile)**. This pastes the table as an image that maintains the precise style and formatting of the table you have created in SPSS. While you can re-size the table by clicking and dragging you cannot then edit the contents of the table directly in your report. To do this you would need to edit the table in SPSS and then re-paste the amended table into your document.

In this case we will use the latter option. Thus, select **Pictures (Window Metafile)** and then click "OK." This pastes in an image of the table as shown in the right-hand image in Figure 4.6.

EXERCISE 4.2

Create a contingency table (**Analyze → Descriptive Statistics → Crosstabs ...**) showing the relationship between sex ("s1gender") and grades achieved in GCSE English ("gradeng"). Edit the chart so that it is also in the same style as the last chart and ready to insert directly into a report. Check what you have done on the companion website. Did you make all of the changes suggested?

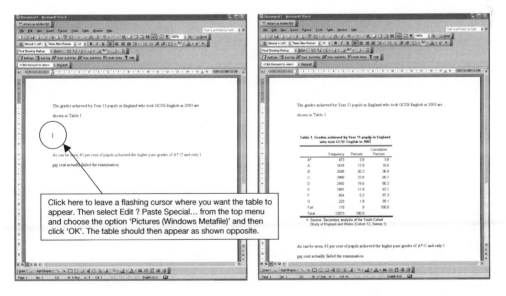

Figure 4.6 Cutting and pasting a table directly into a report

Changing the order of rows and columns

There are a couple of additional functions that SPSS provides in relation to editing tables that are also worth covering briefly. The first is the opportunity that SPSS provides for changing the order of rows and columns. To understand why this may be useful, stay with the **youthcohort.sav** dataset and create a simple frequency table (**Analyze → Descriptive Statistics → Frequencies. . .**) showing the racial/ethnic breakdown of the sample ("ethsfr"). The table you should get is shown in Output 4.2. As before, there is a need to edit the title so that it is more meaningful. In addition, you may wish to remove the category "not answered" and hence also the "Percent" column. Moreover, as we are now dealing with a nominal variable, it makes no sense to have the "Cumulative Percent" column and so this can be removed as well. Try making all of these changes yourself.

Finally, one additional change that may be worth making here is to arrange the order of the racial/ethnic categories so that they correspond to the relative size of each group (i.e. starting with the largest group and finishing with the smallest). This is actually another example of good practice in that it is always desirable, wherever possible, to list nominal categories in some meaningful way to make the table easier to read. In this case we will do it in terms of size. However, there may be other ways. For example, in relation to a contingency table showing the relationship between racial/ethnic background and educational attainment it may be more meaningful to organize the list of racial/ethnic groups by levels of attainment (highest first).

Whichever way we do it the procedure is the same and involves shuffling the rows around until they are in the correct order. To do this in relation to the present example we need to begin by moving the "Other ethnic group" category upwards so that it sits just above the "Indian" category. This is done by clicking on "Other ethnic group" to select it and then dragging and dropping it onto the category "Indian" as shown in Figure 4.7. You are then presented with the option of either directly swapping these two categories

Output 4.2

Ethnicity for c12s1 SFR

		Frequency	Percent	Valid Percent	Cumulative Percent
Valid	White	11242	85.3	87.0	87.0
	Black	373	2.8	2.9	89.9
	Indian	346	2.6	2.7	92.5
	Pakistani	316	2.4	2.4	95.0
	Bangladeshi	134	1.0	1.0	96.0
	Other Asian (inc Chinese)	150	1.1	1.2	97.2
	Other ethnic group (inc. mixed)	364	2.8	2.8	100.0
	Total	12923	98.1	100.0	
Missing	Not answered	255	1.9		
Total		13178	100.0		

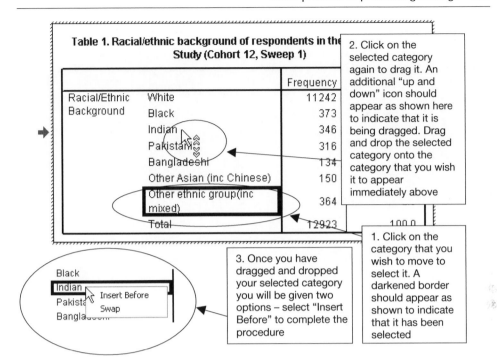

Figure 4.7 Altering the order of rows in a table in SPSS

or inserting "Other ethnic group" immediately before "Indian." Select "Insert Before" as shown in Figure 4.7 to complete the procedure. Next, and in the same way, you need to move "Other Asian" so that it is immediately above "Bangladeshi." Once done, the final order should appear as in Figure 4.8. Exactly the same procedure can be used to alter the order in which columns appear. In this case, should you wish to swap the Frequency and Percent columns you would simply click on one of the column headings to select it and then drag in onto the other.

Changing the appearance of data and text within a table

Finally, you may wish to change the size and style of text or figures in a particular cell of a table. Staying with the same table as shown in Figure 4.8, let us assume that we wish to alter the style and format of the percentage figure for the "White" category (i.e. "87.0"). To do this, click on the figure concerned to select it (as shown in Figure 4.8) and then choose **Format → Cell Properties. . .** to open the **Cell Properties** window also shown in Figure 4.8. As can be seen, it is possible to use this window to change how numbers are displayed (including the number of decimal places and whether commas are added to indicate thousands), how the numbers are aligned in the cell, the spacing around the number within each cell and also whether the cell should be shaded. In a similar vein, it is also possible to change the size and style of the font by choosing **Format → Font. . .** from the top menu. This is equally applicable to cells containing numbers or text.

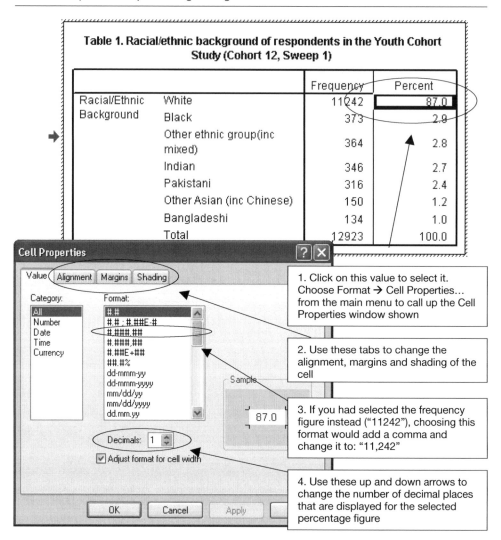

Table 1. Racial/ethnic background of respondents in the Youth Cohort Study (Cohort 12, Sweep 1)

		Frequency	Percent
Racial/Ethnic Background	White	11242	87.0
	Black	373	2.9
	Other ethnic group(inc mixed)	364	2.8
	Indian	346	2.7
	Pakistani	316	2.4
	Other Asian (inc Chinese)	150	1.2
	Bangladeshi	134	1.0
	Total	12923	100.0

Cell Properties

Value | Alignment | Margins | Shading

Category:
All
Number
Date
Time
Currency

Format:
#.#
#.# ; #.##E-#
#,###.##
#.###.##
#.##E+##
##.#%
dd-mmm-yy
dd-mmm-yyyy
mm/dd/yy
mm/dd/yyyy
dd.mm.yy

Sample

87.0

Decimals: 1

☑ Adjust format for cell width

OK   Cancel   Apply

1. Click on this value to select it. Choose Format → Cell Properties... from the main menu to call up the Cell Properties window shown

2. Use these tabs to change the alignment, margins and shading of the cell

3. If you had selected the frequency figure instead ("11242"), choosing this format would add a comma and change it to: "11,242"

4. Use these up and down arrows to change the number of decimal places that are displayed for the selected percentage figure

Figure 4.8 Cell Properties window in SPSS

Generating and editing charts in SPSS

The same three guiding principles discussed above in relation to creating tables—that they should be **self-contained**, **efficient** and **effective**—also apply to charts. In relation to the last principle, we have already considered this briefly in Chapter 2 when we discussed the benefits of using simple bar charts over pie charts (see Figure 2.16). The key issue here is the need to select the type of chart carefully so that it illustrates the key findings from the data as clearly, and thus as effectively, as possible.

As another example of this, let us compare the school grades achieved by boys and girls from kindergarten through to Grade 8 in America (as reported by their parents) using the **afterschools.sav** dataset. We did this originally in Chapter 3 (see Figure 3.7). However, rather than using a clustered bar chart to display the findings it is possible to generate and use what is called a stacked bar chart. Both types of chart are shown in Figure 4.9 for these data. Have a look at both bar charts and ask yourself which one most clearly and effectively displays the differences in school grades attained by boys and girls. It should be fairly obvious that the clustered bar chart does this most effectively given that you can see, at a glance, how boys and girls compare for each level of attainment listed. By comparison, it is more difficult to see this from the stacked bar chart, particularly when the proportions of boys and girls at any one level are fairly similar.

As stated at the beginning of this chapter, the key lesson to learn from this is the need to see the creation of charts as an art form. It is well worthwhile trying out and comparing a number of different ways of displaying your data so that you can identify the most effective way of illustrating the key findings from these. Fortunately, and as we have already seen, SPSS makes it very easy to produce a wide range of charts. As will be shown in this section it is also very straightforward to edit the charts generated so that they are in exactly the style and format required.

To take you through the basics of editing charts we will continue with the above example and create a clustered bar chart from the **afterschools.sav** dataset showing differences between boys and girls ("SEX") in their school grades achieved as reported by their parents ("SEGRADES"). You were actually shown how to generate this particular chart in the last chapter (see Figure 3.6). Before going any further there are two points to stress regarding different versions of SPSS:

- As you will have already seen, in SPSS Version 15.0 this chart is generated by initially selecting **Graphs → Legacy Dialogs → Bar**. For SPSS Version 14.0 and earlier and in Mac versions you simply need to select **Graphs → Bar**. The same actually applies for whatever chart you intend to generate.
- The procedure for then editing the charts generated, as described below, applies only to SPSS Version 13.0 and above. A more simple procedure was used for SPSS Version 12.0 and earlier and Version 11.0 for Macs and earlier and this is described in Appendix 2.

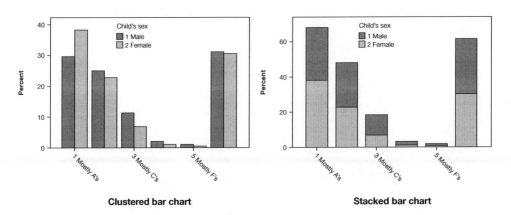

Clustered bar chart   Stacked bar chart

Figure 4.9 Comparison of a clustered bar chart and a stacked bar chart as means of displaying gender differences in school grades achieved by young children in America

The initial chart that you will generate with this procedure is shown in Figure 4.10. Note this time that the category "6 NO LTR GRADES" has been included and thus not defined as missing. Don't forget to weight cases before generating this chart using the variable "WTCORRCT" (see Figure 2.5). As we did earlier in relation to tables, have a look at this chart and, with the three guiding principles in mind (i.e. the chart needs to be **self-contained**, **efficient** and **effective**), try to list what needs to be amended for it to be ready to insert directly into a report.

Hopefully you will have identified at least some of the following amendments that need to be made:

- a title needs to be added to explain what data the chart is displaying;
- a footnote is needed to explain the source of the data;
- the title for the *x*-axis (the horizontal axis) and the value labels need to be amended to remove unnecessary detail (i.e. "SE1" in the main axis title and the numbers preceding the value labels);
- the note indicating that the cases were weighted could also be removed (assuming that this point was made in the methodology section of the report);

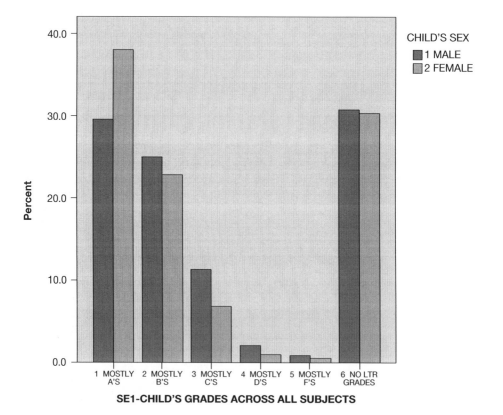

Cases weighted by FINAL ASPA INTV WEIGHT ADJUSTED BY DEFT

Figure 4.10 Clustered bar chart as it first appears in SPSS, comparing the school grades achieved by boys and girls as reported by their parents

- assuming that the report will be printed in greyscale, the colors of the bars need to be changed accordingly;
- finally, it would be useful to generally tidy up the chart a little by moving the legend (i.e. the key to the right of the chart headed "CHILD'S SEX").

As before, it is worth taking you through how to address each of these points in turn as this will give you a good feel for how to use the Chart Editor function in SPSS. In fact, while there are many different types of chart that you can generate in SPSS, the main way that you would edit any particular chart is essentially the same. Just as a reminder before we move on: for those of you with SPSS Version 12.0 and earlier and Version 11.0 for Macs and earlier you should skip the rest of this section and consult Appendix 2 instead.

Opening the Chart Editor window

To get started you need to begin by double-clicking on the chart to open the **Chart Editor** window as shown in Figure 4.11. All the editing you will do in relation to the chart will be done in this window. When you have finished editing the chart all you need to do is to close down the window (by clicking the red cross situated at the top right of the window) to return to the main output window. In doing this you will see that the chart in this main output window will reflect the changes you have made. If you want to make any further changes you just need to double-click on the chart again to re-open the **Chart Editor** window. It is this main output window that you should use to save the chart (and any other output created). Once saved you can always return to and re-open this output file in the future and continue editing the chart if you wish.

The second thing that is useful to do to get started is to click on the icon shown in Figure 4.11 to open the **Properties** window. This window can remain open as you navigate your way around the chart and the particular content of the window will change depending upon what element of the chart you have selected and are thus working on.

Adding a title and a footnote to the chart

To begin with, then, we need to add a title. Once you have opened the **Chart Editor** window, click on the "Insert a title" icon as shown in Figure 4.12. This creates a new text field at the top of the chart as also shown. You can now type the title of your chart directly into this field. In this instance we will call the chart: "Figure 1. Sex differences in school grades attained by American children (Kindergarten through Grade 8) as reported by their parents in 2005." Once done, click anywhere else in the chart to deselect this text field.

Next, we need to add a footnote to explain the source of the data. To do this click on the "Insert a footnote" icon as shown in Figure 4.13. This creates a small text field at the foot of the chart with the word "Footnote" as can also be seen. Delete this word and type in the footnote here. In this instance we will insert: "Source: Secondary analysis of the National Household Education Surveys Program of 2005 (After-School Programs and Activities Survey)."

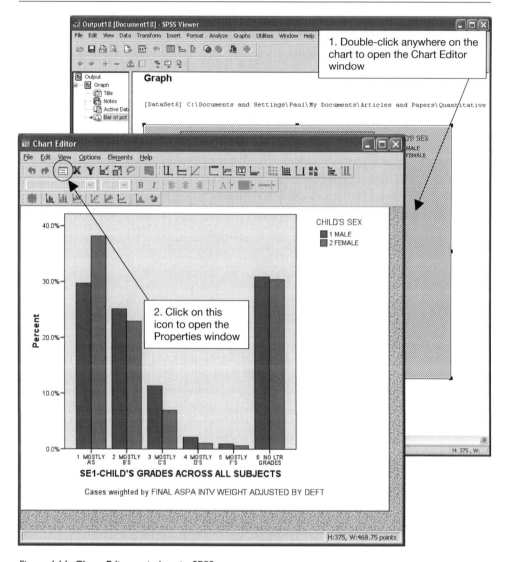

Figure 4.11 Chart Editor window in SPSS

Editing axis titles and value labels and removing text

Following this, we need to amend the title for the "*x*-axis" and the value labels. In relation to the title for the *x*-axis, simply click on the title once to select it (a box will appear around it signifying it has been selected) and then click on it again to change it into edit mode. Just as you have done with the main title and the footnote, you can now edit this text. In this instance we need to clean up the axis title by removing "SE1-" from the beginning. It is also probably better to change the title to lower case as well. Similarly, for the value labels we need to remove the initial numbers that reflect the way the categories have been

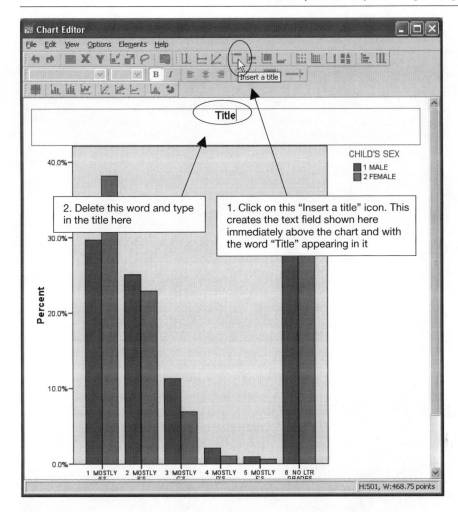

Figure 4.12 Adding a title to a chart in the Chart Editor window in SPSS

coded. To do this, simply click on any of the value labels once. This will result in all of the value labels being selected (denoted again by the appearance of boxes around each of the labels). Click on the first label again and that changes it into edit mode. As before, simply remove the number at the beginning and, for the sake of consistency, change the text to lower case. Repeat the procedure again for the remaining five values.

Do the same for the text in the legend. As before, select the text by clicking on it once to select it and then a further time to change it into edit mode. In this instance remove the numbers before "Male" and "Female" and also change the text to lower case for consistency. Finally, in relation to the note indicating that cases have been weighted, click on this once to select it (a box will appear around it to denote that it has been selected). Once selected, simply press the "Delete" key (or choose **Edit** → **Delete** from the main menu if you still want to make extra work for yourself!).

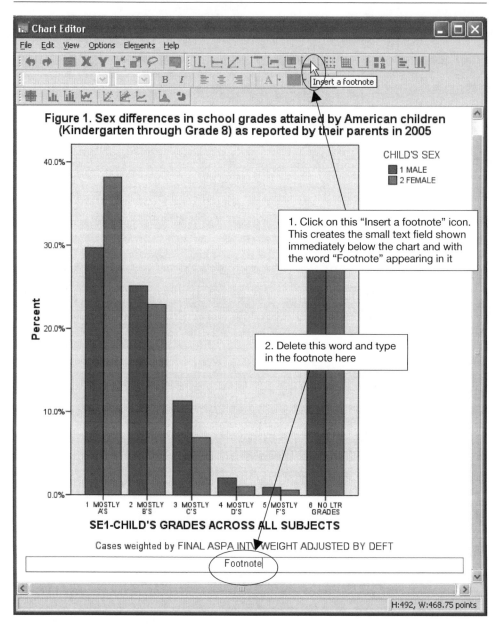

Figure 4.13 Adding a footnote to a chart in the Chart Editor window in SPSS

Changing the colors of the bars in a bar chart

To change the colors of the bars in the chart it is now necessary to have the **Properties** window open. If you have not done so already click on the "Show Properties Window" icon to open the **Properties** window (see Figure 4.11). To change the color of the bars, begin by clicking once on any of the bars. This will select all of the bars (as denoted by a border appearing around them). Once you have done this click on one of the bars for males. This will change the selection to just the male bars as illustrated in Figure 4.14.

In the **Properties** window click on the "Fill & Border" tab. To change the color of the bars click on the square next to "Fill" as shown in Figure 4.14 and then click on an alternative color in the palette to change it. In this instance, and for the sake of clarity, we will change the boys' bars to black. Once you have selected black from the palette click on the "Apply" button to make the change to the chart itself. Repeat the procedure to change the girls' bars to white.

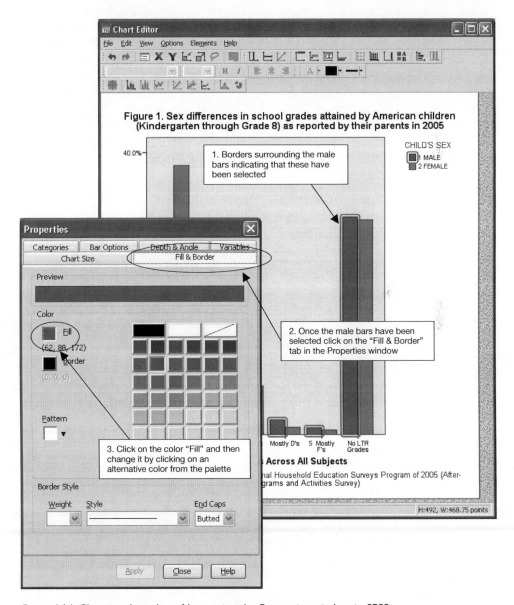

Figure 4.14 Changing the color of bars using the Properties window in SPSS

Removing bars from a bar chart and changing their order

Finally, there are a few things we can do to tidy the chart up a little. While we won't actually do this first one it is worth showing you how to remove any unnecessary bars from a bar chart and also how to change the order they appear in. You may wish to remove bars, for example, that represent missing values or bars that represent groups that you are not interested in for the purposes of your specific analysis. Let us assume for the sake of illustration that you only wish to show the proportions of children who were actually awarded school grades (and, thus, want to remove the category "No LTR Grades"). To remove these bars you need to click anywhere on one of the bars to select them and then go to the **Properties** window. If the **Properties** window is not open click on the "Open Properties window" icon shown in Figure 4.11. Once opened, click on the "Categories" tab to get the view shown in Figure 4.15. To remove the "No LTR Grades" category, first you need to ensure that the relevant variable name is selected using the drop-down menu as shown in Figure 4.15. Having done this, all of the categories will appear in the "Order:" field as shown. Click on "No LTR Grades" and then click on the delete button as shown. This places the category into the "Excluded:" field and thus removes it from the chart. Click "Apply" to remove the bars from the chart. Try this to see what happens. Once done, you can return the bars into the chart by clicking on the button shown in Figure 4.15.

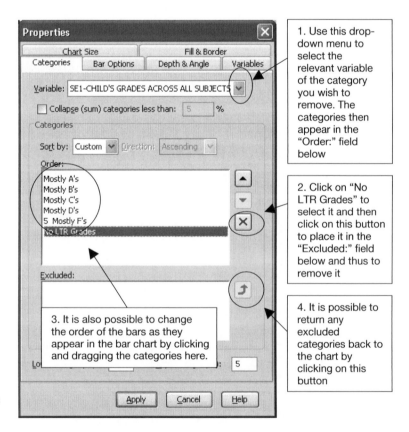

Figure 4.15
Categories view
in the Properties
window in SPSS

The next thing to do is to increase the size of some of the text. To do this, click on the text concerned and then click on the "Text Style" tab in the **Properties** window. This brings up the view shown in Figure 4.16. As can be seen, this allows you to change the style and size of the text as well as the color. In this case we will simply change everything to a 11 point size (except for the footnote, which will be changed to 10 point). One thing you will notice is that when you increase the size of the labels on the *x*-axis they become too crowded together. To prevent this you can change the orientation of the labels. In this case we will change them so that they are vertical. To do this select the labels and click on the "Labels & Ticks" tab in the **Properties** window. Where it says "Label orientation" use the drop-down menu to select "Vertical" and then click the "Apply" button to make the changes to the chart.

We can create a little more space by moving the legend (the key currently located to the right of the chart and headed "CHILD'S SEX"). To do this click somewhere near to the legend as shown in Figure 4.17 but not on the actual text within the legend itself

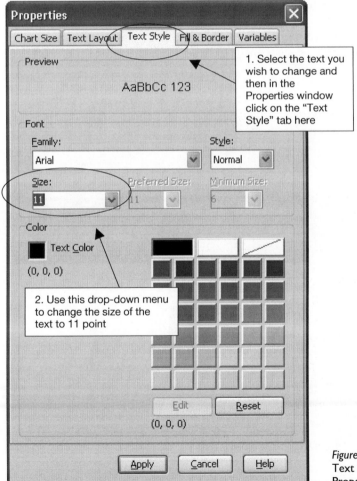

Figure 4.16
Text Style view in the
Properties window in SPSS

as this will then just select the text. Once selected, the border will appear as also shown in Figure 4.17. The border can be re-sized by dragging the handles as indicated. To move the legend itself, hover the cursor over the border (but not over a handle) until the cursor changes into a four-arrowed shape as shown in Figure 4.17. You can then click and drag the legend to where you want it to go (in this case on the chart itself).

Finally, we can re-size the bar chart itself so that it fills the gap that is left to the right-hand side. To do this click anywhere towards the bottom of the chart as shown in Figure 4.18 to select the chart area itself. When you first start to edit charts it will take you a little time to get used to where precisely to click because there are so many different elements of the chart that can be selected. However, you will soon learn. Once you have selected the chart area, hover over one of the handles that appear on the right-hand side of the border as also shown in Figure 4.18 until your cursor turns into a double-arrow. You can now click and drag the chart to stretch it into the area as illustrated.

Once you have done all this you should end up with the chart shown in Figure 4.19. As explained before you can return to the main output window simply by closing the **Chart Edit** window. Once in this main output window you can click on the chart once to select it and then cut and paste it directly into your report just as you were shown with the tables (see Figure 4.6). This time, however, you can just choose **Edit** → **Paste** rather than **Paste Special. . .** as you are already dealing with an image. Once you have pasted the chart into your report you can select the chart and drag its edges to re-size it as you require.

Editing other types of chart

Because of the range of charts available and the many different options to choose from within each type of chart, it is impossible to cover all aspects of how to edit charts here. However, in going through the example above you should have gained an intuitive feel

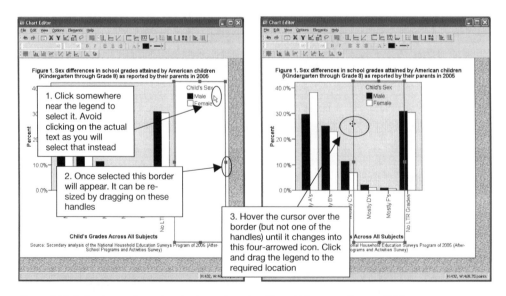

Figure 4.17 Selecting and moving the legend in the Chart Editor window in SPSS

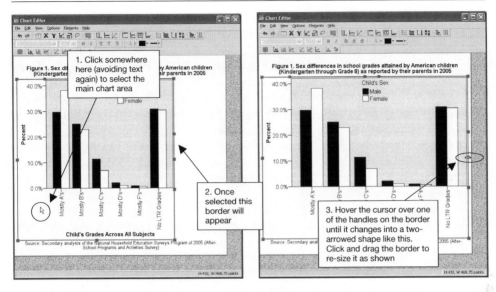

Figure 4.18 Selecting and changing the chart size in the Chart Editor window in SPSS

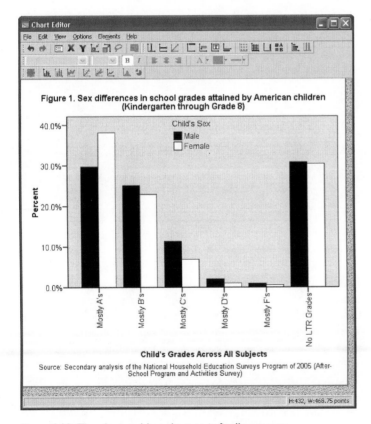

Figure 4.19 The clustered bar chart as it finally appears

for how to edit charts. In fact, whatever the type of chart you are working with the procedures are very similar. In this sense it is worth stressing a few final points:

- Have a good look at the icons across the top of the **Chart Editor** window. We have used some of them in the example above (i.e. adding a title and a footnote). However, there are many more that perform some useful functions. Click on each one to explore what it does. You will learn a lot more by experimenting with the **Chart Editor** window than you will by just reading this book.
- As a general rule, if you wish to alter some specific element of a chart (i.e. the text, the color, the style of lines etc.), you need to click on it once to select it and then make the required changes using the **Properties** window.
- Some elements of the chart can be moved around by selecting and dragging them. We have done this, for example, with the legend. However, it can also be done with the title and any footnotes added as well. As we have seen, it is also possible to re-size the chart area.
- Finally, you can change the overall size of the chart once it has been pasted into your report by selecting it and dragging the handles. However, this can sometimes result in some of the text becoming too small to read. Another option is to change the overall size of the chart in Chart Editor mode by clicking on the "Chart Size" tab in the **Properties** window. Doing it this way enables you to select the exact size you need and then to re-size the text and re-arrange any other elements of the chart as necessary so that they appear precisely as you want them at this size.

EXERCISE 4.3

Take a look at Figure 3.14 from the last chapter. It was created using the **valueadded.sav** dataset. Try to recreate it precisely as it appears (minus the text boxes). See if you can work out how to add the "line of best fit" and also the three reference lines and to change their style so they appear as in Figure 3.11. Check what you did on the companion website.

Chart Builder

SPSS Versions 14.0 onwards include a new function—**Graphs → Chart Builder. . .**—which provides a simple, interactive way of generating charts. Once you have selected the required chart and set the basic elements relating to it, the chart can then be edited as normal using the procedures outlined above. As an example of Chart Builder we will use the **youthcohort.sav** dataset. Open the dataset and weight cases using the variable "s1weight" (see Figure 2.5). Once done, select **Graphs → Chart Builder. . . .**

This will open up an initial window as shown in Figure 4.20. As can be seen, it is essential that you set the measurement levels for each variable correctly (i.e. as either nominal, ordinal or scale) for Chart Builder to work properly. In relation to the datasets used in this book this has already been done. However, do bear this in mind if you subsequently create your own dataset and wish to use Chart Builder.

Once you click on "OK" in this initial window, the main **Chart Builder** window and **Element Properties** window open simultaneously as shown in Figure 4.21. The basic idea here is that you choose a chart type from the gallery at the bottom of the window and drag and drop it into the main field as the instructions suggest. You then simply select your

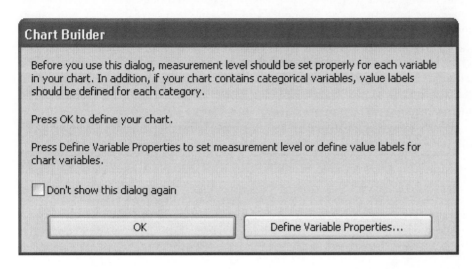

Figure 4.20 Initial Chart Builder dialog window in SPSS

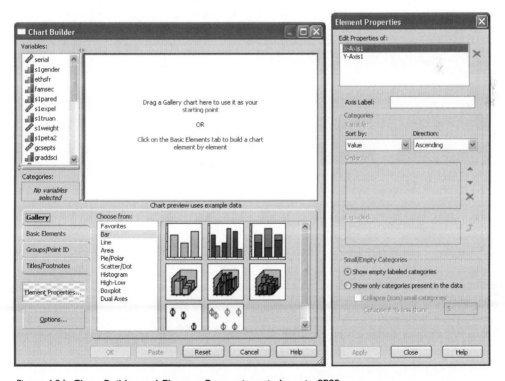

Figure 4.21 Chart Builder and Element Properties windows in SPSS

variables and drag and drop these onto the chart that you have put into the main field and click "OK" to generate your chosen chart. All very simple and actually easier to use than creating charts through the **Graphs → Legacy Dialogs. . .** procedure as we have been doing up to this point.

As an example, let us create a population pyramid comparing the GCSE scores ("gcsepts") of boys and girls ("s1gender") in the sample. I have chosen a population pyramid as we have not encountered one of these before and yet, as will be seen, they are incredibly useful in illustrating differences between two groups in relation to a scale variable. To find the population pyramid chart you need to click on "Histogram" in the list headed "Choose from:" as shown in Figure 4.22. It is definitely worth clicking on and exploring all of the items in this list to get a feel for what charts are available. The population pyramid is basically two histograms arranged back-to-back as also shown in Figure 4.22. Click on the population pyramid icon and then drag and drop it into the main field as illustrated.

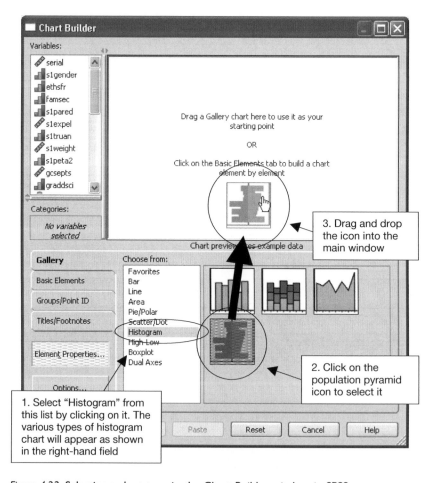

Figure 4.22 Selecting a chart type in the Chart Builder window in SPSS

Once you have chosen the chart you want you then need to select the variables. To do this click on "s1gender" and simply drag and drop it onto the area marked "Split Variable?" as shown in Figure 4.23. You can then do the same for the other variable "gcsepts" by dragging and dropping it onto the area marked "Distribution Variable?" Having done this, have a look at the **Element Properties** window. This is shown in Figure 4.24. As can be seen, it is possible through this window to add normal curves onto the data and also to make a number of other changes to the population pyramid. In this case, we will just select "Display normal curve" and click "Apply." You will see two normal curves superimposed onto the chart in the main **Chart Builder** window.

When you have completed all this, click "OK" in the main **Chart Builder** window. You should get the chart shown in Figure 4.25. You can now edit this chart as you would do any other using the procedures covered earlier. I have used this chart purposely to show just how useful a population pyramid can be in comparing the distribution of scores

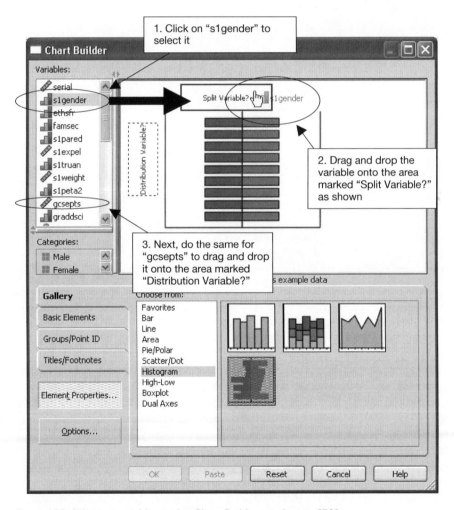

Figure 4.23 Selecting variables in the Chart Builder window in SPSS

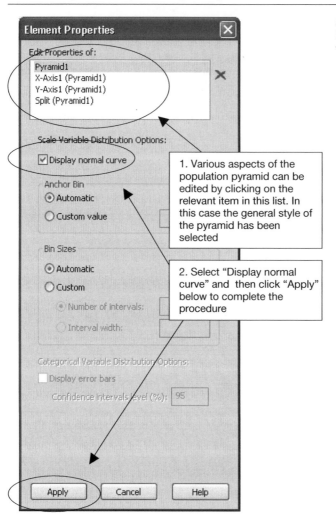

Figure 4.24
Element Properties
window in SPSS

from two groups. In this case we are comparing the examination scores obtained by boys and girls in public examinations (GCSEs) at the end of compulsory schooling in England. This is a particularly useful comparison given the moral panic that continues to arise each year surrounding "boys' underachievement" (see Connolly, 2004). Interestingly, it is a moral panic based particularly around what is perceived to be the "gender gap" in GCSE performance and how boys are continuing to "lag behind" girls. The point to draw from this population pyramid is that there simply isn't a "gap" between boys and girls as commonly professed and thus it makes no sense to describe these data in terms of a "gap." At best if we wished to describe the key features of this chart we would use terms such as "considerable overlap" in GCSE scores between boys and girls and, at best, we would draw attention to "a slight difference" in the median scores for boys and girls. This, therefore, is an excellent example of how the greater use of exploratory data analysis (EDA), and the emphasis placed on graphically displaying and describing the data in words, can help to guard against the generation of crude and misleading statistics.

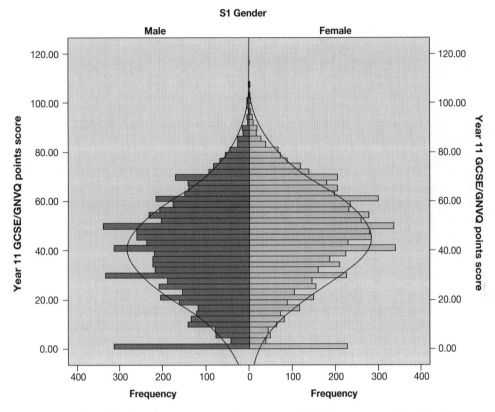

Figure 4.25 Population pyramid showing sex differences in GCSE scores attained by Year 11 pupils in England in 2002

EXERCISE 4.4

Using the **youthcohort.sav** dataset, try creating a boxplot using Chart Builder to illustrate differences between boys and girls ("s1gender") in relation to GCSE points scores. Also try creating a clustered bar chart, using cumulative percentages, illustrating differences between boys and girls in relation to the grades they achieved in GCSE English. Check your method and what you have produced on the companion website.

Conclusions

In this chapter you have learnt the key skills necessary to display data appropriately and effectively using tables and charts. Running throughout the chapter has been the emphasis on three guiding principles that you should bear in mind when considering how to present data. More specifically these relate to ensuring that your tables and charts: make sense in their own right (i.e. are **self-contained**); that they only include the key information necessary (i.e. are **efficient**); and that you select the type of table or chart carefully so that it illustrates your key findings as clearly as possible (i.e. is **effective**). All of this, in turn, indicates that the presentation of quantitative data is essentially an art form and that you need to experiment with different styles and formats and, thus, give the whole process due care and attention. After all, given that you have gone to all the trouble of designing a research study and then collecting and analyzing the data, it is almost criminal to obscure your key findings by producing ill-thought out and poorly constructed tables and charts.

By way of a recap, Box 4.1 includes a checklist of the key issues you need to address when creating a table or chart. When you have created your table/chart, you should be able to tick all the boxes that are relevant to what you have produced. All the questions, bar one, should be familiar to you as they relate to points made in this chapter. The one exception is the third question in the additional checklist for charts that asks about whether the axes you have used begin from zero. I have left this to the end of the chapter to leave

---

Box 4.1 Summary guide: good practice in presenting data in tables and charts

General Checklist

☐ Do you actually need the table or chart? Could the key findings be stated in the text just as clearly and easily?
☐ Would the table/chart make sense to someone who reads it in isolation and has not read any of the accompanying report?
☐ Does the table/chart have a clear title that explains precisely what the data relate to?
☐ Is the title of the table/chart numbered for clarity and to distinguish it from others in the report?
☐ Is there a footnote to acknowledge the source of the data, where appropriate?
☐ Have you removed all references to SPSS variable names and codes for values?
☐ Are all of the labels and values in the table/chart meaningful?
☐ Is all of the information and data in the table/chart absolutely necessary?

Additional Checklist for Tables

☐ Are the categories listed in a meaningful order?
☐ If you are comparing categories, have you place these in rows where possible?
☐ If you are comparing categories have you included percentages?
☐ If your table includes percentages, have they been calculated in the correct direction (i.e. in rows or columns)?
☐ If you have cumulative percentages included, is your variable ordinal?

Additional Checklist for Charts

☐ In relation to a clustered bar chart, are you using percentages to compare categories?
☐ Are all the axes clearly labeled, with measurement units stated where appropriate?
☐ Do your axes begin from zero? If not, could this lead to a misinterpretation of the nature of the relationship or differences being illustrated?
☐ In relation to a scatterplot, if there is reason to assume that there is a causal relationship between two variables, have you put the potential independent variable on the x-axis?

you with a simple but very important lesson about the use of tables and charts. The underlying point to this question is illustrated by the two bar charts shown in Figure 4.26. Both of the charts are technically correct and illustrate the percentage of boys and girls gaining five or more good GCSE passes in England in their final year of compulsory schooling (taken from the **youthcohort.sav** dataset). Hopefully you can see how axes that do not begin from zero can result in a misleading and often exaggerated picture of any differences or trends that exist. It is not surprising therefore that the chart on the right is often referred to as "Gee Whizz" chart. The lesson here is not only that you need to think very carefully about how to present your own findings in a clear but appropriate manner but also the need to read other people's tables and charts critically.

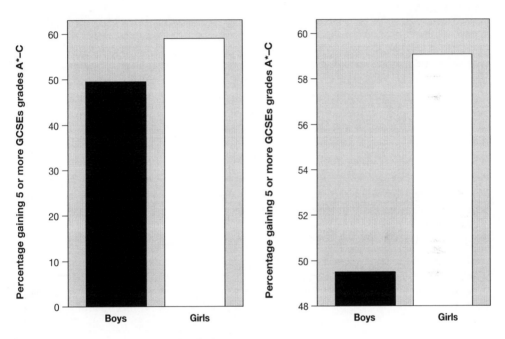

Figure 4.26 Example of a "Gee Whizz" chart

Chapter 5

Confidence intervals and statistical significance

Introduction

By now you should have the knowledge and skills you need to explore, describe and conduct routine analyses of a quantitative dataset. For some of you, this is actually all you will ever want to do. You may, for example, be interested simply in studying the children in your own school. The data you collect could relate to all children in that school (or a particular year group) and you are content just to analyze those data in relation to a particular issue or set of issues you are interested in (i.e. prevalence of bullying; attitudes to different subject lessons; gender differences in end of year tests; and/or attitudes to school meal provision). Alternatively, you may have data for all schools in your own school board or local education authority area and would like to explore and analyze key performance indicators across these schools. Moreover, if you have access to data gathered as part of a census (i.e. a survey of all schools or a survey of all members of a given population) then, again, you already have the knowledge and skills necessary to conduct routine analysis of those data.

However, you will often want to do more than this. In many circumstances, researchers wish to use the findings from their sample to make claims about the likely characteristics of the population as a whole. In other words, they wish to use their findings to make broader generalizations. Unfortunately, you can never just assume that the findings from your sample are representative of the population as a whole. In order to make generalizations you first need to consider the nature of your sample very carefully, and to identify the possible ways in which your findings from the sample may have been affected by a range of factors relating to the sampling procedure used. Once identified you need to acknowledge and address such influences in your analysis.

This, then, provides the focus for this chapter. The chapter begins by considering the range of factors that can introduce bias into a sample. One of these factors relates particularly to random sampling and the possibility that the findings you gain from a sample may just be a quirk of the random nature of the selection procedure rather than representing a real underlying trend in the population as a whole. It is this issue that provides the main focus for the chapter and, in particular, how such an influence might be better understood and incorporated into an analysis of the data in order to provide more solid and robust findings that can be appropriately generalized to the population as a whole. There are, however, a number of controversies surrounding the methods used to do this—particularly the use of confidence intervals and tests for statistical significance—and these controversies will be addressed in the concluding section of this chapter.

By the end of this chapter therefore you will:

- have an understanding of the key issues faced by researchers wishing to use the findings from their sample to make wider generalizations about the population from which it was drawn;
- know what confidence intervals are and be able to calculate them, and also know how to appropriately display them in relation to your own findings;
- have a sound grasp of the notion of statistical significance and related concepts including: hypothesis testing; Type I and Type II errors; statistical power; and one- and two-tailed tests.

It is worth warning you at this stage that this is the chapter that some of you might find most difficult to follow initially. This is not because we are about to dive into complex and nasty mathematical formulae (in fact, have a quick look ahead—you will be relieved to note that it is still all in words). Rather, the reason you may struggle initially with this chapter is because some of the ideas to be discussed here do require you to work through a number of logical arguments to understand them. However, I would still strongly maintain that if you can struggle with other educational and social theories then you are more than capable of handling the ideas to be discussed here. All you need to do is to be patient and expect that you might need to read this chapter (and the next one) more than once. My recommendation is that you read this chapter carefully and try to understand it as best you can. You should then read through the next chapter, which provides a number of practical illustrations of the key concepts to be described here as they are applied in practice. Having read the next chapter you will be in a much better position to re-read and understand this current chapter.

Sources of bias in samples

As indicated above, we often want to do more than just describe and analyze the data drawn from a sample in and of itself. Most commonly, we will often wish to use the findings we have gained from our sample to make some generalizations about the wider population from which that sample has been selected. Thus, for example, if we find that there are gender differences in attainment among a sample of pupils we have selected and studied then we would ideally like to use these findings to make more general claims about gender differences among the population of pupils as a whole. To do this, however, and notwithstanding all of the issues already raised in previous chapters to do with the reliability and validity of the measures used, there are two key issues we need to address.

The first relates to any **systematic bias** that may be associated with our data. Systematic bias is most commonly caused by a sample that is not representative of the population from which it is drawn. This can occur for a variety of reasons:

- We may have selected our sample randomly but not from the entire population. For example, if we only selected from pupils who were present in school this would systematically exclude those who tended to be persistent truants or who were temporarily or permanently excluded from school. It would also exclude any pupils who were actually home tutored. Therefore, before selecting a sample we need to think very carefully about the wider population we are interested in developing generalizations about and whether any sub-groups are likely to be excluded or under-represented in our final sample because of the sampling procedure used. If so, we need to include a proper discussion of the likely effects of this on the findings produced.

• Even if we have selected a sample randomly from the entire population, non-response is likely to introduce bias. More specifically, we know that those who tend not to respond to and/or take part in surveys are likely to have particular characteristics. In relation to the Youth Cohort Study of England and Wales, for example, it is known that there are at least four factors associated with non-response: gender, school type, region and GCSE attainment at Year 11 (NCSR, 1999). Therefore, non-response is likely to result in a biased sample and this, too, needs to be considered carefully in terms of its likely effects on any findings produced and how these might affect the ability to develop generalizations from the sample to the population as a whole.

• While random samples are always preferable, in many cases non-random, oppor-tunistic samples are used. This could involve selecting pupils from schools where the researcher is already known and has worked previously. Alternatively, it could involve surveying teachers by asking those attending professional development courses to complete a questionnaire. Generally, opportunistic samples like these are especially prone to producing biased samples (i.e. samples that are not entirely representative of the population as a whole) and so, again, this needs to be considered carefully before attempting to apply the findings from the sample to the population as a whole.

All of these factors raise questions about the reliability and validity of the data and thus any findings produced from them. However, because of the infinite number of factors that could emerge, each study needs to be considered on a case-by-case basis and cannot be adequately covered in this present book. However, while the issue of systematic bias is not covered in further detail here this should not be read as implying that it is unimportant. Indeed, it is crucial that any report of findings from a quantitative study fully contextualizes those findings in relation to the potential limitations and biases of the sample from which they are derived.

The second issue that needs to be addressed when considering how well one can generalize findings from our samples to the population as a whole is the effect of non-systematic bias or **sampling error**. Notwithstanding all of the potential influences related to systematic bias as touched upon above, there is also the distinct possibility that your findings may be unrepresentative of the population as a whole simply due to the random nature of the way it was selected. In other words, there is always the possibility that while you may have some interesting findings from your sample, these could simply have occurred by chance because of the random sampling procedure used rather than because they reflect a real underlying trend in the population as a whole. It is for this reason that we need to contextualize any findings that we do report in terms of also reporting their margins of error and/or the possibility that these findings could have occurred by chance. This is what the concepts of confidence intervals and statistical significance are all about and it is these that provide the main focus for the remainder of this chapter.

Confidence intervals

We will start with the notion of confidence intervals. There are actually two main types of confidence intervals that we would generally deal with—one relating to the mean that we would calculate for a scale variable, and the other relating to a percentage that we would calculate for a categorical variable (i.e. a nominal or ordinal variable). We will look at each in turn.

Confidence intervals for means

To gain an intuitive feel for what it is all about, we will use the **youthcohort.sav** dataset and focus specifically on the scale variable "gcsepts" that represents each young person's GCSE score. This variable was introduced in the previous chapters and represents a measure of a young person's level of attainment in public examinations at the end of their final year of compulsory schooling. To begin with open up the dataset and, for the purposes of this exercise, *do not* apply the weighting variable ("s1weight"). Use the **Analyze → Descriptive Statistics → Explore. . .** procedure to get an overall feel for this variable. The partial results of this are shown in Output 5.1. From this you will see that the (unweighted) variable ranges from 0 to 117 points with a mean of 49.29 and standard deviation of 19.35. If you have not got these figures then you have most likely applied the weighting variable, so reset Weight Cases and try again. You will also see from the stem and leaf display that is produced by default in SPSS, that the variable largely resembles a normal distribution (except for the "floor effect" noticeable by a slight bunching of cases at "0").

Output 5.1

Descriptives

			Statistic	Std. Error
Year 11 GCSE/GNVQ points score	Mean		49.2865	.16839
	95% Confidence Interval for Mean	Lower Bound	48.9564	
		Upper Bound	49.6165	
	5% Trimmed Mean		49.7825	
	Median		51.0000	
	Variance		374.336	
	Std. Deviation		19.34775	
	Minimum		.00	
	Maximum		117.00	
	Range		117.00	
	Interquartile Range		25.50	
	Skewness		−.390	.021
	Kurtosis		−.105	.043

What we are going to do now is to assume that the 13,201 pupils that comprise this dataset actually represent the population as a whole. Usually, we do not have the resources to survey the whole population (i.e. conduct a census) and so we make do with taking a random sample from the population. The basic idea is that we calculate the mean GCSE score for the sample and use this as an estimate of the likely mean GCSE score for the population as a whole. Let us try this by selecting a random sample of 200 cases from this dataset (if you are using a student version of SPSS then just select 50 cases). To do this, choose **Data → Select Cases. . . .** This opens up the **Select Cases** window you have already been introduced to in the previous chapter, as shown in Figure 5.1. This time, however, choose the third option down—"Random sample of cases"—and click on the "Sample" button. This opens up the additional window also shown in Figure 5.1. Here we will specify that we want SPSS to randomly select a sample of 200 cases from the first 13,201 cases (i.e. the entire dataset). If you have a student version of SPSS then select 50 from the first 1,450. Do this as shown and then click "Continue" to return to the main window. Ensure that the "Filter out unselected cases" option is chosen and then click "OK" to finish. You should notice that most cases have been deselected and that the "Filter On" label has appeared (see Figure 3.3) indicating that only the random sample of 200 cases selected is now active.

Once you have done this, use the **Analyze → Descriptive Statistics → Descriptives** . . . procedure to calculate the mean for your sample of 200 cases. What you should find is that the mean is pretty close to the mean we calculated for the population as a whole

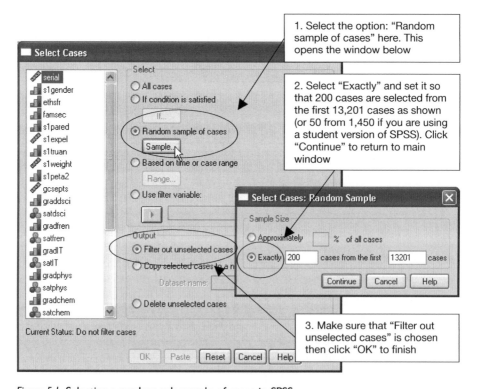

Figure 5.1 Selecting a random sub-sample of cases in SPSS

(which is 49.29) but it is likely to be slightly different from it. Now, do not close the SPSS Output window but just minimize it instead. Return to the main dataset and open up the **Select Cases** window again (**Data** → **Select Cases. . .**). Click on the "Reset" button to reset Select Cases and then go through the same procedure again of selecting another random sample of 200 cases from the entire dataset (i.e. the first 13,201 cases) as explained above (see Figure 5.1). Again, if you have the student version of SPSS then just select another 50 from 1,450. Once you have done this, calculate the mean for this second random sample just as you did for the first. If you have not closed the Output window you will now see the mean for your second sample appear in a table below the table displaying the mean for your first sample.

Repeat this procedure a few times so that you can compare the means of five or six different samples. What can you see happening? Hopefully, you can see that the means from each of your small samples are actually fairly good approximations to the actual mean for the population as a whole, and that they just tend to vary slightly within the range of about two or three points either above or below the actual population mean. In doing this exact procedure 20 times I came up with the 20 sample means shown in Table 5.1.

What we can see from this is that this random sampling procedure tends to produce **unbiased estimates** of the population mean. In other words, there is no systematic bias involved but, rather, the means of the samples tend to be randomly scattered either side of the true population mean. However, what we do see for each sample mean is a certain degree of sampling error in that none of the sample means is precisely the same as the true population mean. Because these are random samples, this is to be expected and is simply a by-product of the vagaries of random selection. Sometimes our sample of 200 cases will tend to include a slightly higher proportion of pupils with lower GCSE point scores than one would expect (and hence we get a sample mean slightly below the population mean) and on other occasions we will get a sample with a slightly higher proportion of pupils with higher GCSE point scores than would be expected (and in this case our sample mean will be slightly above the population mean).

Interestingly, if we look at a histogram displaying these 20 sample means, we can see that they tend to be normally distributed as shown in Figure 5.2. In fact, if we continued with this exercise and created more and more samples then what we would see is that the more samples we create and calculate the means for, the more this histogram would come to approximate to a normal distribution. Moreover, the average of these 20 sample means can be seen to be 49.50, which is getting pretty close to the population mean (of 49.29). In fact, another thing you would notice if you kept on generating more and more samples like this is that the average of the sample means would get closer and closer to that of the population mean of 49.29. By the way, if you understand this so far then you are actually

Table 5.1 The means of 20 samples (n = 200) selected from a population of 13,201 cases where the population mean is 49.29 (SD = 19.35)

47.67	52.51	49.57	49.47
51.24	50.43	48.26	50.13
50.42	49.37	47.77	50.02
48.07	49.41	48.05	50.14
49.82	50.08	48.00	49.52

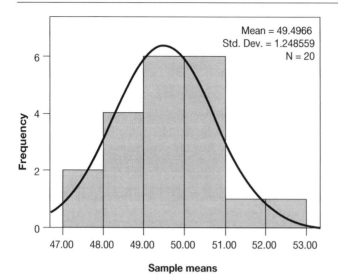

Figure 5.2
Distribution of the means of 20 random samples selected from a population of 13,201 cases with a population mean of 49.29 (SD = 19.35)

understanding some of the key tenets of the **central limit theorem**—an extremely important statistical theory.

So what is the relevance of all of this? There are two key points to draw out here. First of all it should show you that any statistic you generate from a random sample (such as the mean of a variable, or a percentage of another variable) is bound to have some error associated with it simply because of the fact that it is calculated from a randomly selected sample. Second, the histogram in Figure 5.2 gives you some sense of the extent of that error, in this case when you are dealing with a sample of 200. Moreover, as these sample means tend to be normally distributed we already have a way of measuring the extent of that error by calculating the standard deviation for this distribution. The concept of the standard deviation was introduced and discussed in Chapter 2. If it all seems a little hazy to you now then you should go back and re-read the relevant section (including the bit on standard scores) before continuing with this chapter.

It can be seen from Figure 5.2 that the standard deviation for the distribution of these 20 sample means is 1.25. As you were shown in Chapter 2 (see Figure 2.4), we can use this to conclude that if we take a number of random samples of the same size (n = 200) then we can assume that about two-thirds of these (68 percent) will be within one standard deviation of the actual population mean (i.e. ± 1.25 points in this case). Moreover, about 95 percent of these samples will produce a mean within two standard deviations of the population mean (i.e. ± 2.50 points).

The standard deviation of the sample means is an important concept in statistics and actually has a particular name—the **standard error**. It is the standard error that is used, in a similar way to what we have just done above, to create what we call **confidence intervals** for any statistics we produce from a random sample. As an illustration of all of this, open up the **20samples.sav** dataset. This includes the 20 samples I randomly selected (see Table 5.1 and Figure 5.2) which now appear in this dataset as 20 separate variables. What you will see in the dataset is the original "gcsepts" variable appearing first (with data for all 13,201 cases) and then followed by 20 random samples selected from this first variable (each with data for just 200 cases). Following this are the means and confidence intervals (to be explained shortly) for the 20 samples. Please note, this is not a usual dataset—each row does not represent a separate case. Rather, it has been specially constructed for this exercise (with another one to come in the next section).

Now, let us use the **Analyze → Descriptive Statistics → Explore. . .** procedure to explore the first sample. You should get the output shown in Output 5.2. As can be seen, the mean for the sample is 47.67 and the standard error is estimated from the data as 1.34. What we can now do, in line with the above discussion, is to take these figures to make the following points:

- There is a 68 percent chance that the true population mean lies within the range of one standard error of the sample mean (i.e. is captured within the boundaries of 47.67 ± 1.34 or, in other words, between 46.33 and 49.01).
- There is a 95 percent chance that the true population mean is within just under two standard errors of the sample mean (1.96 standard errors to be precise). As 1.96 standard errors is 2.63 (i.e. 1.96 × 1.34) this means there is a 95 percent chance that the population mean is contained within the boundaries 47.67 ± 2.63 (i.e. between 45.04 and 50.30).
- Finally, there is a 99 percent chance that the true population mean is within 2.58 standard errors of the sample mean (i.e. is captured within the boundaries of 47.67 ± 3.46 or, in other words, between 44.21 and 51.13).

What we have actually constructed here, then, are confidence intervals. They provide us with some sense of the margin of error associated with any summary statistic (in this case the mean of a sample). To summarize what we have just done, we have taken a

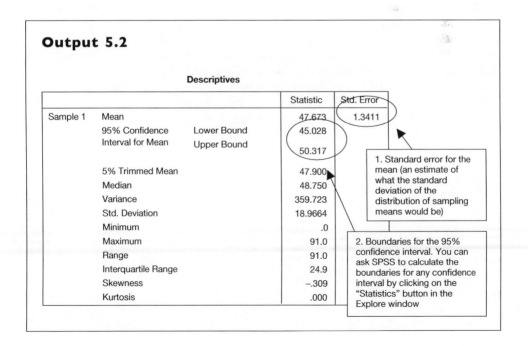

Output 5.2

Descriptives

			Statistic	Std. Error
Sample 1	Mean		47.673	1.3411
	95% Confidence Interval for Mean	Lower Bound	45.028	
		Upper Bound	50.317	
	5% Trimmed Mean		47.900	
	Median		48.750	
	Variance		359.723	
	Std. Deviation		18.9664	
	Minimum		.0	
	Maximum		91.0	
	Range		91.0	
	Interquartile Range		24.9	
	Skewness		–.309	
	Kurtosis		.000	

1. Standard error for the mean (an estimate of what the standard deviation of the distribution of sampling means would be)

2. Boundaries for the 95% confidence interval. You can ask SPSS to calculate the boundaries for any confidence interval by clicking on the "Statistics" button in the Explore window

random sample of 200 young people and calculated their mean GCSE points score. We would now like to use this sample mean as an estimate of the true population mean. However, we know from earlier that because we used a random sample this estimate is unlikely to be completely accurate and there is, thus, likely to be some error attached to it. Using the standard error we can therefore provide the reader with a sense of the margin of error involved in our estimate of the population mean. In this case, and from the above, we can report that we are 95 percent confident that the true population mean is contained within the range 45.04 and 50.30 (i.e. $\pm$ 1.96 standard errors from the sample mean). Not surprisingly, this is actually known as the **95% confidence interval** which SPSS has already calculated for us as shown in Output 5.2 (the figures shown for the lower and upper bounds of the confidence interval are slightly different to what we have calculated by hand due to rounding errors). If we wanted to, we could use the **Analyze → Descriptive Statistics → Explore. . .** procedure to calculate any confidence interval. In the main **Explore** window simply click on the "Statistics" button and set the confidence interval at the level required as shown in Figure 5.3.

EXERCISE 5.1

Try calculating the 99% confidence interval for the mean from this first sample. You should find that it is: 44.185 to 51.160. Similarly, try calculating the 68% confidence interval for the mean. You should find that it is: 46.335 to 49.010.

Another way to understand what is going on here is to display these confidence intervals using what is known as error bars. These are best explained with an example. For the **20samples.sav** dataset, choose **Graphs → Legacy Dialogs → Error Bar. . .** (or just **Graphs → Error Bar. . .** in SPSS Version 14.0 and earlier and Mac versions). An initial window will open up; make sure you select "Simple" and also "Summaries of separate variables" beneath this and then click "Define." This opens the main **Define Simple Error Bar** window shown in Figure 5.4. What we will do is to display error bars for all 20 samples. To do this, select all 20 variables representing these samples and place them into the "Error Bars:" field as shown. Make sure you have the error bars set at the 95% confidence interval level and then click "OK." You should get the chart shown in Figure 5.5 (except for a few minor amendments I have made to it).

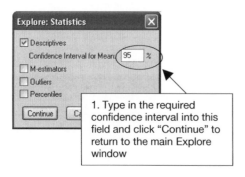

Figure 5.3
Explore: Statistics window in SPSS

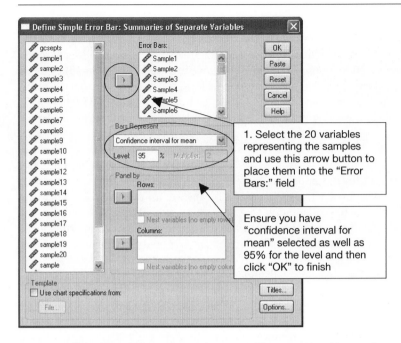

Figure 5.4 Define Simple Error Bar: Summaries of Separate Variables window in SPSS

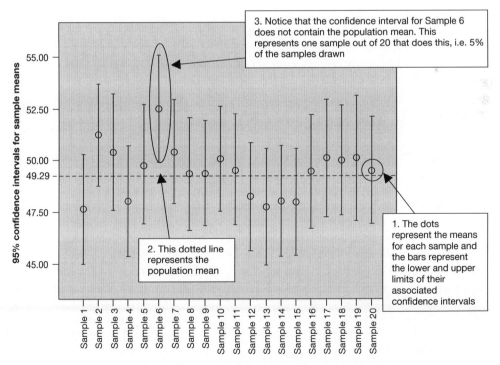

Figure 5.5 Error bars showing 95 percent confidence intervals for the means of 20 samples randomly selected from a population with a mean of 49.29

The error bars are actually very straightforward to interpret. The dots represent the means that have been calculated for each of the 20 samples. The bars protruding from the dots represent the 95% confidence intervals for each of these means with the ends indicating the lower and upper bounds of the confidence interval. Taking Sample 1 as an example, we can read off from the scale that the mean (represented by the dot) is about 47.7 and the lower and upper bounds of the confidence interval are about 45.0 and 50.0, respectively (i.e. the data we derived formally from the **Explore. . .** procedure earlier—see Output 5.2).

What I have done to the chart is to add a reference line (dotted) to indicate the true population mean for the 13,201 cases (i.e. 49.29 points). With this included, the chart provides a very useful illustration of the whole notion of confidence intervals (see also Field, 2005: 19). As can be seen, the 20 sample means are all pretty close to the true population mean and tend to be randomly scattered either side of it. For the confidence intervals associated with these sample means, it will be remembered that we interpret these as telling us that we can be 95 percent confident that the true population mean is contained within these intervals. From SPSS Figure 5.5 it can be seen that this is precisely what we have found. Out of the 20 samples selected randomly, 19 (i.e. 95 percent) do indeed include the true population mean.

By contrast, only one of the samples (Sample 6) has a confidence interval that does not include the true population mean. This, in turn, raises a really important point that we need to grasp. Trying to convey uncertainty is at the heart of statistics. Therefore, we rarely make absolute claims. In this case, the confidence intervals represent precisely what they state, i.e. a 95 percent chance that the true population mean lies within the boundaries stated. However, we can never be absolutely certain. Because our samples are random there is always the chance (a 5 percent chance in this case) that a rogue sample will be selected that will, in turn, produce a bogus result. This is why we should never completely trust the findings from any single survey but should look for corroborating evidence from other surveys for the findings we are interested in. Of course, if we only have the resources to conduct one survey and it is very important that the estimates of the population mean we produce are as accurate as possible then we can always use a different confidence interval, i.e. a 99% confidence interval rather than a 95% confidence interval. This would reduce the risk of a bogus result appearing from 5 percent down to 1 percent. As was seen earlier, while this would not change the value of the sample mean it would increase the size of the confidence interval.

Finally, it is worthwhile looking at an example of where error bars might be used in practice. For this we will go back to the **youthcohort.sav** dataset and examine differences in GCSE scores between different racial/ethnic groups. Open up the dataset and, this time, make sure you Weight Cases using the "s1weight" variable. Once you have done this, choose **Graphs** → **Legacy Dialogs** → **Error Bar. . .** and this will open the initial window that you have already seen. Select "Simple" as before but this time select "Summaries for groups of cases" and then click "Define." This opens up the main **Simple Error Bar** window shown in Figure 5.6. This time place "gcsepts" into the "Variable:" field and "ethsfr" into the "Category Axis:" field as shown. Check that 95% confidence interval has been selected for "Bars Represent" as before and then click "OK." You should obtain the error bar chart shown in Figure 5.7 (notwithstanding a few modifications I have made).

There are three points to make about this chart. First, it can be seen that the size of the error bars (i.e. the 95% confidence intervals) vary between the different racial/ethnic groups. They are clearly very small for the "White" group and largest for the

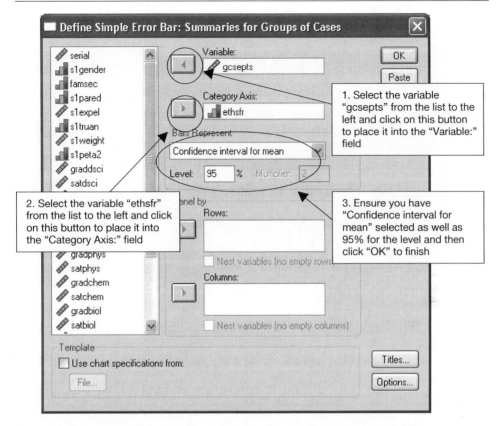

Figure 5.6 Define Simple Error Bar: Summaries for Groups of Cases window in SPSS

"Bangladeshi" and "Other Asian" groups. The reason for this is simply that these means have been calculated on differently sized sub-samples. The reason that the error bar for "White" students is so small is because the mean has been calculated on a very large sub-sample of 11,242 pupils. Given a sub-sample of this size it can be expected that the sample mean will tend to be a very good estimate of the population mean, and so the confidence interval will be very small. Similarly, the fact that the confidence interval for the "Bangladeshi" and "Other Asian" groups are the largest also simply reflects the fact that the means for these groups have been calculated on the smallest sub-samples (n = 134 and 150, respectively). As such it can be expected that there is more room for sampling error and, thus, a larger confidence interval will result.

EXERCISE 5.2

In order to gain a proper sense of the effects of sample size on these estimates, use the "Split File" facility to calculate the lower and upper bounds of the 95% confidence intervals for each of the racial/ethnic groups. Check your method and results on the companion website.

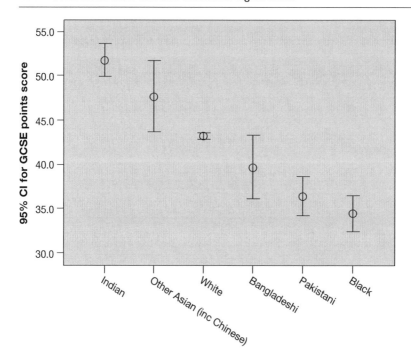

Figure 5.7 Error bars showing differences in mean GCSE point scores between different racial/ethnic groups for Year 11 pupils in England

The second point to make about this chart is that it can be useful in terms of providing a quick indication of whether the means between the different racial/ethnic groups are likely to be different or not. The more the error bars for any two groups overlap, the more this indicates that we cannot be confident in assuming that the means for those groups in the population as a whole are likely to be different. The overlapping error bars would suggest that any difference between the sample means for those two groups may just be a quirk of random sampling rather than representing a real difference in the population as a whole. However, and having said this, it is difficult to draw firm conclusions from just a visual inspection of an error bar chart, especially when error bars only partially overlap. While they may provide an initial indicator of how the means of different groups compare, we need to use more specific statistical tests to assess whether there is sufficient evidence to indicate that the population means of the two or more groups are likely to be different or not. This is something we will explore in the next chapter.

The third and final point to make about this chart is that it tells us nothing about the distribution of scores between differing racial/ethnic groups. In fact, because it focuses solely on the mean for each group, it can tend to provide a misleading picture that emphasizes the differences and fails to show the overlapping nature of the actual scores between different groups. In this sense, a better way to display GCSE scores for different racial/ethnic groups is via the use of boxplots as illustrated in Chapter 3 for these particular data (see Figure 3.10). The boxplots still allow a comparison of the average levels of attainment between racial/ethnic groups (by comparing the median lines for each box) but also give a more holistic and grounded sense of the level of overlap between groups.

Confidence intervals for proportions

Alongside creating confidence intervals for means, you may also need to provide confidence intervals for summary statistics generated from categorical variables (whether nominal or ordinal variables). Most commonly, this will involve providing confidence intervals for percentage figures you may calculate. In fact, this is where you might well have seen confidence intervals reported in the past, especially in relation to opinion polls. In these cases it is not uncommon to find a statistic reported along the lines of "23 percent of those surveyed supported the government's new education bill" and then to see a note stating that the margin of error for this figure is ± 3%. This is actually just another example of a confidence interval and, unless stated otherwise, it can be assumed that it is a 95% confidence interval. In other words, therefore, we can take from this that there is a 95 percent chance that the true proportion of people in the population as a whole supporting the government's new education bill is contained within the range 23 ± 3%, i.e. between 20 percent and 26 percent.

Unfortunately, there is no obvious way of calculating standard errors for percentages in SPSS Version 15.0 (or earlier versions). As such this is one of the only occasions in the book when you will have to face your demons and tackle an equation and calculate the standard errors by hand. Fortunately, the formula is pretty straightforward and so if you've got this far then you shouldn't find it a problem. Basically, let us assume you have a finding from your analysis expressed as a percentage. We will call that percentage "p". Also, we will assume that this percentage was calculated on a sub-sample of a size we will call "n". From this, the formula for calculating the standard error of that proportion is:

$$\text{Standard error of a percentage } (p) = \sqrt{\frac{p\,(100-p)}{n}}\,.$$

To put this in words, you: (1) subtract the percentage you are interested in from 100; (2) multiply the figure you get by the original percentage; (3) divide the result of this by the size of your sub-sample; and then (4) take the square root of this final figure. To illustrate this, let us take an example from the **bullying.sav** dataset. It will be remembered that these data were based upon a survey of a random sample of 819 young people in Northern Ireland. One of the questions they were asked was whether they had ever been bullied in school. Open up the dataset and run the **Analyze → Descriptive Statistics → Crosstabs. . .** procedure to examine the proportions of boys and girls in the sample who reported having been bullied. The variable you are interested in here is "unbullsch" and you should get the output shown in Output 5.3.

If we focus on girls for the purposes of this example it can be seen that 32.6 percent of girls stated that they had been bullied. Now, figures like this can have important implications for policy and practice. It is, therefore, important when reporting these that we also give some indication of the likely margins of error involved. To do this we need to use the above formula as follows. First, we need to identify what the values for "p" and "n" are. From Output 5.3 we can see that the percentage we are interested in is 32.6 percent and so this is "p". We then need to ask what this is a percentage of. In this case it is a percentage of all girls in the sample who answered the question and, thus, is a percentage of a total of 472 girls: so, "n" = 472. We can now put these figures into the formula as follows:

Output 5.3

Q1 - Are you male or female? * Q26 - Have you yourself ever been bullied in school?
Crosstabulation

			Q26 - Have you yourself ever been bullied in school?		
			Yes	No	Total
Q1 - Are you male or female?	Male	Count	90	239	329
		% within Q1 - Are you male or female?	27.4%	72.6%	100.0%
	Female	Count	154	318	472
		% within Q1 - Are you male or female?	32.6%	67.4%	100.0%
Total		Count	244	557	801
		% within Q1 - Are you male or female?	30.5%	69.5%	100.0%

1. The percentage we are interested in here (i.e. "p") is 32.6%

2. This percentage relates to a total of 472 girls (i.e. it is 32.6% of all 472 girls and thus "n" = 472

$$\text{Standard error} = \sqrt{\frac{32.6\,(100-32.6)}{472}}.$$

If we follow the steps outlined above then first we subtract 32.6 from 100 and this gives 67.4. We then multiply 67.4 by 32.6 which gives 2197.24 and divide this by 472 as shown:

$$\text{Standard error} = \sqrt{\frac{30.4\,(67.4)}{472}} = \sqrt{\frac{2197.24}{472}} = \sqrt{4.655}.$$

Finally, using a calculator, the square root of 4.655 is 2.158. Thus, the standard error for this percentage figure of 32.6 percent is 2.158. All we need to do now is to create our confidence interval using this standard error as we did in the previous section for our sample means. Thus for the 32.6 percent finding:

- a 95% confidence interval $= \pm 1.96$ standard errors, i.e. $\pm 1.96 \times 2.158 = \pm 4.23$
- a 99% confidence interval $= \pm 2.58$ standard errors, i.e. $\pm 2.58 \times 2.158 = \pm 5.57$

From these figures we can conclude that we are 95 percent confident that the true proportion of girls who would report being bullied in school lies within the range of 32.6% $\pm 4.2\%$, i.e. between 28.4 percent and 36.8 percent. Of course, this figure assumes that it is based upon a simple random sample with a 100 percent response rate. It also assumes that all of the young people shared the same definition of bullying when answering the question. All we can really draw from this is that if these two conditions have been met then our estimated proportion with the associated margin of error is as reported above. In reality we will be faced with non-response and so we need to also consider the likely effects of this on the findings reported. In addition, and in this case, we would need to consider the possible confusion over the interpretation of the question and the effect this may have had on the young people's answers. Of course, while non-response is a difficult problem to deal with, making sure you use clear and unambiguous questions is something that you do have much more control over.

Finally, while SPSS does not calculate standard errors for percentage estimates, it does have the facility to allow you to display their associated confidence intervals in bar charts. However, unfortunately this is only available in Version 14.0 on upwards (Version 13.0 for Macs). To illustrate this let us stay with the same example and create a bar chart to show the proportions of boys and girls answering "yes" and "no" to the question: "Have you yourself ever been bullied in school?" Here we need to use the **Graphs** → **Legacy Dialogs** → **Bar. . .** procedure covered in Chapter 3 to create a clustered bar chart (see Figure 3.6). We need to place "unbullsch" in the "Category Axis:" field and "rsex" in the "Define Clusters by:" field. Alongside selecting "% of cases" for "Bars Represent", the only other thing we need to do to include error bars is to click on the "Options" button in the main **Define Clustered Bar** window. This calls up the additional **Options** window shown in Figure 5.8. Select the "Display error bars" option and set the level for the confidence intervals by typing "95" into the field as shown. Click "Continue" to return to the main window and then "OK" in the main window to complete the procedure. This should produce the clustered bar chart shown in Figure 5.9 (give or take a few minor amendments I have made to it). As can be seen, the error bars can be interpreted in very much the same way as those described in the last section. The top of each of the main bars represents the actual percentages of boys and girls responding yes and no to the question. The error bars superimposed on these indicate the 95% confidence intervals and their lower and upper bounds just as before.

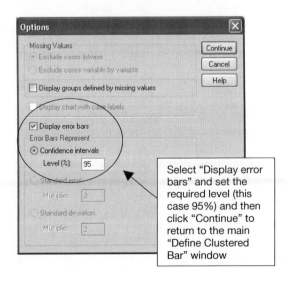

Select "Display error bars" and set the required level (this case 95%) and then click "Continue" to return to the main "Define Clustered Bar" window

Figure 5.8
Options window for Define Clustered Bar window in SPSS

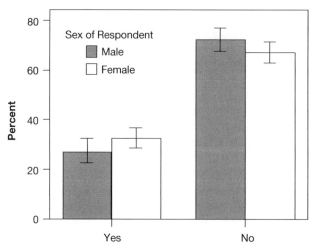

Figure 5.9
Clustered bar chart with 95 percent confidence intervals added, showing sex differences in proportions of pupils stating that they had been bullied in schools in Northern Ireland in 2005

Interestingly in this case, while more girls reported that they had been bullied compared to boys (32.6 percent compared to 27.4 percent, respectively), it can be seen that there is considerable overlapping of the error bars. It could be the case, therefore, that due to the random nature of the sample selected it just happened to have slightly more girls that were bullied than one would expect from the population as a whole, and also slightly fewer boys that had been bullied than one expect. While, as before, we need to be careful not to base our conclusions on a visual inspection of the error bars alone, this does at least encourage us to examine this issue further. In fact, trying to determine whether a finding derived from a sample does actually reflect a real pattern among the wider population, rather than just being a quirk of the random nature of the sample selected, is what lies at the heart of the concept of statistical significance and it is to this that we now turn.

The concept of statistical significance

If you have ever read any published research based upon quantitative methods you may well have noticed an excessive use of the word "significant" to describe findings, even when they do not seem that striking or practically significant to you. You will have also seen the letter "p" being dropped in all over the place, often in the form of "$p < 0.05$" or "$p = 0.023$" and so on. All of this relates to the concept of **statistical significance** which is about assessing how confident we can be in using a finding taken from a sample to generalize to the population as a whole. It is not an exaggeration to say that quantitative research in education and the social sciences more generally tends to be obsessed with the notion of statistical significance and yet, for the most part, the concept seems to remain widely misunderstood and inappropriately used. In this section we will focus on developing an intuitive grasp of the concept itself and then, in the next section, we will examine how it tends to be applied in research more formally through an approach known as hypothesis testing. In the concluding section of the chapter we will take a step back and assess how the concept of statistical significance can be used more appropriately within educational research, and will highlight some of the dangers to look out for in the way it is used by others.

To begin with, therefore, let us try to understand the notion of statistical significance intuitively. To do this we will take a scenario whereby a researcher working in a large university is interested in assessing whether there are any differences in the proportions of male and female students who said that if their professors made their lectures available as podcasts (i.e. as audio recordings available to listen to and/or download from the internet) they would use this service. Let us assume that there are 30,000 students and the researcher has a complete list of all of the students' names and contact details. The researcher does not have the resources to question every student individually and so she needs to take a sample.

The researcher begins by selecting just five male students and five female students randomly from her list (Scenario 1). The results of this initial survey are shown in Table 5.2. As can be seen, three out of the five male students said they would use podcasts of lectures if available, while two out of the five female students responded in the same way. If we turned these figures into percentages then this would give us the finding that male students are more likely to want to use the service than females; with 60 percent of males stating they would compared to 40 percent of females. The key question is: how confident can we be about this finding? If it was presented to you, would you feel that you had sufficient evidence of an underlying difference between male and female students in the university?

Hopefully your answer to this is "no," you would not have much confidence in these findings. The second question that follows on from this, then, is: why are you not confident in these findings? Presumably the main reason you feel you cannot trust these findings is because they are based upon such a small sample. All it would take is just one of the students in the sample to change their view for the findings to be completely altered. If, for example, just one of the male students who said "yes" had actually said "no" then this would alter the findings altogether with the result that male and female students would now be equally likely to want to use the podcast lecture service.

Therefore the problem here is that because the sample size is so small and we are also selecting it completely randomly, there is a high chance that we could find a difference like this in our sample even if there is actually no difference between males and females in the population as a whole. One of the ways we can think about this is to ask ourselves: what are the chances of coming up with a difference like this if there was actually no such difference in the population as a whole (i.e. if males and females were equally likely to state that they would use lecture podcasts)? Have a think about this particular example

Table 5.2 Scenario 1: Proportions of male and female university students indicating that they would use podcasts of lectures if they were made available (Total sample = 10)

	Yes		No		Total	
	n	%	n	%	n	%
Male students	3	60	2	40	5	100
Female students	2	40	3	60	5	100
Total	5	50	5	50	10	100

involving just five male and five female students. Assuming that there are no gender differences in the population as a whole, what do you think the chance would be of still getting a finding like this from a sample of just ten students selected randomly? Try to express it as a percentage (i.e. a 10 percent chance or a 50 percent chance or a 90 percent chance, and so on).

When I have discussed a similar scenario to this in class with my own students they have tended to argue that there is a very high chance of this occurring and have suggested a figure as high as 90 percent. In this sense what they are arguing is that because of the really small size of the sample, there is a 90 percent chance of selecting a sample that gives you a finding like this one, even if there are no such differences in the population of students as a whole. In other words, there is a 90 percent chance that your finding is a bogus one; representing a quirk of the random sampling procedure rather than a real underlying trend in the population of students as a whole.

Now, rather than having a total sample of just ten, what if the researcher had originally selected a sample of 20 instead (i.e. ten male students and ten female students). Let's call this Scenario 2. Supposing that the findings were as before, and as illustrated in Table 5.3, would you feel any more confident in these results? When I asked my own students this question their responses tended to be that they would possibly feel a little more confident but only marginally so. The sample is still very small and, thus, they would still not trust the findings. Looking at it the other way, what do you think the chances are now of getting the findings you have here from a sample of 20 students if there are actually no underlying gender differences in the student population as a whole? Again, my own students tended to feel it was still highly likely and suggested that there was about an 80 percent chance of this being a bogus result.

This time, let us double the sample size again. What about a scenario where the researcher had originally selected 40 students randomly in total, producing the results shown in Table 5.4. Now that these percentages are based upon 20 male students and 20 female students can we be any more confident in these results? For my own students they said that they would have a little more confidence in these results. More specifically, they felt that it probably could be seen as representing an underlying trend but that there is still a good chance that the results are bogus. The figure they put on it this time was about a 50 percent chance. In other words, while they felt that there may be something notable emerging from a survey of 40 students, there was still a 50 percent chance that it could be a bogus result reflecting a quirk of the random sampling procedure and thus still could not really be trusted.

Table 5.3 Scenario 2: Proportions of male and female university students indicating that they would use podcasts of lectures if they were made available (Total sample = 20)

	Yes		No		Total				
	n	%	n	%			n	%	
Male students	6	60	4	40			10	100	
Female students	4	40	6	60			10	100	
Total	10	50	10	50			20	100	

Table 5.4 Scenario 3: Proportions of male and female university students indicating that they would use podcasts of lectures if they were made available (Total sample = 40)

	Yes	No		Total				
	n	%		n	%		n	%
Male students	12	60		8	40		20	100
Female students	8	40		12	60		20	100
Total	20	50		20	50		40	100

We could carry on with this, doubling the sample size each time and asking the same questions. Rather than doing this, let me ask you just one more question: at what point would you feel confident enough in the findings? In other words, what sample size would you feel you needed in order that you would trust that the difference in the sample between male and female students (the 60 percent to 40 percent difference) actually reflected a real underlying difference in the student population as a whole? For my own students they started to show more confidence in a random sample of 80 students (40 males and 40 females) but still felt there was a chance (they suggested a 15 percent chance) that the findings could be bogus. However, when the sample size was doubled again to 160 students (80 males and 80 females) they felt that they could now trust the findings and that there was only a very small chance that these findings could have resulted simply from a quirk of the random sampling procedure. When asked what they thought the chance could be that these findings could be bogus, based as they were on a total sample of 160 students, many of them said that it would be less than a 5 percent chance (an interesting figure for them to choose as we will see shortly).

So why have we gone through all this? Well, if you have understood the logic so far then you have basically understood the principles underlying the concept of statistical significance. All of this weighing up of evidence that we have done here, and the assessments of whether findings taken from a sample are likely to reflect real underlying trends in the population as a whole rather than just a quirk of the random sampling procedure (i.e. sampling error) are at the heart of the notion of statistical significance. There are just three minor differences to the way all of this is done in practice by researchers using real-life data:

• Rather than having to guess what the chances are that a finding may be bogus and just the result of sampling error, the chances can be calculated formally and accurately using a number of different statistical tests (many of which we will see in the next chapter).

• Rather than reporting the chances as percentages (i.e. a 30 percent chance), these statistical tests report them as probabilities in the form of "p = 0.30". Probabilities run from "0" (indicating there is no chance whatsoever) to "1" (indicating that there is a definite, 100 percent chance). As illustrated in Table 5.5, you can convert chances expressed as percentages to probabilities simply by dividing by 100. For every type of finding you may generate from your data, there is a statistical test you can use to calculate the probability that the finding has occurred by chance as a result of the random nature of the sample, assuming that there is no actual and corresponding trend within the population as a whole.

• By convention, a cut-off point of p = 0.05 (or a 5 percent chance) is used to determine whether we can have confidence in a finding derived from our sample or not. Thus, if the chances of our finding being just the result of the random nature of our sample is 5 percent or less (i.e. "p" is less than or equal to 0.05—often denoted as "p < 0.05") then we tend to conclude that the chances are so small that, on balance, we can have sufficient confidence (i.e. at least 95 percent confidence, in fact) that the finding reflects a real underlying trend in the population as a whole. It is in cases like this that we refer to the finding being "statistically significant."

With all of this in mind, we can now go back to the scenarios we have been discussing and see what the actual probabilities are that findings such as these could have occurred by chance, assuming that no such differences exist in the wider student population. The probabilities are given in Table 5.6 and you will be shown how to calculate these particular probabilities in the next chapter. For now it is interesting simply to note the actual probabilities listed and, in particular, how they tend to be smaller than we would tend to have guessed intuitively. While we may feel that a sample of 160 is small, statistically we can see that it allows us to be very confident that the finding produced represents a real underlying trend in the population as a whole. In fact, the figures suggest we can actually be 98.9 percent confident in these findings (i.e. if there is a 1.1 percent chance of the finding being bogus then there is a 100 – 1.1 = 98.9 percent chance that it is not).

Table 5.5 Percentage chances of events occurring expressed as probabilities

Chances that an event will occur, expressed as a percentage	Associated probabilities that the event will occur
0% chance	p = 0
5% chance	p = 0.05
10% chance	p = 0.10
25% chance	p = 0.25
50% chance	p = 0.50
75% chance	p = 0.75
95% chance	p = 0.95
100% chance	p = 1.00

Table 5.6 Percentage chances and probabilities that findings derived from a sample may have occurred by chance assuming that there are no such differences in the population as a whole

Finding	Sample size	% Chance*	Probability*
60% of male students answered 'yes', compared to 40% of female students	20 (10 females and 10 males)	37.1	p = 0.371
	40 (20 females and 20 males)	20.6	p = 0.206
	80 (40 females and 40 males)	7.4	p = 0.074
	160 (80 females and 80 males)	1.1	p = 0.011
	320 (160 females and 160 males)	< 0.1	p < 0.001

*Derived from Chi-Square tests (see Chapter 5 for more details)

Testing for statistical significance

While the main conceptual basis of the notion of statistical significance has been outlined above, there are a few more details just to run through briefly in order to complete the general picture. More specifically, there are four issues to explain here that will each be dealt with in turn: **hypothesis testing**; **Type I and Type II errors**; **statistical power**; and **one- and two-tailed tests**. Beyond this, you will find in the next chapter a number of specific examples of how all of this is put together and applied in practice that will help to consolidate your understanding.

Hypothesis testing

There is a particular procedure known as hypothesis testing that is used in the analysis of statistical significance. It comprises a series of logical steps and simply helps to formalize the more intuitive approach outlined above. The main steps of hypothesis testing will simply be outlined here and these will then be illustrated extensively in the next chapter:

- *Step One: Derive a hypothesis that you wish to test.* The hypothesis should be clear and specific and something that can actually be measured and thus tested. For the purposes of this book, it will tend to take the form of a hypothesis about the relationship between two variables. An example could be: "There is a difference in the proportions of boys and girls who report being bullied in school." This is known as the **alternative hypothesis** (sometimes denoted by: "H_1"). You should note that a hypothesis is a statement of what is believed to be the case. This is different from the research questions asked in the last chapter which are more general in nature.

- *Step Two: State the null-hypothesis associated with alternative hypothesis that you wish to test.* The null-hypothesis is basically the assumption that there are no differences or relationships between the variables you are interested in. In this particular case the **null-hypothesis** (sometimes denoted by: "H_0") is simply stated as: "There is no difference in the proportions of boys and girls who report being bullied in school."

- *Step Three: Identify the two variables you wish to use to test your hypothesis.* Much of the previous chapter was spent running through examples where we had to find valid and reliable variables to address particular research questions we asked ourselves. While you are now concerned with addressing a particular hypothesis rather than a more general research question, you still need to identify and use appropriate variables in the same way. In the case of the hypothesis stated above we can use two variables from the **bullying.sav** dataset: sex of pupil ("rsex") and also their responses to the question as to whether they have been bullied in school ("ubullsch").

- *Step Four: Select an appropriate statistical test to use.* There are a range of different tests that can be used and that have been specifically designed for analyzing relationships between different types of variable. You shouldn't be surprised by this stage to know that the particular test you choose will depend upon the types of variables you are analyzing (i.e. nominal, ordinal or scale). How to choose the correct statistical test is actually very straightforward and is covered in the next chapter. However, just in case you are interested, in relation to our current example we are dealing with two nominal variables and thus the appropriate test would be the Chi-Square test.

- *Step Five: Use the statistical test to calculate the significance level of the relationship found between the two variables.* Again, this is the focus for the next chapter where you will be shown, step by step, how to undertake all of the main statistical tests. For now you will remember that the relationship between these two variables was actually explored earlier in this chapter (see Output 5.3) on a relatively large sample (n = 801). In this instance we found that girls were only slightly more likely to report being bullied in school than boys (32.6 percent to 27.4 percent, respectively). A Chi-Square test conducted on these findings produced a significance level of $p = 0.111$. In other words, this tells us that there is an 11.1 percent chance that these differences were simply a result of the random nature of the sampling procedure rather than representing a real difference between boys and girls in the underlying pupil population.

- *Step Six: Use the findings from the statistical test to decide whether there is sufficient evidence to reject the null-hypothesis (and thus accept the alternative hypothesis) or not.* The key point to note here is that the probability of 0.111 has been calculated on the assumption that the null-hypothesis is true. In other words, and as the reasoning has gone, if we assume that there are no gender differences in the wider pupil population (i.e. assume the null-hypothesis is correct), what is the probability of selecting a sample by chance with the differences found between boys and girls? Assuming that we are using the conventional 5 percent significance level as a cut-off point to make a decision, then there are just one of two outcomes to our test:

- *If $p < 0.05$* (i.e. the significance level calculated is less than or equal to 0.05) then we would conclude that there is sufficient evidence to reject the null-hypothesis and thus accept the alternative hypothesis. To explain this another way, what we are basically doing is concluding that the possibility that there are no differences between boys and girls in the population as a whole, and thus that the findings in our sample have occurred by chance, are so small (i.e. only 5 percent chance or less) that this is therefore unlikely to have occurred by chance. This is why we then reject the null-hypothesis. Moreover, if it hasn't occurred by chance then it is likely to have occurred because there is actually a real underlying difference between boys and girls in the population as a whole. This, in turn, is why we then accept the alternative hypothesis.
- *If $p > 0.05$* (i.e. is greater than 0.05) then you would conclude that there is not sufficient evidence to reject the null-hypothesis. In other words, while you may have found a difference between boys and girls in your sample you cannot be confident enough that it represents a real underlying difference in the population as a whole, rather than just having occurred by chance. This is actually the outcome of the present example where we found that there was a relatively high chance—an 11.1 percent chance—that our findings could have simply been the result of sampling error. In this present case the most appropriate option here, therefore, is not to actually report the substantive findings that indicate a difference between boys and girls, as we do not have sufficient confidence in these. Rather, we would just report that no evidence was found of a difference/relationship between boys and girls, and then report the results of our significance test.

In reality, the interpretation of the significance level calculated for any finding derived from a sample is not always as straightforward as this. However, we will save discussion of this until the concluding section of this chapter.

Type I and Type II errors

One of the key issues to grasp in relation to hypothesis testing is that it can never produce absolute results. For example, and as stressed earlier, even when a difference in our sample has an associated significance level as small as $p = 0.011$ we cannot be completely certain that the difference found in our sample does, in fact, reflect a difference within the population as a whole. As the significance level indicates, there is still a small risk (a 1.1 percent chance, in fact) that our finding is bogus. In such cases, claiming that a difference exists within the population when in reality there is no difference is known as committing a **Type I error**. In this case the risk of committing a Type I error is just 1.1 percent.

We control the level of risk associated with committing such an error by setting our significance level accordingly; sometimes labelled as "α" or alpha. As mentioned earlier, the general convention is to set the cut-off point at 5 percent (i.e. $\alpha = 0.05$). As such what we are actually doing is setting the level of risk of committing a Type I error at 5 percent or less (i.e. $p \leq 0.05$). We then use this criterion to decide whether to accept that a finding from our sample is likely to be "real" or not. Thus, for example, if a statistical test shows that the statistical significance of our finding is $p = 0.085$ (i.e. an 8.5 percent possibility of the finding simply having occurred by chance) then if we concluded that the finding is "real" we would be taking a higher risk (an 8.5 percent risk) than we have decided is acceptable. As such, we should conclude that there is not sufficient evidence to claim that such a finding is likely to reflect an underlying trend in the population as a whole.

Of course, it is important to realize that this 5 percent cut-off point is essentially arbitrary and we only tend to use it because of convention. There will be occasions, especially in medical trials of new drug treatments, when a 5 percent risk of producing bogus results is unacceptably high. In such circumstances it is not uncommon to find researchers setting a much higher and more stringent threshold, maybe a 1 percent significance level ($p < 0.01$) or even less. On the other hand, a researcher may just be conducting an exploratory study with a relatively small sample. His or her intention may be to test a few initial hypotheses and, if there is sufficient evidence to support these, to then attempt to confirm these findings using a much larger survey. In this case it may well be appropriate to loosen the level of risk of committing a Type I error, especially as the intention is to verify any findings in the larger survey to follow. As such it would make sense for the researcher to maybe set the significance level at a less stringent level, possibly at a 10 percent level (i.e. $p \leq 0.10$). As always, the point is that there are no absolutes in statistical analysis. Rather, any statistical finding is a result of a series of subjective judgments made by the researcher.

One of the consequences of making the significance level more stringent (i.e. by reducing it from 5 percent to 1 percent) is that we then increase the risk of rejecting a finding from our sample even though it may actually reflect a real underlying trend in the population. This is what is known as committing a **Type II error**. It may be, for example, that a real difference does exist in the population as a whole. Moreover, you may have also detected that difference in your sample and used a statistical test to show that there is just a 1.5 percent possibility of that difference occurring by chance (i.e. $p = 0.015$).

Now, if you used the conventional 5 percent cut-off level you would correctly accept this difference as reflecting a real difference in the population as a whole. However, consider a scenario where you decided to use a much more stringent cut-off point of 1 percent significance (i.e. $p = 0.01$). In this case by adopting a stricter criterion you would have to reject the finding from your sample and conclude that you do not have sufficient evidence that it reflects a real difference in the population.

The key point here then is that your decision as to where to set the statistical significance level involves a trade-off between committing a Type I error and a Type II error. This relationship between the two types of error is summarized in Table 5.7. As mentioned earlier, in making a final decision as to where to set the cut-off level you will need to take into account the relative risks and consequences of committing either of these errors. In most circumstances, however, the conventional 5 percent level seems to work more than adequately.

Statistical power

Another concept to mention briefly here in relation to Type II errors is the notion of **statistical power**. The power of a statistical test is defined as its ability to detect a difference or relationship if one does actually exist in the population as a whole. It is also expressed as a probability and is sometimes labeled as "β" or beta. Thus, if the power of a test is $\beta = 0.60$ then this means that there is a 60 percent chance that the test will detect a difference or relationship in a sample if one does actually exist in the wider population. By "detect" we mean that the difference or relationship will be found to be statistically significant at the level we have defined. Following on from this, if the power of a test is 0.60 and thus there is a 60 percent chance of detecting a difference/relationship if one exists, then it stands to reason that there is a 40 percent chance that the test would not detect that difference/relationship even though it exists in the population. In other words there is a 40 percent chance, or a probability of 0.40, of committing a Type II error. As can be seen, once we know the statistical power of a test (β) we can easily calculate the chances of committing a Type II error, which is just $1 - \beta$. As a general rule, researchers tend to aim for a test that has statistical power of at least 0.80. In other words, they tend to want to limit the chances of committing a Type II error to 0.20 (i.e. $1 - 0.80$) or 20 percent.

Table 5.7 Type I and Type II errors

Conclusions drawn from a hypothesis test conducted on data derived from a sample	Actual characteristics of the population	
	No difference exists in the population	A difference does exist in the population
There is no evidence to reject the null-hypothesis (i.e. continue to assume that no differences exist in the population)	Correct	Type II error $(1 - \beta)$
Reject the null-hypothesis and accept the alternative hypothesis (i.e. assume that a difference does exist in the population)	Type I error (α)	Correct

There are three factors that influence the statistical power of a test:

- the size of the sample upon which the test is to be conducted;
- the level of statistical significance (α) set;
- the size of the relationship/difference to be detected (i.e. the effect size—a concept that will be covered in the next chapter).

If you have information on these three factors it is possible to calculate the statistical power of the test. Unfortunately, the current version of SPSS (Version 15.0) does not have a facility to do this for most tests. However, there are a number of software packages that have been developed to calculate the statistical power for a given test. Perhaps the most useful is **G*Power** not just because it is freely available to download from the web but also because it is relatively user-friendly and there are useful guides and tutorials on how to use the software available, also free, on the website. Further information and a link to the website can be found on the companion website. A practical example of how the notion of statistical power is used in practice is provided in the next chapter.

One- and two-tailed tests

The final key element to understand in relation to testing for statistical significance is the distinction between **one- and two-tailed tests**. The difference between these two types of test derives from the way in which the initial alternative hypothesis is stated. Essentially there are two types of hypothesis:

- *A non-directional (or two-tailed) hypothesis.* This is where it is hypothesized only that a difference or relationship exists between two variables. The hypothesis does not extend to what the nature of that difference or relationship is. An example of a non-directional hypothesis is: "There is a difference in levels of educational attainment between male and female students." What is not included in this hypothesis is any sense of whether it is believed that female attainment is likely to be higher than male attainment or vice versa; only that they will be different. In this sense there is no indication as to what the *direction* of the difference is.
- *A directional (or one-tailed) hypothesis.* This is where a hypothesis specifies the nature of the difference or relationship that exists between two variables. Taking the last example, a directional version of this hypothesis would be: "The educational attainment of female students is higher than male students." As can be seen, there is now a direction included in the hypothesis (that one group is more than the other).

In practical terms, the type of hypothesis you use will determine how you interpret the significance levels that SPSS calculates for you (as will be explained in the next chapter). In essence, all of the calculations undertaken by SPSS assume that you are using a two-tailed (i.e. non-directional) test. If this is the case then you simply take the significance levels that are calculated and report them as they are. However, and this is the crucial point, *if you are testing a one-tailed (directional) hypothesis then you divide the significance levels calculated by two before considering them.* You will see this in operation in the next chapter. For those of you who still feel pretty shaky when it comes to numbers and statistics then this is all you need to know. You can skip the next bit and jump straight to the conclusions. However, if you who would like to know why we do this (and why we have labeled these one- and two-tailed tests) then read on.

To understand what is going on here it is necessary to explain in a little more detail how a statistical test works. To illustrate this we will take another example, this time focusing on whether there are any differences in the scores attained by boys and girls in a French examination. Let's assume that the scores are measured as a scale variable and are normally distributed. To work out whether there is a difference we could simply calculate the mean exam score for boys and subtract this from the mean exam score for girls. If we get zero then clearly there are no underlying differences between boys and girls in the sample (other than individual variation). However, if we get a positive value then this would indicate that the girls' mean score is higher than the boys'. Similarly, if we get a negative value then this would indicate the opposite; that the boys' mean score is higher than the girls'.

Now, let's assume that there are no differences in the exam scores obtained by boys and girls in the school population as a whole (i.e. let's assume the null-hypothesis). If we select a random sample of pupils from this population and compare the mean exam scores for boys and girls then, because of the random nature of the sampling process, it is likely that the mean scores in the sample will not be exactly the same. Rather, there would probably be a small difference. If we now go ahead and select a large number of samples and calculate the difference between the mean scores for boys and girls in each case then these differences will be normally distributed (assuming that the size of our samples is relatively large). In other words the differences would tend to be small and bunched around zero with some being positive (indicating as explained above that girls had a higher mean score than boys in those particular samples) and others being negative (i.e. indicating that boys had a higher mean score than girls in those samples). Moreover, if we selected a large number of samples then we would find a few rogue ones where the differences would be larger.

All of this is illustrated in Figure 5.10. Assuming that the null-hypothesis is true the distribution would look something like the two here with most of the differences bunched around zero and tails running off either side indicating the few rogue samples mentioned.

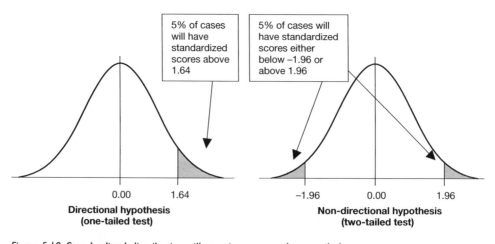

Figure 5.10 Standardized distributions illustrating one- and two-tailed tests

The only thing to note about these histograms is that we have converted the raw difference between the mean scores for boys and girls into a standardized score. This standardized score is called the **test statistic**. This is done so that we can calculate exactly where in the distribution the difference we have found from our sample sits (if this doesn't make sense to you then go back to Chapter 2 and read the section on standardized scores again).

Basically, once we have calculated a test statistic based upon the difference we have found in our sample we can use it to calculate the exact probability of that difference occurring by chance assuming that there are no differences in the underlying population. This, in turn, forms the basis of our statistical test. To explain, let's begin with a directional hypothesis; in this case that the mean exam score for girls in French will be higher than that for boys. If we use the conventional 5 percent significance level, then we need to identify where the most extreme 5 percent of cases will lie in the distribution. In this example, as we are dealing with a directional hypothesis, then we need to focus only on those most extreme 5 percent of cases where girls' scores are higher than boys' (i.e., the most extreme 5 percent of positive values). We already know from standardized scores that for a normal distribution 5 percent of cases will lie on or above +1.64. This is illustrated in the left-hand histogram in Figure 5.10. These most extreme 5 percent of cases are depicted by the shaded area and this shaded area is actually known as the **critical region**. If our test statistic falls into this region then we know that there is only a 5 percent or less chance that we would get girls' scores being as high as this compared to boys' if no such differences were evident in the population as a whole. As such, and going by the logic of hypothesis testing explained earlier, we would therefore reject the null-hypothesis and accept the alternative hypothesis (that girls' scores are actually likely, therefore, to be higher than boys' in the school population). This, then, is why the directional hypothesis is also called a one-tailed hypothesis, as the critical region is located in one tail.

Now, consider the example of a non-directional hypothesis. Here we are simply hypothesizing that there is a difference between boys and girls but we are not stating what that difference could be. In this case when we wish to identify the most extreme 5 percent of cases we have to "hedge our bets" and create two critical regions as shown in the histogram on the right-hand side of Figure 5.10. Here we have identified the largest 2.5 percent of the distribution (i.e. those with differences resulting in test statistics above +1.96) and also the lowest 2.5 percent of the distribution (i.e. those with test statistics below −1.96). Together these two areas form the critical region whereby only 5 percent of samples will have differences so large that their test statistics will fall into one or other of these two areas; and hence the reason it is called a two-tailed test. Thus, if we find a difference between boys and girls in the sample that is either greater than +1.96 or less than −1.96 then this would place it into the most extreme 5 percent of cases and, by the logic of hypothesis testing, we would reject the null-hypothesis and accept the alternative hypothesis.

So, given all of this, why can we divide the significance level that SPSS calculates by two if we decide to use a one-tailed test? Well, let's take an example whereby the mean exam score for girls in a sample was found to be higher than for boys. Suppose SPSS calculated that the chance of this occurring simply as a result of sampling error was 5 percent (i.e. $p = 0.05$). Now, as explained earlier, this probability will have been calculated on the basis of a non-directional hypothesis. In other words this figure of 5 percent includes not only those potential outcomes where the girls' mean scores are greater than the boys' but also where boys' mean scores are greater than girls'. Thus only half of this 5 percent actually relates to girls having a higher mean score than boys. Therefore, if we had begun with a directional hypothesis that the mean score for girls will be higher than that for the boys, this would place this difference found within the top 2.5 percent of the most extreme cases (of girls having higher mean scores than boys). It is for this reason that we need to divide the probability calculated by SPSS by two before we then interpret and report it.

The key point to note in relation to all of this is that you must decide whether you wish to conduct a directional or non-directional hypothesis at the beginning, before you collect and analyze your data. Unfortunately, it is tantamount to cheating to change your mind once you have the results. Take, for example, a case where you begin with a non-directional hypothesis and after running a statistical test the probability comes out as $p = 0.09$ (i.e. a 9 percent chance that your finding could have been the result of sampling error). What you cannot do at this point is suddenly decide to turn it into a directional hypothesis so that you can halve the probability (thus changing it to $p = 0.045$) and thus, in turn, magically making it statistically significant. As with all quantitative analysis, everything you do must be grounded and justified theoretically and this includes deciding upon the type of hypotheses you wish to test. If you have grounds to suggest using a directional hypothesis (based upon existing research evidence and/or theories) then you should go ahead and use a one-tailed test. Otherwise, if you suspect a relationship between two variables but have no prior knowledge of what the nature of that relationship could be then you should stick with using a two-tailed test.

Conclusions

From my own experience of working with students over a number of years, my guess is that many of you will feel your heads spinning a little after having read this chapter. If these ideas are completely new to you then there are quite a few concepts for you to grasp and, unfortunately, they have had to be explained so far at quite an abstract level. However, in the next chapter we will run through all of the major statistical tests using real-life examples and this will help you considerably in terms of making sense of the concepts discussed here. As stated in the introduction to this chapter, you may find it useful to re-read this chapter once you have worked your way through the next. In this way you will have a much greater practical sense of what is going on to help you fully understand the underlying concepts involved.

I also mentioned at the beginning of this chapter that there is considerable controversy surrounding the use of hypothesis testing. This controversy tends to rest on two fundamental issues:

- the tendency for hypothesis testing to completely dominate social and educational research, with the need to detect statistically significant findings becoming the end in itself rather than the beginning of a more thorough analysis of the data; and
- questions concerning the relevance of doing this type of hypothesis testing at all when dealing with samples that are either not random or have such a substantial level of non-response that they cannot really be considered to be random (which actually tends to describe most cases of social and educational research).

Unfortunately, what seems to be emerging now among some sections of the educational research community is a move to replace one orthodoxy—the zealous use of hypothesis testing—with another equally unhelpful orthodoxy—the rejection of hypothesis testing altogether for most purposes (for an example of the latter see Gorard, 2001, 2006a). While I would share the concerns raised over the use and abuse of hypothesis testing in social and educational research I would also want to make a plea for a more balanced and considered stance that recognizes the uses of hypothesis testing but is also acutely aware of its limitations. With this in mind, there are a number of general points to draw out from the material covered in this chapter by way of a summary:

1   *Hypothesis testing should be used even if you are dealing with non-random samples (or random samples with notable proportions of non-response)*. I recognize that this is a contentious argument, especially as all of the statistical tests developed are based upon the assumptions of random sampling. However, and in defence of this argument, let's go back to the beginning of this chapter where we discussed sources of bias in findings. It will be remembered that we made the distinction between systematic bias and non-systematic bias (or sampling error). Now let us suppose that we have used a purposive sample rather than a random one. We could, quite legitimately, forget hypothesis testing altogether. What we would be left with is a set of findings that we would then have to interpret very carefully in the light of the different forms of systematic bias that are likely to exist. In other words we would report the findings but then suggest how we need to treat these cautiously given the likely biases that are associated with our sample because it was not selected randomly (or was selected randomly but has suffered from a notable level of non-response).

This is fine at one level. However we are missing an additional piece of information that would be useful to provide readers to help them further contextualize and make sense of the findings produced. In this sense, while you may have addressed any systematic bias in relation to interpreting your results, there is still the question of whether those results could have simply occurred by chance. To take an example, let's suppose you are using a purposive sample of pupils from just three local schools. This, in turn, raises questions concerning systematic bias and how representative the pupils in these schools are of the wider population. This is certainly something you can address in your discussion and interpretation of the results. However, and beyond this, there remains random variation and fluctuation between schools and from year to year in each school. Thus even if you can establish that your schools are broadly representative of the population you are interested in, there is still the possibility that the particular group of children you are studying may be slightly different from others just because they include—by chance—a slightly higher proportion of children in that school, and/or for that year, with above-average reading ability or increased behavioral problems. This type of random fluctuation is well known to teachers (and college and university professors) who tend to notice slight differences in their children or students from year to year, and is reflected in comments such as: "I've got a particularly good class this year" or "They seem to be struggling more with the lessons this year than my previous classes."

Thus, even though the sample may not be randomly selected, it is surely still useful just to test whether the findings you have produced could have occurred by chance. In this sense hypothesis testing provides a useful approximate method to answering this question. To take an example, let's stick with the scenario of a study of pupils in three local schools. Perhaps you conducted a survey of attitudes to schoolwork and found that while 10 percent of girls stated that they found schoolwork "dull and boring," 18 percent of boys did. In reporting and interpreting the results you have considered any systematic biases that may exist in relation to your sample because of the three schools chosen and how these may have influenced these results. Even with such systematic biases considered you may still reach the conclusion that this difference between boys and girls remains important and cannot simply be explained by the biases you have highlighted. So is it an important finding? Well, let's suppose we then run a statistical test and find that if you assumed that there were no differences between boys and girls generally in relation to their attitudes to schoolwork, there was a 30 percent chance that you could have got this finding simply due to random variation (between schools and/or from year to year). In such circumstances, this would surely make you wary of reporting such a finding and claiming much from it.

It is for this reason that I would recommend the continued use of hypothesis testing, even if some of the fundamental assumptions (about random selection) upon which it is based are not met. As can be seen from the above example, it still provides us with useful information in the form of: "even controlling for the systematic biases identified, the chances of this finding occurring by random variation within the population is . . . ." Having argued this, however, I am acutely aware of the problems and dangers associated with the use of hypothesis testing in social and educational research to date and this leads onto the next few summary points.

2   *Remember that the results of a hypothesis test only help you determine whether a finding could have occurred by sampling error and/or random variation. It tells you nothing about the nature of the finding or its practical importance.* For reasons outlined above, hypothesis testing is useful as a means of just ruling out the possibility that the findings you have gained could simply be an artifact of the particular sample you have, and the random variation within it. While this is clearly useful, it should only be the starting point for your analysis. If you find that there is a high chance that your findings could be the result of sampling error then that is probably sufficient for you to stop your analysis at that point as you cannot have any confidence in your findings. However, if you conclude that they are "statistically significant," you still need to then consider the actual findings themselves and their substantive importance.

One of the big problems in hypothesis testing is that people get hung up on calculating and reporting the probabilities associated with findings as if they are an end in themselves. Thus it is not uncommon to find reports where researchers note that their finding(s) are "statistically significant" but then fail to adequately discuss the nature of the findings themselves. As a general rule, therefore, you should treat hypothesis testing as an extremely useful procedure but one that addresses just one specific issue. Once you have confirmed that you have sufficient confidence in your findings you still need to actually interpret and discuss them.

3   *Try to avoid using the term "significant" wherever you can.* Following on from the last point, this obsession with just reporting the results of hypothesis testing has meant that research reports can often confuse the lay reader. This is particularly true given the tendency for researchers to describe their findings as "significant" or, even worse, as "highly significant." How many times have you seen reports making claims such as "our research found a significant difference between boys and girls in relation to reading scores." What this actually means is that the researchers found a difference between

boys and girls and that they are sufficiently confident that this difference reflects a real difference among boys and girls in the population as a whole rather than being the result of sampling error. What we still need to know, however, is what the nature and size of this difference is.

Unfortunately, the careless use of the term "significant" in this way (meaning "statistically significant") can easily mislead readers into thinking that the difference between boys and girls is practically or substantially significant. Of course it means nothing of the sort. Have a look back at Table 5.6. Here we have the same substantive finding but produced from samples of different sizes. In each case, as will be remembered, 60 percent of male students said they would make use of lecture podcasts if available, compared to 40 percent of female students. However, based on a sample of 40 students we would conclude that "no significant differences were found between male and female students," which is clearly misleading. In actual fact, a notable difference was found but we cannot be sufficiently confident with it given the relatively small size of the sample upon which it was based. However, equally misleading would be the claim (based upon the sample of 320 students) that a "highly significant difference was found between male and female students." Yes, there is a difference but it is not huge as the term "highly significant" would imply to the lay reader. As can be seen, the statistical significance of the finding bears no relationship to its practical significance or importance.

So, what can we do to address this problem? My own suggestion is that you should definitely avoid using the term "significant" on its own when describing findings, and even try to avoid using the term "statistically significant" wherever possible. In practical terms, this would mean:

- *For findings that are statistically significant:* Just reporting your findings and including the results of a hypothesis test discretely in brackets in the text (or even as a footnote). You need not mention the fact that the results are "statistically significant" at all. This would be much better for the lay reader (who will tend to just accept your findings at face value in any case) and also will be sufficient for the more specialist reader (who can still verify that your findings are statistically significant).
- *For findings that are not statistically significant:* You have a choice of not reporting the findings at all and simply noting, for example, that your research found no evidence of a difference between male and female students' views on lecture podcasts. Alternatively, you can report the findings but then explain in lay terms, as I have done above, that while you found differences they need to be treated with caution (or even extreme caution) as they could have easily occurred by chance due to the random nature of the sample selection.

Alongside this, you should get into the routine practice of reporting what are known as **effect sizes**, which give some standardized measure of the actual size of the relationship of difference found between two variables. This is something covered in the next chapter.

4   *Don't become obsessive about the 5 percent cut-off point.* The final danger inherent in hypothesis testing, worth briefly mentioning here, is the obsessive focus on the 5 percent ($p = 0.05$) cut-off point and the rigid application of it. It is not uncommon to see researchers claiming that their findings are not statistically significant even when their hypothesis tests have produced a probability as low as $p = 0.06$ or 0.07. If you think about it logically,

these values may not have quite reached the magical figure of $p = 0.05$ but they are very close. In practical terms they are indicating that the chances of your finding having occurred by sampling error are as low as 6 or 7 percent. It would therefore be wrong simply to dismiss these findings because of the rigid application of the 5 percent cut-off point. Rather, a more grounded approach would be to report the findings and claim that they are "reaching statistical significance" (one of the only times where it may be necessary to use the term "statistical significance"). You can then accompany this claim with the probability value and other essential details from the statistical test (see the next chapter).

With all of these points in mind we can now move on, in the next chapter, to see how all this can be applied in practice.

Chapter 6

Conducting statistical tests and calculating effect sizes

Introduction

In the last chapter you were provided with an overview of the key concepts and issues associated with the notion of statistical significance. If your head is still spinning a little after reading through all of this then don't worry. The purpose of this chapter is to bring the discussion right down to a very practical level. Through the use of a range of examples we will see how we actually go about conducting statistical tests using real-world educational data. Not only will this give you a much better understanding of how all of the concepts and issues covered in the last chapter are applied in practice, but you will also be taught the practical skills necessary to choose the right statistical test and then how to run each of these using SPSS. Moreover, you will be shown how to interpret the output that is produced as well as how, precisely, you should report these findings.

By the end of this chapter therefore you will:

- have consolidated your understanding of the concept of statistical significance and how it is applied in practice;
- know how to select the most appropriate statistical test for the data you are analyzing;
- be able to run and interpret the output for the following statistical tests: Chi-Square test; Mann-Whitney U test; Kruskal-Wallis test; independent and related samples t-tests; one-way ANOVA; Friedman test; Wilcoxon test; and Spearman and Pearson correlations.
- understand the basic principles behind simple experimental designs and how to analyze these;
- have developed a practical sense of the key issues and controversies surrounding the use of statistical significance testing covered in the last chapter.

The chapter begins with an outline of how to select the appropriate statistical test. Each test is then covered in turn with a practical example that provides a step-by-step guide as to how to run the test in SPSS, how to interpret the output and then how to report the key findings from this.

Selecting the appropriate statistical test

There are a number of different statistical tests that have been developed for use with particular types and combinations of variables. The first thing we must do therefore is to ensure we have selected the right test for the variables we are interested in. Box 6.1 provides an outline of all of the different combinations of variables you could be interested in analyzing and which statistical test you should use in relation to each combination. For example, let us take the simple analysis discussed in the last chapter of whether there is a relationship between a student's sex and whether they have been bullied in school or not. In this case we have two variables—the student's sex (i.e. a nominal variable) and whether they have been bullied or not (as this is only coded "yes" or "no" then we treat this as a nominal variable as well). From Box 6.1 it can be seen that if we are dealing with two nominal variables then our appropriate statistical test to use is the Chi-Square test.

Similarly, let us consider an analysis of whether there is a relationship between students' racial/ethnic background and their educational attainment. Furthermore, for educational attainment let us assume we are using an ordinal variable with categories summarizing their school achievement in terms of: "Mostly A's," "Mostly B's," "Mostly C's" and so on. In this case we are therefore dealing with a nominal variable (racial/ethnic background) and an ordinal variable (educational attainment). From Box 6.1 it can be seen that when dealing with a nominal and an ordinal variable we need to identify how many categories of the nominal variable we are interested in comparing before we then choose the appropriate statistical test. If, for example, we were just comparing two categories (i.e. "White, Non-Hispanic" and "Black, Non-Hispanic") then we can see that the appropriate test to use would be the Mann-Whitney U test. However, if we were comparing three categories (i.e. "White, Non-Hispanic," "Black, Non-Hispanic" and "Hispanic") then we would choose the Kruskal-Wallis test.

For the remainder of this chapter we will look at each test in turn and use one or more real-life examples for each to show precisely how you should go about running these tests in practice. What follows is, therefore, a largely mechanistic account of how to actually undertake each of the tests concerned. Rather than focusing on the statistics involved, the emphasis will be placed on how to actually interpret and make sense of the substantive findings that the tests produce. I therefore apologize at this point to those of you who would actually like to "look under the bonnet" to see what is actually going on with each of these tests. It is with you in mind that I have recommended a number of excellent books in the next chapter where you can go on and do precisely this.

For now it is more than sufficient for you to know what each of the tests is doing in principle. Regardless of the actual statistical test concerned, each one tends to follow the same logic:

- Each statistical test involves a calculation that produces what is known as a **test statistic**. This test statistic summarizes in one number the nature and size of the relationship between the two variables concerned.
- The test statistic is either already standardized or can be standardized once we know what are called the **degrees of freedom** ("df") for that statistic.
- With each test statistic (and its associated degrees of freedom where relevant), the statistical test is then used to calculate the probability of the findings concerned having occurred by chance, assuming that no relationship actually exists between the two variables in reality. This is the "p" value or what tends to be referred to in the SPSS output as the "Sig." (i.e. the statistical significance of the finding).
- It is this last bit of information, the statistical significance of the finding, that is important. However, when we report it we also need to provide the reader with the

Box 6.1 Summary guide for selecting the appropriate statistical test

Types of Variable	Additional Conditions	Appropriate Statistical Test to Use
Nominal and Nominal	None	Chi Square Test
Nominal and Ordinal	Comparing just 2 categories of the nominal variable	Mann Whitney U Test
	Comparing 3 or more categories of the nominal variable	Kruskal-Wallis Test
Nominal and Scale	Comparing just 2 categories of the nominal variable	Independent Samples T-Test
	Comparing 3 or more categories of the nominal variable	One-Way ANOVA
Ordinal and Ordinal	Dealing with two different variables	Spearman Correlation Test
	Dealing with the same variable but where measures have been taken at two different points in time for each case (i.e. repeated measures)	Wilcoxon Test
Ordinal and Scale	None	Spearman Correlation Test
Scale and Scale	Dealing with two different variables	Pearson Correlation Test
	Dealing with the same variable but where measures have been taken at two different points in time for each case (i.e. repeated measures)	Related Samples T-Test

other bits of data upon which it is based (i.e. the value of the test statistic concerned and its associated degrees of freedom where necessary).

• Finally, alongside reporting that a finding is "statistically significant" it was stressed in the last chapter that it is also important to provide some sense of the actual, substantive importance of the finding. It is for this reason that we also tend to calculate and report the associated **effect size**. You have already come across one example of an effect size in relation to the correlation coefficient in Chapter 3. As you will remember, what the correlation coefficient does is to provide an indication of the strength of the relationship between two variables on a standardized scale between 0 and 1 (or –1 for negative correlations). Values close to "0" indicate a weak relationship whereas values that get nearer to 1 (or –1) indicate an increasingly strong relationship. What you will see is that we can calculate effect sizes for each of the tests used in order to give a similar standardized picture of the size of the effect associated with any particular finding.

With this in mind, let us now see how this works in practice for each of the statistical tests listed in Box 6.1. Following this we will conclude the chapter with a consideration of what tests to use to analyze data from simple experimental designs.

Chi-Square test

The first example we will use to illustrate the Chi-Square test is the one discussed in the previous chapter concerning the relationship between a pupil's sex and their likelihood of being bullied. As explained in the last chapter, the first step is to derive the hypothesis (the alternative hypothesis—H_1) we wish to test and the second, related step, is to then state our corresponding null-hypothesis (H_0). In this case the hypotheses are:

• H_1: There is a difference between male and female students in terms of their likelihood of reporting being bullied in school.
• H_0: There is no difference between male and female students in terms of their likelihood of reporting being bullied in school.

As can be seen, we are dealing with a non-directional, two-tailed hypothesis in this case, as we are not providing any indication of what the differences are likely to be (i.e. is it male students who are more likely to report being bullied than female students or vice versa?). The third step is to identify what two variables we are dealing with. Clearly one variable relates to the students' sex and the other to whether they have been bullied or not. From the **bullying.sav** dataset we will obviously use "RSEX" for the students' sex and "UBULLSCH" for whether they have been bullied or not. The first variable, "RSEX" is clearly a nominal variable. As for the second variable, as it only has two categories (i.e. students reporting "yes" or "no" when asked whether they have been bullied in school) then we also treat this as a nominal variable.

Having identified our two variables the fourth step is to choose an appropriate statistical test to use. From Box 6.1 we can see that as we are dealing with two nominal variables, we should use the Chi-Square test. The fifth step is to actually run the Chi-Square test.

Open the **bullying.sav** dataset and then select **Analyze → Descriptive Statistics → Crosstabs. . . .** This brings up the main **Crosstabs** window shown in Figure 6.1, which

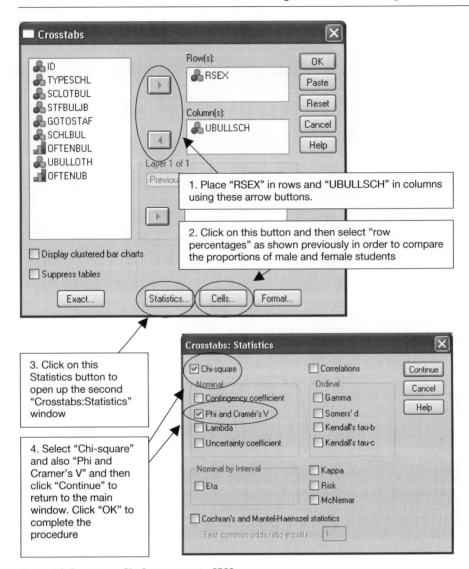

Figure 6.1 Running a Chi-Square test in SPSS

you should by now be familiar with. Place "RSEX" in the "Row(s):" field and "UBULLSCH" in the "Column(s):" field as shown. Use the "Cell" button to select "Row Percentages" to allow comparisons between male and female students. After this, click on the "Statistics . . ." button to open up the second window also shown in Figure 6.1. Here you should select "Chi-Square" to instruct SPSS to run a Chi-Square test and also select "Phi and Cramer's V" to instruct SPSS to also produce measures of effect sizes (to be discussed and explained shortly). Once you have done all this, click the "Continue" button to return to the main window and then the "OK" button to complete the procedure. The resultant SPSS output, minus the actual contingency table that you have already seen (see Output 5.3), is shown in Output 6.1.

Output 6.1

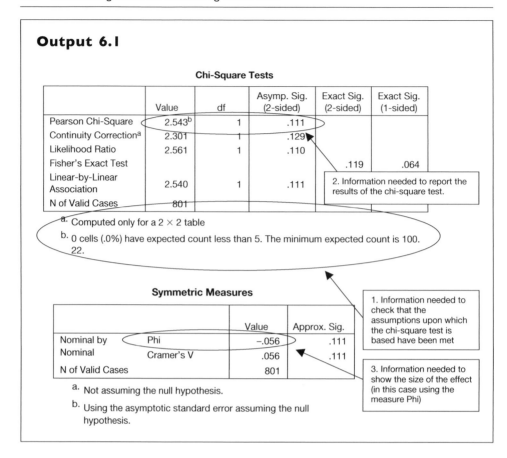

Chi-Square Tests

	Value	df	Asymp. Sig. (2-sided)	Exact Sig. (2-sided)	Exact Sig. (1-sided)
Pearson Chi-Square	2.543[b]	1	.111		
Continuity Correction[a]	2.301	1	.129		
Likelihood Ratio	2.561	1	.110		
Fisher's Exact Test				.119	.064
Linear-by-Linear Association	2.540	1	.111		
N of Valid Cases	801				

2. Information needed to report the results of the chi-square test.

a. Computed only for a 2 × 2 table

b. 0 cells (.0%) have expected count less than 5. The minimum expected count is 100.22.

Symmetric Measures

		Value	Approx. Sig.
Nominal by Nominal	Phi	−.056	.111
	Cramer's V	.056	.111
N of Valid Cases		801	

a. Not assuming the null hypothesis.

b. Using the asymptotic standard error assuming the null hypothesis.

1. Information needed to check that the assumptions upon which the chi-square test is based have been met

2. Information needed to report the results of the chi-square test.

3. Information needed to show the size of the effect (in this case using the measure Phi)

There are three pieces of information we need to draw from this output. The first relates to the need to check that the assumptions upon which the Chi-Square test are based have been met. Basically, we should only use the Chi-Square test if two conditions are met:

- no more than 20 percent of cells in the contingency table should have expected values less than five;
- no cell has an expected value of less than one.

For now you do not need to understand what these two conditions mean—you just need to ensure that they are met. Fortunately, the SPSS output tells us whether these two conditions have been met. As can be seen in Output 6.1, the information provided as a footnote to the Chi-Square tests table indicates that both conditions have been met. More specifically it can be seen that no cell has an expected count less than five and the minimum expected count is actually 100.22. We can, therefore, go ahead and use the actual test statistic. In the next example we will look at what you should do if one or both of these conditions is not met.

The actual test statistic calculated for this particular test is the Pearson Chi-Square statistic and, from Output 6.1, it can be seen that it has the value of 2.543. For the Chi-Square test we also need to quote the degrees of freedom associated with this statistic and this is also given in the output (in this case, df = 1). As mentioned earlier, the final and most important piece of information is the probability that is also provided in the output as indicated under the column headed "Asymp. Sig.". In this case it can be seen that p = 0.111. Finally, for a contingency table that only has four cells (i.e. only two categories for each of the two variables) we use Phi as the effect size measure. For any tables larger than this we would use Cramer's V. In this case we can see that the effect size associated with our findings is very small (Phi = 0.056). When dealing with Phi, we can ignore the minus sign.

Step six is to use this evidence to decide whether to accept the alternative hypothesis or not. In this case, as p = 0.111 we can see there is an 11.1 percent possibility of this finding having occurred by chance. As this is greater than our conventional level of 5 percent (or p = 0.05) we must conclude that there is no evidence to reject the null-hypothesis and thus no evidence of a relationship between a student's sex and their likelihood of reporting being bullied in school.

The final step in the process is to actually report these findings. As there is no evidence of a relationship between sex and levels of bullying we would usually just report this without the need to report the actual percentage findings (i.e. 32.6 percent of female students reported being bullied compared to 27.4 percent of male students) or the associated effect size. The problem with reporting these specific findings is that it may encourage the reader to see a difference even though our statistical test has confirmed that we cannot be confident that this difference is not just a product of chance. In these circumstances, therefore, when our findings are not statistically significant we simply report this and also the p value and associated test statistic upon which this conclusion is based. One way of doing this in your report is therefore:

> The survey produced no evidence of any differences between male and female students in terms of their likelihood of reporting having been bullied in school (p = 0.111, Chi-Square = 2.543, df = 1).

If the findings were statistically significant then you would report the actual findings (and maybe display these in a chart or table) and their associated effect size. You would also still report the three bits of information shown above in brackets at the point where you explain that the findings you are reporting are statistically significant. We will see how this is done a little later.

For the next example we will use the **earlychildhood.sav** dataset to assess whether there is a relationship between a young child's racial/ethnic background and their likelihood of being diagnosed with attention deficit disorder in America. The alternative and null hypotheses this time are:

- H_1: There are racial/ethnic differences in the proportions of young children in America who are diagnosed with attention deficit disorder (ADD or ADHD).
- H_0: There are no racial/ethnic differences in the proportions of young children in America who are diagnosed with attention deficit disorder (ADD or ADHD).

As before, the next step is to select the variables to be used to test these hypotheses. From the **earlychildhood.sav** dataset there are two that can be used: the racial/ethnic background of the child ("RACEETH2") and whether they have been diagnosed as having attention deficit disorder ("HDADD"). "RACEETH2" is clearly a nominal variable and "HDADD" consists of three categories: "not applicable" (in that the child has not been diagnosed with any disability); "yes" (indicating that they have been diagnosed with attention deficit disorder); and "no" (indicating that they have not been diagnosed with this disorder but have been diagnosed with another disability).

Before beginning the analysis, make sure you Weight Cases using the "WTCORRCT" variable. Once done, run the **Analyze → Descriptive Statistics → Crosstabs...** procedure, placing "RACEETH2" in rows and "HDADD" in columns and making all of the selections outlined in the last example (i.e. select row percentages, select "Chi-Square" and also "Phi and Cramer's V"). The contingency table that you should obtain is shown in Output 6.2. If you don't get this check to see whether the first category (-1) is defined as missing. As can be seen, there would appear to be a slightly higher chance that young children from minority racial/ethnic backgrounds are likely to be diagnosed with attention deficit disorder than white, non-Hispanic children. However, the output from the associated Chi-Square test of these findings as shown in Output 6.3 indicates that one of the conditions of the Chi-Square test has not been met. As can be seen, the minimum expected count is reported as 0.85 which fails to meet the requirement that no cell has an expected value less than 1.

When one or both of the conditions for using a Chi-Square test are not met like this we cannot use the test statistic itself or, by extension, the probability calculated (in this case

Output 6.2

D-DETAILED RACE-ETHNICITY OF CHILD * PT2I-CHILD HAS ADD OR ADHD Crosstabulation

| | | | PT2I-CHILD HAS ADD OR ADHD | | | |
			-1 INAPPLIC ABLE	1 YES	2 NO	Total
D-DETAILED RACE-ETHNICITY OF CHILD	1 WHITE, NON-HISPANIC	Count	1122	13	909	2044
		% within D-DETAILED RACE-ETHNICITY OF CHILD	54.9%	.6%	44.5%	100.0%
	2 BLACK, NON-HISPANIC	Count	307	5	216	528
		% within D-DETAILED RACE-ETHNICITY OF CHILD	58.1%	.9%	40.9%	100.0%
	3 HISPANIC	Count	437	6	319	762
		% within D-DETAILED RACE-ETHNICITY OF CHILD	57.3%	.8%	41.9%	100.0%
	4 ASIAN OR PACIFIC ISLANDER	Count	66	1	49	116
		% within D-DETAILED RACE-ETHNICITY OF CHILD	56.9%	.9%	42.2%	100.0%
	5 ALL OTHER RACES	Count	129	2	96	227
		% within D-DETAILED RACE-ETHNICITY OF CHILD	56.8%	.9%	42.3%	100.0%
Total		Count	2061	27	1589	3677
		% within D-DETAILED RACE-ETHNICITY OF CHILD	56.1%	.7%	43.2%	100.0%

Output 6.3

Chi-Square Tests

	Value	df	Asymp. Sig. (2-sided)
Pearson Chi-Square	3.675 ^a	8	.885
Likelihood Ratio	3.660	8	.886
Linear-by-Linear Association	1.372	1	.241
N of Valid Cases	3677		

a. 3 cells (20.0%) have expected count less than 5. The minimum expected count is .85.

The conditions for the Chi Square test have not been met

it can be seen that it is p = 0.885). In such circumstances what we need to do is to conflate some of the categories of one or both of the variables so that the frequencies in each cell are increased. In this current example, one simple way of doing this is to recode the "RACEETH2" variable so that it consists of just two categories: "White, Non-Hispanic" and "All Other Racial/Ethnic Groups." This is what we will do by creating a new variable: "RACEETH3" with just these two categories. You have already been shown how to recode variables in Chapter 3 (see Figure 3.1). Try doing this yourself using the following two recoding commands:

$1 \rightarrow 1$
$2 \text{ thru } 5 \rightarrow 2$

Once you have done this, do not forget to add a title and labels for your new variable, "RACEETH3." With this new variable created you can now re-run the same analysis but using "RACEETH3" rather than "RACEETH2." The output you should get from the analysis this time is shown in Output 6.4. As can be seen, the findings from the sample suggest that young children from minority racial/ethnic backgrounds are more likely to be diagnosed with attention deficit disorder than their white, non-Hispanic counterparts. Indeed, the findings suggest that they are 1.5 times (or 50 percent) more likely to be diagnosed (i.e. 0.9/0.6 = 1.5).

However, before we can confidently report this finding we need to check whether it is statistically significant. As the footnote to the second table in Output 6.4 indicates, the two conditions upon which a Chi-Square test depend have now been met and so we can go ahead and use the test statistic and associated significance level calculated from it. As can

Output 6.4

D-RACE-ETHNICITY OF CHILD * PT2I-CHILD HAS ADD OR ADHD Crosstabulation

			PT2I-CHILD HAS ADD OR ADHD			Total
			-1 INAPPLIC ABLE	1 YES	2 NO	
D-RACE-ETHNICITY OF CHILD	1 WHITE, NON-HISPANIC	Count	1122	13	909	2044
		% within D-RACE-ETHNICITY OF CHILD	54.9%	.6%	44.5%	100.0%
	4 ALL OTHER RACES	Count	940	14	680	1634
		% within D-RACE-ETHNICITY OF CHILD	57.5%	.9%	41.6%	100.0%
Total		Count	2062	27	1589	3678
		% within D-RACE-ETHNICITY OF CHILD	56.1%	.7%	43.2%	100.0%

Chi-Square Tests

	Value	df	Asymp. Sig. (2-sided)
Pearson Chi-Square	3.442[a]	2	.179
Likelihood Ratio	3.440	2	.179
Linear-by-Linear Association	2.726	1	.099
N of Valid Cases	3678		

a. 0 cells (.0%) have expected count less than 5. The minimum expected count is 12.00.

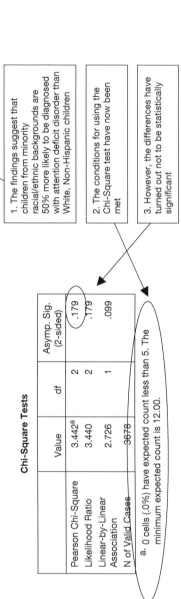

1. The findings suggest that children from minority racial/ethnic backgrounds are 50% more likely to be diagnosed with attention deficit disorder than White, Non-Hispanic children

2. The conditions for using the Chi-Square test have now been met

3. However, the differences have turned out not to be statistically significant

be seen, the findings are not statistically significant (p = 0.179). There is actually a 17.9 percent chance that these differences could have just arisen as a quirk of random sampling rather than reflecting a real underlying difference in the population as a whole. As before, therefore, we would report the results as follows:

No evidence was found of any racial/ethnic differences between young children in terms of their likelihood of being diagnosed with attention deficit disorder (ADD or ADHD) (p = 0.179, Chi-Square = 3.442, df = 2).

There are two very important points to draw out from this finding. The first is that it would be misleading to report the actual finding given that it has been found to be not statistically significant. The finding that young children from minority racial/ethnic backgrounds are 50 percent more likely to be diagnosed with attention deficit disorder than their white, non-Hispanic peers is a matter of concern. However, the results of the Chi-Square test suggest that we just cannot be confident that these findings reflect a real underlying trend in the population as a whole. In fact, there is a 17.9 percent chance that they could have occurred by chance and that there is actually no such underlying trend.

Second, all that we can conclude from this analysis is that this present sample has not provided sufficient evidence of a relationship between a young child's racial/ethnic background and their likelihood of being diagnosed with attention deficit disorder. This is very different to claiming that the survey has proven that no such relationship exists. In fact, as we have seen, the survey does suggest that a relationship might be evident but the actual numbers involved (i.e. just 13 white, non-Hispanic children and 14 children from other racial/ethnic groups) mean that we cannot be sufficiently confident that this reflects a real underlying trend in the population as a whole. The fact that the present finding is not statistically significant, therefore, could possibly reflect the fact that no such underlying relationship exists. However, it could equally reflect a weakness in the survey design; in this case a lack of power to detect such a small difference in proportions. It is because of this, therefore, that it is never possible using hypothesis testing to actually prove a null-hypothesis.

One final technique worth showing you in relation to the Chi-Square test is how to calculate the test statistic and effect size in circumstances where you only have the data summarized in a table rather than having access to the original dataset. As an example let us take the findings shown in Table 6.1 which compare the proportions of male and female school leavers in England in 2002 achieving five or more good passes in public

Table 6.1 Proportions of male and female school leavers in England achieving five or more GCSE Grades A*–C or their equivalent, 2002

	5 or more		Less than 5		Total	
	n	*%*	*n*	*%*	*n*	*%*
Males	3,300	49.5	3,366	50.5	6,666	100
Females	3,848	59.1	2,665	40.9	6,513	100
Total	7,148	54.2	6,031	45.8	13,179	100

Source: Youth Cohort Study of England and Wales (Cohort 12, Sweep 1)

examinations. These data are actually taken from the **youthcohort.sav** dataset (with the weighting variable "s1weight" applied and using the variables "s1gender" and "s1peta2"). However, for the moment let us assume that all we have is the summary shown in Table 6.1. The question is, how can we tell if these differences are statistically significant and also, if they are, how can we calculate the effect size for these?

The answer is to create a special dataset in SPSS as follows. First of all, open up a new dataset by selecting **File → New → Data**. Next, define three variables as follows:

"sex"	1 = "Males"
	2 = "Females"
"exams"	1 = "5 or more passes"
	2 = "Less than 5 passes"
"count"	No labels

Once you have set these three new variables, go to Data View and code the first four cases as shown in Figure 6.2. Once you have done this click on the "Value Labels" icon as shown to view the actual label names. To view the labels fully you can drag and widen the column for the "exams" variable. As can be seen from the second window shown in Figure 6.2, you now basically have four categories reflecting the four main cells in Table 6.1 (i.e. males achieving five or more passes; males achieving fewer than five passes; females achieving five or more passes; and females achieving fewer than 5 passes). What you need to do now is to type in the actual cell frequencies from Table 6.1 into the corresponding cells for the "count" variable as shown in Figure 6.2.

The final thing you need to do before you can actually analyze the data is to use the **Data → Weight Cases. . .** procedure to weight cases by the "count" variable. Once you have done this you can analyze the data in the usual way. Try running the **Analyze → Descriptive Statistics → Crosstabs. . .** procedure, placing "sex" into rows and "exams" into columns and making all of the selections outlined in the previous two examples (i.e. select "Row percentages," select "Chi-Square" and also "Phi and Cramer's V"). The output you should obtain from this is shown in Output 6.5.

As can be seen, the same substantive contingency table is reproduced as originally shown in Table 6.1. From the Chi-Square tests table below this, it can be seen that both conditions have been met for the test and that the substantive findings are statistically significant (which is not surprising given the large numbers involved). When SPSS reports the statistical significance level in this way (i.e. $p = 0.000$) this does not mean that it is actually zero. Rather, it means that it is so small that it is less than 0.001 and so should be reported as "$p < 0.001$."

With such a low statistical significance level, findings such as these can often be reported as showing that the differences between male and female attainment are "highly statistically significant" or even just "highly significant." However, as stressed in the last chapter, they are only "highly statistically significant" because of the very large sample used. In this sense, all we are saying here is that these differences are highly unlikely to have occurred by chance. However, using phrases such as "highly significant" in this way can be very misleading. This is why we need to also report the effect size. As mentioned earlier, when dealing with a small 2×2 contingency table as in this case (where there are only two categories for each variable and thus only four cells) we tend to use Phi as the measure of effect size. For all other types of table we should use Cramer's V. In both

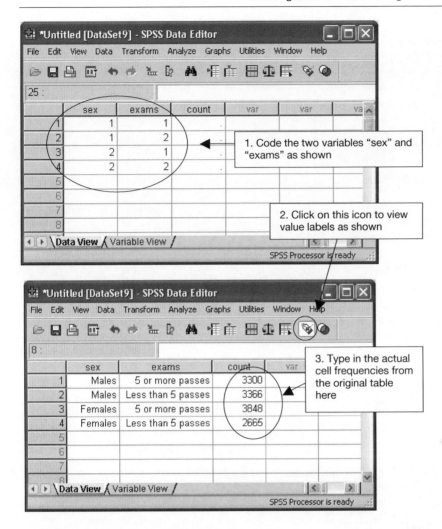

Figure 6.2 Creating a 2 × 2 contingency table in SPSS

cases, and just as with the correlation coefficient, they both provide standardized measures of the size of the effect and can take values between "0" (indicating there is no relationship at all) and "1" (indicating there is a perfect relationship between sex and examination performance). In this case, as Phi = 0.096 (ignoring the minus sign), we can conclude from this that the relationship is only a weak one.

Reporting effect sizes in this way certainly helps to counter any possibility of misleading the reader by focusing solely on the "significance" of the findings. An example of how all of these findings may be reported is as follows. Note how we have avoided using the term "statistically significant" at all:

A higher proportion of female students (59.1 percent) achieved five or more good examination passes compared to their male peers (49.5 percent) in the sample

Output 6.5

sex * exams Crosstabulation

			exams		
			5 or More Passes	Less Than 5 Passes	Total
sex	Male	Count	3300	3366	6666
		% within sex	49.5%	50.5%	100.0%
	Female	Count	3848	2665	6513
		% within sex	59.1%	40.9%	100.0%
Total		Count	7148	6031	13179
		% within sex	54.2%	45.8%	100.0%

2. The findings are statistically significant

Chi-Square Tests

	Value	df	Asymp. Sig. (2-sided)	Exact Sig. (2-sided)	Exact Sig. (1-sided)
Pearson Chi-Square	121.732[b]	1	.000		
Continuity Correction[a]	121.346	1	.000		
Likelihood Ratio	121.941	1	.000		
Fisher's Exact Test				.000	.000
Linear-by-Linear Association	121.722	1	.000		
N of Valid Cases	13179				

a. Computed only for a 2 × 2 table.

b. 0 cells (.0%) have expected count less than 5. The minimum expected count is 2980.49.

Symmetric Measures

		Value	Approx. Sig.
Nominal by Nominal	Phi	-.096	.000
	Cramer's V	.096	.000
N of Valid Cases		13179	

a. Not assuming the null hypothesis.

b. Using the asymptotic standard error assuming the null hypothesis.

1. The conditions for the Chi-Square test have been met

3. The effect size, Phi, is fairly small at 0.096

($p < 0.001$, Chi-Square $= 121.732$, df $= 1$). However, the strength of this relationship between sex and educational attainment was found to be relatively weak (Phi $= 0.096$).

Finally, there are two points worth noting about this general technique for analyzing contingency tables. The first is that it can be adapted for use with any sized contingency table. All that you would need to do is to increase the categories for each of the variables accordingly so that you have the required number of cells. The second point is that in order to calculate a valid Chi-Square statistic it is necessary to work with cell frequencies rather than percentages. However, if all you are interested in doing is calculating the effect size for a particular finding then you can type in percentages rather than frequencies in the "count" variable. While the resultant Chi-Square statistic would be incorrect, the effect size measures (whether Phi or Cramer's V) would both be accurate.

EXERCISE 6.1

Using the **timeseries.sav** dataset (see Figure 3.21) create a new variable called "Phi". For each year use the percentage figures to calculate the effect size, Phi, and type these figures into the dataset. Create a new line chart and compare this to the line chart you created using the cross-product ratio (see Figure 3.22). Do they both give the same picture of trends in gender differences over time? Check your method and answers on the companion website.

Mann-Whitney U test

To demonstrate this statistical test we will return to the example covered in Chapter 3 that considered the relationship between a child's sex and the overall school grades their parent(s) reported that they were achieving in America. You should therefore begin by opening the **afterschools.sav** dataset and Weight Cases using the "WTCORRCT" variable. It will be remembered from the analysis in Chapter 3 (see Figure 3.7) that there certainly appeared to be a difference between boys and girls, with girls tending to achieve higher school grade profiles than boys. What we wish to do here is to formally test whether this difference is likely to reflect an underlying trend in the population of school children in America or could have occurred by chance. Our first step, as usual, is to specify the (alternative) hypothesis we wish to test and then to state the associated null-hypothesis. In this case these are:

- H_1: There are differences between boys and girls in America in relation to the school grades they achieve.
- H_0: There are no differences between boys and girls in America in relation to the school grades they achieve.

You could ask why we are using a non-directional (two-tailed) hypothesis here. As we have seen from the bar charts in Chapter 3 (Figure 3.7) that girls are achieving better grades than boys then surely it would be better to state a directional (one-tailed) hypothesis in this case? The problem here is that you can only state and use a directional hypothesis before you begin analyzing your data. As it is, we have already looked at the data to identify what the differences are. As such we need to stay with a non-directional hypothesis.

The next step in our analysis is to identify the variables we wish to use. As we are working with the **afterschools.sav** dataset we therefore have "SEX" (nominal variable) and "SEGRADES" which is an ordinal variable and consists of parents indicating what their child's school grades are by choosing from a number of categories such as: "Mostly A's"; "Mostly B's"; "Mostly C's" and so on. As discussed in Chapter 3, there are clearly questions as to the validity of this measure of a child's performance given it is based upon the reports of parents. However, we will put these concerns to one side for the moment.

The next step is to choose the appropriate statistical test to use. In this case we are dealing with one nominal and one ordinal variable. As shown in Box 6.1 there are actually two different tests that can be used for this combination of variables with the final choice depending on how many categories of the nominal variable we are interested in comparing. In this case our nominal variable only has two categories ("male" and "female") and so we can see from Box 6.1 that we should choose the Mann-Whitney U test.

One important thing to note before running this test is that we need to ensure that all of the categories of the ordinal variable can actually be rank ordered. If, for example, you looked at the categories for "SEGRADES" you will see that it is coded as follows:

-9 = "-9 NOT ASCERTAINED"
-8 = "-8 DK"
-7 = "-7 REFUSED"
-1 = "-1 INAPPLICABLE"
1 = "1 MOSTLY A'S"
2 = "2 MOSTLY B'S"
3 = "3 MOSTLY C'S"
4 = "4 MOSTLY D'S"
5 = "5 MOSTLY F'S"
6 = "6 NO LTR GRADES"

If we simply run a Mann-Whitney U test on this variable as it is then it will treat all of these categories as being rank ordered. It will, therefore, obviously treat "Mostly A's" as above "Mostly B's" and so on. However, it will also treat "Refused" as above "Inapplicable" as above "Mostly A's." It would also treat "Mostly F's" as above "No

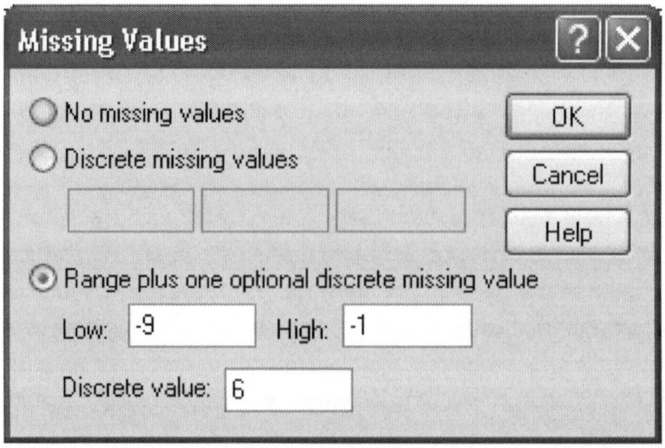

Figure 6.3
Defining categories for the variable "SEGRADES" as "Missing" in SPSS

LTR Grades" whereas in fact it can be seen from the original questionnaire that this last category refers to those children whose schools do not give grades. It is therefore wrong to treat this category as below "Mostly F's." Because of this, before we actually conduct the Mann-Whitney U test we need to go to Variable View and ensure that the categories that are coded: "-9," "-8," "-7," "-1" and also "6" are listed as "Missing" so that they are effectively removed from the analysis. The simplest way of doing this, using the **Missing Values** window (as introduced in Chapter 1) can be seen in Figure 6.3.

Once we have done this we need to run the actual test. To do this, select **Analyze** → **Nonparametric Tests** → **2 Independent Samples. . .** and this opens the **Two-Independent Samples Tests** window shown in Figure 6.4. Select the variable "SEGRADES" and use the arrow button to place it into the "Test Variable List:" field as shown. Similarly, select the variable "SEX" and place it in the "Grouping Variable:" window as also shown. Once you have done this you need to tell SPSS which two groups within the nominal variable you wish it to compare for the test. This may seem obvious in the present example where there are only two categories. However, it is worth noting that you may have a nominal variable with more than two categories but you only wish to compare two of them (i.e. you could use the "RACEETHN" variable but only wish to compare the first two categories of "White, Non-Hispanic" and "Black, Non-Hispanic").

To define the two categories you wish to compare, click the "Define Groups. . ." button and this opens a second window as shown. To decide which codes to type into this second window you need to refer back to the original variable and how it is coded. In this case

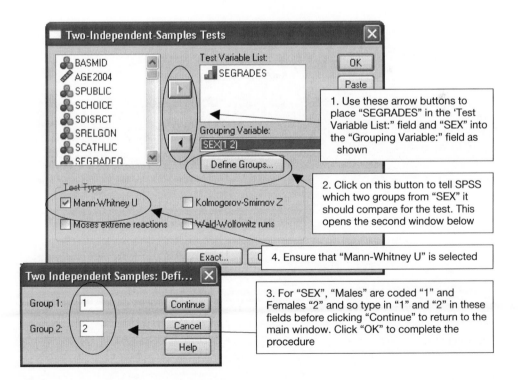

Figure 6.4 Running a Mann-Whitney U test in SPSS

"Males" have been coded "1" and Females have been coded "2" and as these are the two groups you wish to compare you therefore type in "1" and "2" into the fields shown. Click "Continue" to return to the main window and then "OK" to complete the procedure. The output you should obtain is shown in Output 6.6 (if you do not get this then check that you have applied Weight Cases using the variable "WTCORRCT").

Before looking at the test statistic, we can gain some idea of what the nature of the differences in school grades achieved between boys and girls (as reported by their parents) are from the mean ranks shown. To interpret these it should be remembered that high grades were given low ranks (i.e. "Mostly A's" were coded as "1," "Mostly B's" coded as "2" and so on). Thus, as girls had a lower mean rank (1,408.50) than boys (1,614.62), this indicates that they achieved higher reported grades, on average, than boys.

To assess whether this difference is statistically significant we need to derive three pieces of information from the output. The first, as usual, is the actual test statistic, in this case the Mann-Whitney U value (989,669). This statistic is actually converted into a Z score (in this case –7.067) which is the second piece of information to pull out from this output. Finally, we also need the actual probability associated with the finding as calculated from the test statistic (in this case it is "$p = 0.000$" which, as explained before, should be reported as "$p < 0.001$"). What we can see from these results is that the likelihood of these findings occurring by chance is so small ($p < 0.001$ or less than a 0.1 percent chance) that we can reject the null-hypothesis and thus accept the alternative hypothesis that there are differences between boys and girls in America in relation to the school grades their parents report they have attained.

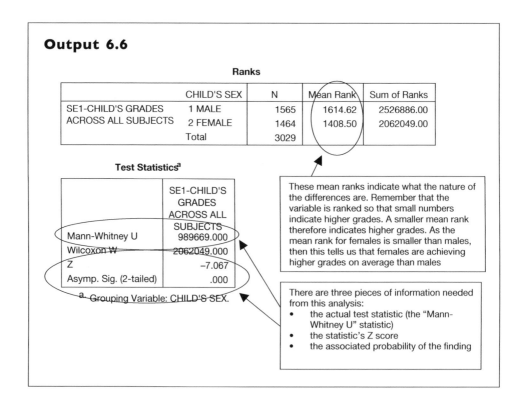

Output 6.6

Ranks

	CHILD'S SEX	N	Mean Rank	Sum of Ranks
SE1-CHILD'S GRADES ACROSS ALL SUBJECTS	1 MALE	1565	1614.62	2526886.00
	2 FEMALE	1464	1408.50	2062049.00
	Total	3029		

Test Statistics[a]

	SE1-CHILD'S GRADES ACROSS ALL SUBJECTS
Mann-Whitney U	989669.000
Wilcoxon W	2062049.000
Z	–7.067
Asymp. Sig. (2-tailed)	.000

a. Grouping Variable: CHILD'S SEX.

These mean ranks indicate what the nature of the differences are. Remember that the variable is ranked so that small numbers indicate higher grades. A smaller mean rank therefore indicates higher grades. As the mean rank for females is smaller than males, then this tells us that females are achieving higher grades on average than males

There are three pieces of information needed from this analysis:
- the actual test statistic (the "Mann-Whitney U" statistic)
- the statistic's Z score
- the associated probability of the finding

Before we report all of this, one final thing we need to calculate is the effect size associated with this finding. Unfortunately, SPSS does not calculate the effect size directly and so we need to calculate it ourselves. It is actually very straightforward to do and is just calculated by dividing the Z score by the square root of the total sample size. More formally the effect size is:

$$\text{Effect size, } r = \frac{Z}{\sqrt{n}}.$$

Thus in this present case, as $Z = 7.067$ (we can ignore the minus sign) and $n = 3,029$ (see Output 6.6 for where to find this figure):

$$\text{Effect size, } r = \frac{7.067}{\sqrt{3029}} = \frac{7.067}{55.036} = 0.128.$$

To identify the nature of the differences involved it is necessary to examine the data as we did in Chapter 3 (see Figure 3.7). When reporting the findings it would certainly be useful in this case to display them in a bar chart and make reference to it. With this in mind, one way of reporting these findings would be as follows:

> Differences were found between boys and girls in relation to the average school grades that their parents reported they had achieved ($p < 0.001$, Mann-Whitney U = 989,669, Z = 7.067). As can be seen from Figure 3.7 girls tended to achieve higher grades than boys on average with 38.2 percent of girls, for example, achieving "Mostly A's" compared to 29.7 percent of boys. The strength of this relationship between sex and school grades reported was found to be fairly weak however ($r = 0.128$).

There are a few things to note from how the findings have been reported above:

- Note how we have, once again, avoided using the term "statistically significant." Those who are technically minded will see that the findings are statistically significant from the detail provided in the brackets. Most readers, however, will be left to assess the practical importance of the findings for themselves.
- As we have displayed the findings in a bar chart there is no need to report all of the findings again in words here. However, it is sometimes worth just drawing out a key finding (in this case the proportions achieving "Mostly A's") and reporting this.
- We have also described the data more accurately as the proportions of school grades achieved as reported by parents. While we are using this variable as a measure of school grades achieved there are the questions of validity posed by the fact that they rely upon the reports of parents. It is better to be clear and up-front about the nature of the data you have. Thus, even when reporting the findings try to describe the actual data you have rather than what they are meant to represent. The discussion you provide after reporting these findings can then consider how valid this is as a measure of educational attainment in schools.

- The inclusion of reference to the effect size helps to provide a more grounded sense of the strength of the relationship between sex and school grades reported by parents.

EXERCISE 6.2

Using the **youthcohort.sav** dataset, test the hypothesis that there are gender differences ("s1gender") in relation to grades achieved in maths GCSE examination ("gradmath"). Test the hypothesis again in relation to a few of the other GCSE subjects. Using effect sizes, which examination resulted in the biggest difference between male and female students? Check your methods and findings on the companion website.

Kruskal-Wallis test

To demonstrate the Kruskal-Wallis test we will stay with the **afterschools.sav** dataset and the variable "SEGRADES." However, this time we will see whether there is a relationship between the racial/ethnic background of children and the school grades they achieve, as reported by their parents. For racial/ethnic background we will use the variable "RACEETHN" which comprises four categories: "1 = White, Non-Hispanic," "2 = Black, Non-Hispanic," "3 = Hispanic" and "4 = All Other Races." This time, while we are still dealing with a nominal ("RACEETHN") and an ordinal ("SEGRADES") variable, the nominal variable now has more than two categories that we wish to compare and so, from Box 6.1, we can see that the appropriate test this time is the Kruskal-Wallis test. The alternative and null-hypotheses this time are:

- H_1: There are differences between children from differing racial/ethnic backgrounds in America in relation to the school grades they achieve.
- H_0: There are no differences between children from differing racial/ethnic backgrounds in America in relation to the school grades they achieve.

After selecting our two variables to test this hypothesis, as we have already done, the next steps are to select and then run the statistical test—in this case the Kruskal-Wallis test. One question we need to consider is what racial/ethnic groups we wish to compare within the variable "RACEETHN." We could obviously compare all four groups. However, one problem here is that the fourth group—"all other races"—is so broad and diverse that any findings we derive from this are going to be practically impossible to interpret. One option, which we will follow for this present example, is to focus our comparisons on just the three main groups—"White, Non-Hispanic," "Black, Non-Hispanic" and "Hispanic."

Before running the Kruskal-Wallis test make sure you have weighted the sample using the "WTCORRCT" variable. Also check that you have defined the category "6 NO LTR GRADES" as missing. Having done this we can now run the test by choosing **Analyze**

→ **Nonparametric Tests** → **K Independent Samples...** which opens the window shown in Figure 6.5. Use the arrow buttons to place "SEGRADES" and "RACEETHN" into the "Test Variable List:" and "Grouping Variable:" fields respectively as shown. Once done click the "Define Range..." button to tell SPSS which groups to compare for the test. In this case, as already explained, the three groups we are interested in are coded "1," "2" and "3" and so we define the range accordingly as shown in Figure 6.5. Once you have done this, click "Continue" to return to the main window. Check that "Kruskal-Wallis H" has been selected and then click "OK" to complete the procedure. The output that this produces is shown in Output 6.7.

As with the Mann-Whitney U test, we can begin by examining the mean ranks for each group to gain some sense of what the average differences are. Remembering that lower mean ranks indicate higher grades achieved, it can be seen that white, non-Hispanic children tend to achieve the highest grades as reported by their parents (mean rank = 1,322.00), followed by Hispanic children (mean rank = 1,482.94) and then black, non-Hispanic children (mean rank = 1,550.40).

To ascertain whether these differences are statistically significant we now need to look at the results of the Kruskal-Wallis test itself. From the "Test Statistics" table there are three pieces of information we need to derive and report. The first is the test statistic itself. In this case the Kruskal-Wallis H statistic = 48.672 (SPSS labels it "Chi-Square" because this statistic actually follows a Chi-Square distribution). We also need the degrees of

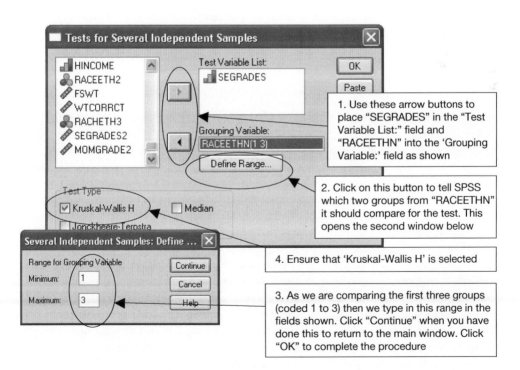

Figure 6.5 Running a Kruskal-Wallis test in SPSS

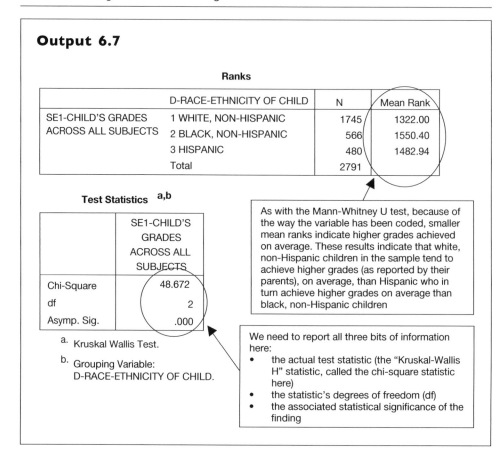

Output 6.7

Ranks

	D-RACE-ETHNICITY OF CHILD	N	Mean Rank
SE1-CHILD'S GRADES ACROSS ALL SUBJECTS	1 WHITE, NON-HISPANIC	1745	1322.00
	2 BLACK, NON-HISPANIC	566	1550.40
	3 HISPANIC	480	1482.94
	Total	2791	

Test Statistics a,b

	SE1-CHILD'S GRADES ACROSS ALL SUBJECTS
Chi-Square	48.672
df	2
Asymp. Sig.	.000

a. Kruskal Wallis Test.

b. Grouping Variable: D-RACE-ETHNICITY OF CHILD.

> As with the Mann-Whitney U test, because of the way the variable has been coded, smaller mean ranks indicate higher grades achieved on average. These results indicate that white, non-Hispanic children in the sample tend to achieve higher grades (as reported by their parents), on average, than Hispanic who in turn achieve higher grades on average than black, non-Hispanic children

> We need to report all three bits of information here:
> * the actual test statistic (the "Kruskal-Wallis H" statistic, called the chi-square statistic here)
> * the statistic's degrees of freedom (df)
> * the associated statistical significance of the finding

freedom (in this case df = 2) and finally the actual probability associated with the findings which, as can be seen, is reported as "0.000" (or p < 0.001). We can conclude, therefore, that there is sufficient evidence to reject the null-hypothesis and to accept the alternative hypothesis or, in other words, to conclude that there are differences between racial/ethnic groups in relation to their school grades achieved as reported by their parents.

Unfortunately, SPSS does not calculate an effect size for this. Moreover, it is not straightforward to calculate an effect size from the information given here. To be honest, it is actually not that informative to do so either. The reason for this is that all that this finding tells us is that there are at least some statistically significant differences in school grades reported by parents between these three racial/ethnic groups of children. Unfortunately, we cannot conclude anything more specific from this, such as that white, non-Hispanic children achieve higher reported school grades than their black, non-Hispanic peers and/or that black, non-Hispanic children achieve higher grades than their Hispanic peers. Any effect size calculated from the Kruskal-Wallis test would, therefore, simply represent some global measure of the association between children's race/ethnicity and school grades reported. What we tend to be more interested in is the size of the differences between specific groups.

Overall, therefore, all that the Kruskal-Wallis test tells us is that there are at least some statistically significant differences between the three racial/ethnic groups of children here. With this finding we can now examine what the specific differences might be. One obvious way of doing this is to conduct three Mann-Whitney U tests for the three pairs of variables, i.e.:

- "White, Non-Hispanic" and "Black, Non-Hispanic"
- "White, Non-Hispanic" and "Hispanic"
- "Black Non-Hispanic" and "Hispanic"

The main problem in conducting multiple tests like this is that it increases the chances of making a Type I error (see Chapter 5 for a discussion of what this means). To explain it another way, for each test, if we use the 5 percent level, then if the difference turns out to be statistically significant we can be 95 percent confident that this reflects a real underlying trend in the population as a whole. However, in this case our ultimate findings that we report are based not just on one test but three. While we can be 95 percent confident in each of the three tests individually, we can only be 85.7 percent confident that the results of all three tests can be trusted (i.e. $0.95 \times 0.95 \times 0.95 = 0.857$ or 85.7 percent). In other words, there is now a 14.3 percent possibility of committing a Type I error in relation to at least one of the three findings.

While we can go ahead and use multiple Mann-Whitney U tests we do need to address this problem first. The simplest way of doing so is to use a stricter level of statistical significance so that the overall level remains no higher than 5 percent. To do this we can apply what is known as the **Bonferroni Correction**. This consists of simply setting the statistical significance level to be used by dividing 5 percent by the total number of tests you intend to use. Thus, if we planned to use three Mann-Whitney U tests then the statistical significance level we would use would be $5/3 = 1.7$ percent (or $p = 0.017$). Similarly, if we decided to use only two Mann-Whitney U tests then the statistical significance level would be $5/2 = 2.5$ percent (or $p = 0.025$).

One of the limitations of doing this is that if we need to conduct more than two or three separate tests then we will be forced to use a very strict level for statistical significance and, unless we are dealing with very large samples, we run a much greater risk of not detecting real differences in the population when they actually might exist (know as a Type II error as explained in Chapter 5). It is advisable, therefore, to pick the tests you need to do carefully. In the present example, we do not really need to conduct all three tests. Rather, it would be sufficient to conduct the following two comparisons:

- "White, Non-Hispanic" and "Hispanic"
- "Hispanic" and "Black Non-Hispanic"

If both of these turn out to be statistically significant then we can assume that the third comparison ("White, Non-Hispanic" with "Black, Non-Hispanic") will be statistically significant as well.

With this in mind, try running two Mann-Whitney U tests; the first comparing white, non-Hispanic children with Hispanic children (i.e. those coded "1" and "3" for the variable "RACEETHN") and the second comparing black, non-Hispanic children with Hispanic children (i.e. those coded "2" and "3"). When considering the findings in both cases, remember we are now using a cut-off point of $p < 0.025$ rather than the convention cut-off point of $p < 0.05$. Thus, even if one of the tests produces a result of $p = 0.030$, because we are applying a stricter criteria we have to conclude that the finding is not statistically significant as it does not fall below $p = 0.025$.

After running the tests you should find that the difference between white, non-Hispanic and Hispanic children is statistically significant ($p < 0.001$, Mann-Whitney $U = 370,445$, $Z = 4.257$). However, the difference between black, non-Hispanic and Hispanic children is not statistically significant ($p = 0.145$, Mann-Whitney $U = 129,214$, $Z = 1.458$). To gain a more concrete feel for these differences it is useful to explore the results using the **Analyze → Descriptive Statistics → Crosstabs. . .** procedure and, for the purposes of reporting the findings, possibly use a clustered bar chart. The output from the **Crosstabs . . .** procedure is shown in Output 6.8. As can be seen, a notably larger proportion of white, non-Hispanic children (53.5 percent) are reported as having achieved mostly A's compared to their Hispanic (40.1 percent) and black, non-Hispanic (37.6 percent) peers. While there is a difference between these latter two groups it can be seen that the difference is small and thus it is not surprising that it is not statistically significant. Remember, however, that just because the differences between black, non-Hispanic and Hispanic children were found not to be statistically significant, this does not mean we can interpret this as providing evidence that no differences exist. Again, it may simply be due to the smaller sub-samples used in the survey.

Assuming that a bar chart is provided as part of the report, one way of reporting all of these findings is as follows:

> There is evidence of differences between children from different racial/ethnic backgrounds in the average school grades reported by parents ($p < 0.001$, Kruskal Wallis $H = 48.672$, $df = 2$). On further inspection it was found that white, non-Hispanic children were achieving higher reported grades than their nearest other group, Hispanic children ($p < 0.001$, Mann-Whitney $U = 370,445$, $Z = 4.257$). However, no evidence was found of any differences between black, non-Hispanic and Hispanic children ($p = 0.145$, Mann-Whitney $U = 129,214$, $Z = 1.458$). These differences are illustrated in Figure X. As can be seen, while 53.5 percent of white, non-Hispanic children are reported as having achieved mostly A's, only 40.1 percent of Hispanic children and 37.6 percent of black, non-Hispanic (37.6 percent) children were reported as achieving the same. The effect size for the difference between white, non-Hispanic and Hispanic children was found to be relatively small however ($r = 0.090$).

EXERCISE 6.3

Using the **youthcohort.sav** dataset, test the hypothesis that there are differences in levels of truancy ("s1truan") between different racial/ethnic groups ("ethsfr"). Check your method and findings on the companion website.

Output 6.8

D-RACE-ETHNICITY OF CHILD * SE1-CHILD'S GRADES ACROSS ALL SUBJECTS Crosstabulation

			SE1-CHILD'S GRADES ACROSS ALL SUBJECTS					Total
			1 MOSTLY A'S	2 MOSTLY B'S	3 MOSTLY C'S	4 MOSTLY D'S	5 MOSTLY F'S	
D-RACE-ETHNICITY OF CHILD	1 WHITE, NON-HISPANIC	Count	1224	741	262	41	19	2287
		% within D-RACE-ETHNICITY OF CHILD	53.5%	32.4%	11.5%	1.8%	.8%	100.0%
	2 BLACK, NON-HISPANIC	Count	256	266	129	16	13	680
		% within D-RACE-ETHNICITY OF CHILD	37.6%	39.1%	19.0%	2.4%	1.9%	100.0%
	3 HISPANIC	Count	301	302	107	29	11	750
		% within D-RACE-ETHNICITY OF CHILD	40.1%	40.3%	14.3%	3.9%	1.5%	100.0%
	4 ALL OTHER RACES	Count	184	92	38	7	2	323
		% within D-RACE-ETHNICITY OF CHILD	57.0%	28.5%	11.8%	2.2%	.6%	100.0%
Total		Count	1965	1401	536	93	45	4040
		% within D-RACE-ETHNICITY OF CHILD	48.6%	34.7%	13.3%	2.3%	1.1%	100.0%

Independent samples t-test

For this next example we will use the **valueadded.sav** dataset and, for the purposes of illustrating this and the following statistical test, we will assume that the schools in the dataset are samples that have been randomly selected from the four local education authorities (LEAs). For this first test our focus will be on comparing the academic performance of pupils in schools between just two of these LEAs—the City of York and the City of Leeds LEAs. The measure of performance that will be used is measured at school-level and is simply the GCSE Benchmark that used to form the basis of the construction of school league tables in England, i.e. the percentage of pupils at each school achieving five or more good passes in public examinations in their final year of compulsory schooling (i.e. GCSEs Grades A*–C). The hypothesis we will test and its associated null-hypothesis are:

- H_1: There is a difference between the City of Leeds and the City of York LEAs in terms of the academic performance of pupils in their schools.
- H_0: There is no difference between the City of Leeds and the City of York in terms of the academic performance of pupils in their schools.

The two variables we will use from the dataset are the nominal variable "lea" (that includes the two LEAs in question) and the scale variable "gcse" (that represents the percentage of pupils in each school gaining five or more GCSEs Grades A*–C). In using this latter measure it needs to be stressed that the comparison is based simply on the academic performance of pupils in schools in the two LEAs. It would certainly be wrong to interpret this as a measure of school performance in and of itself or, by extension, a measure of the performance of the two LEAs in any sense.

In terms of selecting an appropriate test, it can be seen from Box 6.1 that there are two options when examining the relationship between a nominal and scale variable. The choice of option depends upon how many categories of the nominal variable we are interested in comparing. In this case, as there are just two categories that we wish to compare, we can see that we should choose the independent samples t-test. However, before we press ahead and use this test we need to check that the assumptions upon which the test is based have been met. The three main ones are:

- that we are comparing the scores of two independent groups on a scale variable;
- that the scale variable is approximately normally distributed;
- that the spread (variances) of the scores for both groups on the scale variable are roughly equal.

The first assumption is met as the variable "gcse" is a scale variable. The third assumption is something we can ignore for now as it is checked as part of the independent samples t-test procedure in SPSS. It is the second assumption—that "gcse" is approximately normally distributed—that we need to check here before we continue. We can do this visually using a histogram. The result is shown in Figure 6.6 for the whole sample. As can be seen, the data look as if they conform approximately to a normal distribution. However there is a slight "ceiling effect" noticeable by the peak at the top end of the distribution reflecting the fact that 100 percent is the absolute maximum.

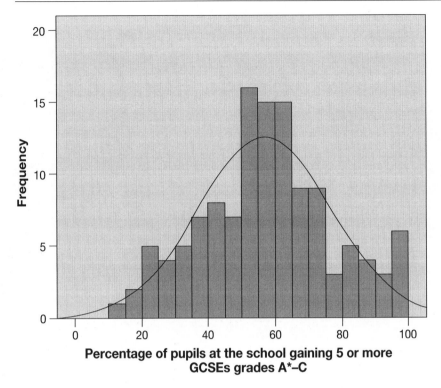

Figure 6.6 Distribution of the "gcse" variable in the valueadded.sav dataset

This visual inspection would actually be sufficient in this case. However, it can be tested formally using the one-sample Kolmogorov-Smirnov test. This test simply calculates the probability of the sample having the distribution it has assuming that it has been drawn from a normal distribution. To run the test select **Analyze → Nonparametric tests → 1-Sample K-S . . .** This opens the **One-Sample Kolmogorov-Smirnov Test** window shown in Figure 6.7. Place the variable in question—"score"—into the "Test Variable List:" field as shown and then check that the "Normal" test distribution has been selected before clicking "OK." The output you should get from this is shown in Output 6.9.

As can be seen, the output includes some summary statistics relating to the variable itself including its mean (56.9) and standard deviation (19.8). The main piece of information we are interested in here is the probability ("Asymp. Sig."). This is the probability of getting a distribution such as this one assuming it has been selected from a population that is normally distributed. As can be seen, even with the slight ceiling effect there is still an 89.2 percent chance of getting a distribution like this if selected randomly from a normally distributed population. As such we can conclude that our sample is sufficiently normally distributed.

If this probability had been less than 0.05 we would have to conclude that the chances are that it has not actually been selected from a population that is normally distributed. If this turns out to be the case then one of the key assumptions upon which the t-test is based

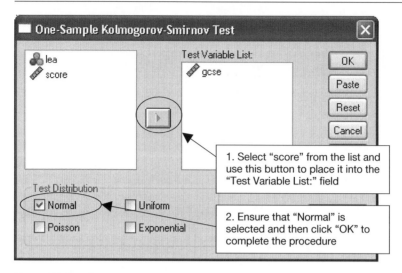

Figure 6.7 One-Sample Kolmogorov-Smirnov Test window in SPSS

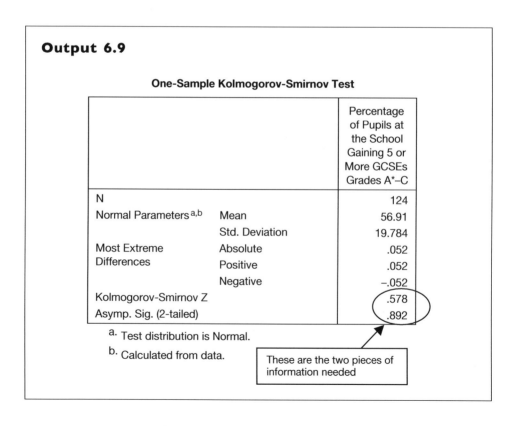

Output 6.9

One-Sample Kolmogorov-Smirnov Test

		Percentage of Pupils at the School Gaining 5 or More GCSEs Grades A*–C
N		124
Normal Parameters [a,b]	Mean	56.91
	Std. Deviation	19.784
Most Extreme Differences	Absolute	.052
	Positive	.052
	Negative	−.052
Kolmogorov-Smirnov Z		.578
Asymp. Sig. (2-tailed)		.892

a. Test distribution is Normal.

b. Calculated from data.

These are the two pieces of information needed

has been violated and so you would need to choose an alternative test instead (in this case the Mann-Whitney U test). In this present example, however, the normality of the distribution has been confirmed and we can report this finding using the probability value and the associated Z score above it as follows:

> The distribution of the proportion of pupils gaining five or more GCSE grades A*–C across schools in the sample was found to be approximately normally distributed (p = 0.892, Kolmogorov-Smirnov Z = 0.578).

We can now move on to run the independent samples t-test. To do this select **Analyze → Compare Means → Independent-Samples T Test. . . .** This opens the window shown in Figure 6.8. Just as with the Mann-Whitney U test previously, you should use the arrow buttons to place the scale variable ("gcse") into the "Test Variable(s):" field and "lea" into the "Grouping Variable:" field. Once done, click on the "Define Groups. . ." button to open the second window shown. Use this to tell SPSS which two groups within "lea" it should conduct the analysis on. In this case, as City of York is coded "1" and City of Leeds "2," type these values into the relevant fields as shown. Finally, click "Continue" to return to the main window and "OK" to complete the procedure. The output produced from this is shown in Output 6.10.

The first table in the output—"Group Statistics"—provides a summary of the mean school-level achievement and their respective standard deviations for schools in both

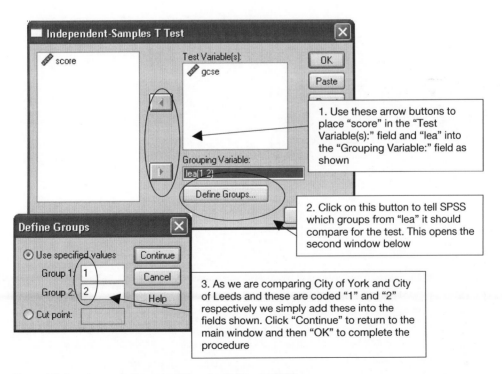

Figure 6.8 Running an Independent-Samples T Test in SPSS

Output 6.10

Group Statistics

	Local Education Authority	N	Mean	Std. Deviation	Std. Error Mean
Percentage of Pupils at the School Gaining 5 or More GCSEs Grades A*–C	City of York	12	59.00	22.111	6.383
	City of Leeds	44	48.20	20.380	3.072

1. Summary statistics showing the different mean scores for schools in the two LEAs. As can be seen, the mean score is higher for the City of York compared to the City of Leeds

Independent Samples Test

		Levene's Test for Equality of Variances		t-test for E
		F	Sig.	t	df	Sig. (2-tailed)
Percentage of Pupils at the School Gaining 5 or More GCSEs Grades A*–C	Equal variances assumed	.201	.655	1.598	54	.116
	Equal variances not assumed			1.524	16.461	.147

2. Before looking at the results of the independent t-test we need to check whether the third condition for the test mentioned earlier – that the spread of scores in the two groups (i.e. their variances) are roughly equal or not. We do this by checking the statistical significance of Levene's Test for Equality of Variances. As shown here, the statistical significance is ".655"

4. As the statistical significance for the Levene's Test in this case is greater than 0.05, we assume that the variances are different and thus we use the results shown on the top line

| | 10.795 | 7.084 | –4.188 | 25.779 |

3. There are two sets of results for the Independent samples t-test and the choice of which to use depends upon the outcome of Levene's Test:
- If the statistical significance for Levene's Test, p > 0.05 then we assume that there are equal variances and use the results from the top row
- If the statistical significance, p ≤ 0.05 then we assume that the variances are different and we use the results from the bottom row (that include a correction to account for the fact that the variances are different)

LEAs. As can be seen, schools in the City of York do appear to have pupils achieving at a higher level on average than those in the City of Leeds. The next task is to determine whether these differences are statistically significant or not. To do this we consult the second table provided in the output—Independent Samples Test—for the results of the independent samples t-test. While deriving the required pieces of information from this second table is not difficult, you do need to follow a number of steps carefully otherwise it is easy to make a mistake.

It can be seen that SPSS actually provides two sets of results, one for when "equal variances are assumed" and the other for when "equal variances are not assumed." These actually relate to the third of the three conditions that need to be met before an independent samples t-test can be used (i.e. that the spread of scores or variances for the two groups are roughly equal). Basically, if the variances are found not to be roughly equal then SPSS makes some adjustments to the results to compensate for this. With all this in mind, therefore, we now need to take the following steps:

- Check the statistical significance of Levene's test for equality of variances. This is the test that SPSS uses to check whether the variances of the two groups are roughly equal or not. If the statistical significance of Levene's test is greater than 0.05 (i.e. $p > 0.05$) then we can assume that the variances are equal (and thus use the top line for the results of the independent samples t-test). However, if the statistical significance of Levene's test is less than or equal to 0.05 (i.e. $p \leq 0.05$) then we assume that the variances are not equal and thus use the bottom line of results.
- In this particular case, as indicated, the statistical significance of Levene's test is given as "0.655" (in other words $p = 0.655$). As such it is greater than 0.05 and thus we can assume that the variances are equal. With this in mind we need to consult the results for the independent samples t-test on the top line as shown in Output 6.10.
- The three pieces of information to glean from the results of the test are: the test statistic itself (i.e. $t = 1.598$); the degrees of freedom associated with this (i.e. $df = 54$); and finally the actual statistical significance of the finding (i.e. "0.116" or $p = 0.116$).

As can be seen, while there is a difference in the mean school-level achievement scores of pupils in the two LEAs these results are not statistically significant. Now it would be quite common practice to stop at this point and simply conclude the following:

No evidence was found of a difference between the City of York and the City of Leeds LEAs in relation to school-level achievement ($p = 0.116$, $t = 1.598$, $df = 54$).

However, the question is whether this feels intuitively right. We are concluding that there is no evidence of any difference between the York and Leeds LEAs but the summary statistics reported in Output 6.10 indicate that there is actually a 10.8 percentage point gap between the mean scores of schools in the two LEAs (i.e. $59.0 - 48.2$). This is a good example of how you need to always remain connected to your actual data and not just reply simply and mechanically on the findings of statistical tests. One of the possible reasons for this difference could well be the small size of the sample drawn from York LEA ($n = 12$). In this sense the difference may represent a real underlying difference between the population of schools in the two LEAs but we have simply not been able to detect this because our sample size is too small. If you remember from the last chapter this would be an example of a Type II error (if you don't remember then it may be useful for you to go back and read the section on Type I and II errors and also on statistical power).

One way of checking whether this is the case is to calculate the statistical power of the test. As explained in the last chapter, the statistical power of the test is the probability that a difference will be detected in the sample assuming that one actually exists in the population as a whole. By "detected" we mean finding that it is statistically significant. Unfortunately, SPSS Version 15.0 (and earlier versions) does not provide a facility for calculating statistical power and so we have to use specialist software to do this. One such program is G*Power, which is available to download free from the web. Full details on this are provided on the companion website. As I write this book, G*Power is due to launch a new version of the software that represents a major development upon the current version available (Version 2). Rather than provide step-by-step guides as to how to use this current version here, therefore, guidance will be provided on the companion website in relation to the new version as soon as it becomes publicly available. For now, we will just focus on the way to use and interpret the statistical power relating to this current test. Details on how this was calculated using the current version of G*Power, including a step-by-step guide, are provided on the companion website.

It will be remembered from the last chapter that we need three pieces of information to calculate the statistical power of a test: the sample size; the effect size found; and the significance level being used (usually the conventional 5 percent significance level). In this case, G*Power calculates its own version of the effect size using information you provide on the means and standard deviations of the two groups of schools. Thus, with information provided in Output 6.10 we can input this into G*Power and this then tells us that the statistical power of this current independent samples t-test is $\beta = 0.334$. As explained in the last chapter we can use this to calculate the probability of committing a Type II error, which is simply equal to $1 - \beta$ (i.e. 0.666). Thus, in this case, given the relatively small number of schools involved, there is actually a high chance (a 66.6 percent chance) that even if this difference was real then this particular test would be unable to detect it (and thus show that it is statistically significant).

Given that we usually aim for a power level of 80 percent, this lack of power (being only at 33.4 percent) brings into question the validity of the findings of this statistical test. In fact, it is difficult to draw any conclusions from this test given the high chance that a Type II error has been committed here. In such circumstances it is probably better not to rely on the statistical test but to report the findings and explain that a test for statistical significance has not been carried out because of the low levels of statistical power involved. An example of how this can be done in practice will be provided shortly. However, as we are now going to report the findings, we do need to calculate the associated effect size. Unfortunately, SPSS does not produce a measure of effect size with the output but we can calculate one very easily using some of the information provided in the output. While there are a number of different measures of effect size we could use, the most common being Cohen's d, perhaps the simplest to calculate is as follows using the t statistic (in this case t = 1.598) and its associated degrees of freedom (again, in our case df = 54):

$$\text{Effect size, } r = \sqrt{\frac{t^2}{t^2 + df}}.$$

Thus, putting the values into this formula we get:

$$\text{Effect size, } r = \sqrt{\frac{1.598^2}{1.598^2 + 54}} = \sqrt{\frac{2.5536}{56.5536}} = 0.212.$$

Just as with the correlation coefficient, the value of this effect size measure, r, runs from "0" (indicating that there is no relationship between the LEA that a school is located in and the proportion of their pupils gaining five or more GCSE grades A*–C) and "1" (indicating that there is a perfect relationship). Interestingly, the similarities between this measure of effect size and the correlation coefficient are not an accident. In fact, the effect size measure discussed here is the same as the Pearson correlation coefficient calculated between the scale variable and the dichotomous nominal variable concerned (because one of the variables is dichotomous then this coefficient has a special name—the **point biserial correlation**—but let's not get too distracted here!).

If you would like to avoid calculating the effect size by hand, you can calculate it using the **Analyze → Correlate → Bivariate. . .** procedure and computing the Pearson correlation coefficient for the two variables "gcse" and "lea." Before doing this, however, you need to use the **Data → Select Cases. . .** procedure to ensure that only the first two categories of "lea" are included (i.e. York and Leeds). Try running the correlation procedure. You should get the output shown in Output 6.11. As can be seen, we get the same result (i.e. r = 0.212) as when we calculated the effect size by hand. Also note that the significance level reported in this output is actually the same as that for the independent samples t-test (i.e. p = 0.116).

Output 6.11

Correlations

		Local Education Authority	Percentage of Pupils at the School Gaining 5 or More GCSEs Grades A*–C
Local Education Authority	Pearson Correlation	1	−.212
	Sig. (2-tailed)		.116
	N	56	56
Percentage of Pupils at the School Gaining 5 or More GCSEs Grades A*–C	Pearson Correlation	−.212	1
	Sig. (2-tailed)	.116	
	N	56	124

So, where does this all leave us? What started as a simple statistical test has clearly got quite complicated. In summary, we have found a difference in school-level achievement between the two LEAs. While we have also found that this difference is not statistically significant, the power calculations suggest that we should be extremely cautious in reading anything into this. In fact, as suggested, when the power is as small as this (and thus the chances of committing a Type II error are so high) then we would tend to ignore the results of the independent samples t-test altogether and report the findings along the following lines:

> A difference was found in relation to school-level achievement between the City of York and the City of Leeds LEAs. The mean proportion of pupils gaining five or more GCSE Grades A*–C in schools in York was 59.0 (SD = 22.1) and this compared to 48.2 (SD = 20.4) for Leeds. The size of this difference was found to be relatively small (r = 0.212). Because of low statistical power (β = 0.334), it was not possible to undertake a reliable test for statistical significance on these findings. These findings should therefore be treated with some caution.

EXERCISE 6.4

Using the **youthcohort.sav** dataset, test the hypothesis that there are differences between boys and girls ("slgender") in relation to the GCSE points score they achieved in the public examinations they took at the end of compulsory schooling ("gcsepts"). Check your method and results on the companion website.

One-way ANOVA

To demonstrate the one-way ANOVA (or one-way analysis of variance to give its full name) we will stay with the **valueadded.sav** dataset and will continue to assume that the dataset represents samples of schools randomly selected from four LEAs. This time, however, we will examine what differences exist between all four LEAs rather than just two. The alternative and null-hypotheses can therefore be stated as follows:

- H_1: There is a difference between the four LEAs in terms of the academic performance of pupils in their schools.
- H_0: There is no difference between the four LEAs in terms of the academic performance of pupils in their schools.

This time we are dealing with a nominal variable ("lea") and a scale variable ("gcse"). As we are wishing to compare four categories, Box 6.1 indicates that we should therefore use the one-way ANOVA (analysis of variance) test. The assumptions upon which the one-way ANOVA is based are actually the same as for the independent samples t-test:

- that we are comparing the scores of three or more independent groups on a scale variable;

- that the scale variable is approximately normally distributed;
- that the spread (variances) of the scores for the groups on the scale variable are roughly equal.

Fortunately, we have already confirmed that the first two assumptions have been met for the scale variable "gcse" and the third assumption is checked as part of the one-way ANOVA procedure in SPSS. As such we can go straight on to run the statistical test. To do this select **Analyze** → **Compare Means** → **One-Way ANOVA. . . .** This opens up the window shown in Figure 6.9. Use the arrow buttons to place the scale variable "gcse" into the "Dependent List:" field and the nominal variable "lea" into the "Factor:" window as shown. Click on the "Post Hoc. . ." button to call up the additional window shown and select "Hochberg's GT2" (to be explained shortly) and then click "Continue" to return to the main window. Click on the "Options. . ." button to call up the additional window shown in Figure 6.9. Select "Descriptive" to ensure the output includes descriptive statistics for each of the groups and also "Homogeneity of variance test" (that is a test of whether the third assumption listed above is met or not) and then click "Continue" to return to the main window. Finally, click "OK" in the main window to complete the

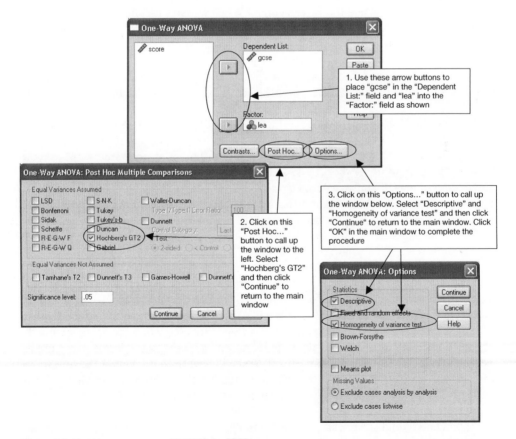

Figure 6.9 Running a one-way ANOVA in SPSS

procedure. The first part of the output SPSS produces from this procedure is shown in Output 6.12.

As can be seen, because we selected "Descriptive" the output begins with a table providing summary statistics for each of the LEAs. Alongside the mean score and associated standard deviation for each LEA, the table also includes a 95 percent confidence interval for each mean and also the minimum and maximum individual scores found within each group. Before we consider the results of the one-way ANOVA, however, we need to check that the third assumption underpinning this test has been met—that the variances of the scores for four LEAs are roughly the same. This is checked by the Levene's test just as with the independent samples t-test and the results are provided in the second table headed "Test of Homogeneity of Variances." As before:

- if the significance of Levene's test is greater than 0.05, we can assume that the assumption of equal variances has been met;
- if the significance of Levene's test is 0.05 or less, we have to conclude that the assumption of equal variances has not been met. As such we would need to select an alternative statistical test (in this case the Kruskal-Wallis test).

In this case, as can be seen from Output 6.12, the result of Levene's test is $p = 0.133$ and so, as it is greater than 0.05, we can conclude that we have met this third assumption. We can now go on to consider the actual results of the one-way ANOVA as presented in the third table in Output 6.12. Basically, the three pieces of information we need to derive from this and report are: the test statistic, F (in this case 5.249); the associated degrees of freedom (in this case both the between groups and within groups degrees of freedom—3 and 120); and finally the statistical significance of the finding (in this case ".002" or $p = 0.002$).

As can be seen, as the statistical significance is below 5 percent we can conclude that there is sufficient evidence to reject the null-hypothesis and accept the alternative hypothesis, i.e. accept that there are differences in levels of academic achievement between at least some of the LEAs. Just as with the Kruskal-Wallis test, however, this finding in itself is only of limited value. All it actually tells us is that there are at least some statistically significant differences between the four LEAs that provide the focus of analysis here. What it does not tell us is where these statistically significant differences actually lie.

One option we have, again just as with the Kruskal-Wallis test, is to run multiple independent samples t-tests comparing the means of two groups at a time. However, as there are four groups, 12 comparisons would be needed in total and the resultant Bonferroni correction required will reduce the statistical significance level to an unacceptably strict degree (i.e. $0.05/12 = 0.004$). Fortunately, there is a number of what are called "post-hoc" tests that have been developed that have been designed to simultaneously make all possible pair-wise comparisons between groups while maintaining the overall risk of a Type I error to 5 percent. You will have seen from Figure 6.9 that there are many different tests that can be used and each has its merits and limitations. Field (2005: 341) provides some useful advice on the actual choice of post-hoc test:

- if you have equal sample sizes choose **Tukey**;
- if the sample sizes are slightly different choose **Gabriel**;

Output 6.12

Descriptives

Percentage of Pupils at the School Gaining 5 or More GCSEs Grades A*–C

	N	Mean	Std. Deviation	Std. Error	95% Confidence Interval for Mean		Minimum	Maximum
					Lower Bound	Upper Bound		
City of York	12	59.00	22.111	6.383	44.95	73.05	22	98
City of Leeds	44	48.20	20.380	3.072	42.01	54.40	12	98
East Riding of Yorkshire	19	58.74	14.813	3.398	51.60	65.88	30	91
North Yorkshire	49	63.51	17.895	2.556	58.37	68.65	21	99
Total	124	56.91	19.784	1.777	53.39	60.43	12	99

1. Summary statistics for the groups being compared showing the mean GCSE point score for each group together with its standard deviation, a 95% Confidence Interval for the mean and maximum and minimum values

Test of Homogeneity of Variances

Percentage of Pupils at the School Gaining 5 or More GCSEs Grades A*–C

Levene Statistic	df1	df2	Sig.
1.903	3	120	.133

2. Before looking at the results of the one-way ANOVA it is important to check the third assumption of equal variances between the four groups. Significance values above 0.05 (as here) indicate that we have met the assumption. Values of 0.05 or below would indicate that the assumption has been violated

ANOVA

Percentage of Pupils at the School Gaining 5 or More GCSEs Grades A*–C

	Sum of Squares	df	Mean Square	F	Sig.
Between Groups	5584.936	3	1861.645	5.249	.002
Within Groups	42557.088	120	354.642		
Total	48142.024	123			

3. The key information to derive from these results of the one-way ANOVA are the two degrees of freedom, the actual test statistic (F) and the statistical significance of this statistic

- if the sample sizes are very different use **Hochberg's GT2**;
- if there is some doubt that the variances are sufficiently equal choose **Games-Howell**.

From the output you will find a Multiple Comparisons table providing the results of all possible pair-wise comparisons between the four LEAs. This table is shown in Output 6.13. It may look a little daunting initially but the only column we really need to look at is that headed "Sig." As the name suggests, the figures in this column represent the statistical significance values for the differences between each of the groups listed. If the value is 0.05 or below, we can conclude that the difference between the mean scores for the two groups concerned is statistically significant. Similarly, if the value is above 0.05, we conclude that there is no evidence from our sample to suggest that the mean scores for the two groups are different.

If we start at the very top we can see that the first section compares York LEA with each of the other LEAs in turn. Using the values in the "Sig." column we can see from this that there are no statistically significant differences between the mean score for York and any of the other three LEAs. Working our way down the table we find that the only statistically significant difference is between Leeds and North Yorkshire LEAs (p = 0.001) which actually have the lowest and highest mean scores, respectively. What this means in practice, then, is that there are no statistically significant differences between Leeds, East Riding of Yorkshire and York LEAs. Similarly, as can be picked out from the Multiple Comparisons table in Output 6.13, there are no differences between East Riding of Yorkshire, York and North Yorkshire LEAs. This is actually confirmed by the second table in Output 6.13 that lists the number of sub-sets of LEAs where the means between them are found not to be statistically significant.

One final thing to do here is to calculate the effect size of the one difference that has emerged—that between Leeds and North Yorkshire LEAs. Using the Pearson correlation between these two variables (with just these two LEA categories selected) this gives an effect size of r = 0.375. With all this information we are now in a position to report the results. One way of doing this is as follows:

> Some evidence was found of a relationship between LEAs and school-level achievement (p = 0.002, F = 5.249, df = 3, 120). However, further analysis revealed that only the difference between Leeds and North Yorkshire LEAs was notable with the mean proportion of pupils gaining five or more GCSE Grades A*–C in Leeds being 48.2 (SD = 20.4) compared to 63.5 (SD = 17.9) in North Yorkshire. The size of this difference was found to be moderate (r = 0.375).

As with the independent samples t-test it should be noted that these results depend upon some sub-samples that are actually quite small. It would, therefore, be worth calculating the statistical power of this one-way ANOVA to check that these results are reliable (i.e. the chances of a Type II error having been committed here are not too high). More generally, it is worth remembering that any results gained from tests such as this are reliant upon the size of the sub-samples involved. In this present case, if you increased the sample sizes sufficiently then all of these differences would eventually become statistically significant. Equally, all you would have to do is to halve the current sample sizes to find that the one-way ANOVA indicates that there are no statistically significant differences between the four LEAs at all.

Output 6.13

Multiple Comparisons

Dependent Variable: Percentage of Pupils at the School Gaining 5 or More GCSEs Grades A*–C

Hochberg

(I) Local Education Authority	(J) Local Education Authority	Mean Difference (I–J)	Std. Error	Sig.	95% Confidence Interval	
					Lower Bound	Upper Bound
City of York	City of Leeds	10.795	6.133	.393	−5.60	27.19
	East Riding of Yorkshire	.263	6.944	1.000	−18.30	18.83
	North Yorkshire	−4.510	6.066	.974	−20.72	11.70
City of Leeds	City of York	−10.795	6.133	.393	−27.19	5.60
	East Riding of Yorkshire	−10.532	5.170	.233	−24.35	3.29
	North Yorkshire	−15.306*	3.911	.001	−25.76	−4.85
East Riding of Yorkshire	City of York	−.263	6.944	1.000	−18.83	18.30
	City of Leeds	10.532	5.170	.233	−3.29	24.35
	North Yorkshire	−4.773	5.089	.922	−18.38	8.83
North Yorkshire	City of York	4.510	6.066	.974	−11.70	20.72
	City of Leeds	15.306*	3.911	.001	4.85	25.76
	East Riding of Yorkshire	4.773	5.089	.922	−8.83	18.38

* The mean difference is significant at the .05 level.

Percentage of Pupils at the School Gaining 5 or More GCSEs Grades A*–C

Hochberg[a,b]

Local Education Authority	N	Subset for alpha = .05	
		1	2
City of Leeds	44	48.20	
East Riding of Yorkshire	19	58.74	58.74
City of York	12	59.00	59.00
North Yorkshire	49		63.51
Sig.		.297	.951

Means for groups in homogeneous subsets are displayed.

a. Uses Harmonic Mean Sample Size = 22.334.

b. The group sizes are unequal. The harmonic mean of the group sizes is used. Type I error levels are not guaranteed.

1. Use this column to consider where the differences lie. Values of 0.05 or below indicate a statistically significant difference while those above 0.05 indicate that the difference is not statistically significant. Here we can see that the only difference that is statistically significant is the one between the LEAs with the top and bottom mean scores i.e. North Yorkshire and City of Leeds. We have no evidence that there are differences between any of the other LEAs

2. This finding is confirmed in this final table that shows that the four LEAs can be split into two overlapping groups. For each group there is no evidence of any difference in their mean scores

The key point arising from the above discussion concerning how to interpret the results of a one-way ANOVA and its post-hoc tests is that you must always remain close to the actual data in order to interpret the results of the tests properly. This, in turn, requires you to do two things before taking any findings at face value:

- Always check the size of the sub-samples upon which the findings are based. Very small sub-samples are likely to increase the risk of Type II errors (and thus suggest that no differences exist when in actual fact they do).
- Always calculate effect sizes for differences that turn out to be statistically significant and use these as a basis for describing and interpreting the findings. Especially with large samples, even very small differences that are negligible in practical terms will become statistically significant.

EXERCISE 6.5

Using the **value-added.sav** data explore the impact of different sample sizes on the results of the one-way ANOVA and the post-hoc tests you have just conducted. To do this, create a new variable and call it "weight." For each school give it the same value (start initially with "2"). Once you have this new variable (which should just comprise a column of 2's), use **Data → Weight Cases. . .** to weight the sample by this variable. In this present case this will have the result of doubling the sample sizes. Now try running the statistical tests again as described in this section to see what happens. Try this again but this time with a different value for the weight variable. You can change the value of the weight variable using the **Transform → Recode into Same Variables. . .** procedure. By what factor must you increase the sample sizes to make every difference statistically significant? Similarly, by what factor must you reduce the sample sizes to make everything not statistically significant? Check your methods and results on the companion website.

Spearman and Pearson correlations

Conducting tests for statistical significance on correlations (whether Spearman or Pearson) is actually the most straightforward procedure of all. As you may have noticed in earlier chapters (see, for example, Output 3.7) not only does the **Analyze → Correlate → Bivariate. . .** procedure give you the correlation coefficient (which is actually the effect size in this case) but it also calculates the statistical significance of this by default as well.

We have actually already analyzed a fair few correlations. To do something a little different we will use the **earlychildhood.sav** dataset and examine the nature of the correlation between the age of a child's mother and their father. Here, we would expect to find a positive correlation and so we can use a directional hypothesis:

- H_1: There is a positive correlation between the ages of a young child's mother and father in America.

- H_0: There is no correlation between the ages of a young child's mother and father in America.

The two relevant variables in the **earlychildhood.sav** dataset are "MOMAGE1" and "DADAGE1." As both of these are scale variables and these variables are different (rather than being the same variable representing measurements taken at two points in time taken on the same cases) we can see from Box 6.1 that we would use a Pearson correlation. As explained in Chapter 3, however, before we calculate the Pearson correlation coefficient we need to satisfy ourselves that the relationship between these two variables is linear. We can do this with a scatterplot. Using the **Graphs → Legacy Dialogs → Scatter/Dot. . .** procedure (or just **Graphs → Scatter/Dot. . .** in SPSS Version 14.0 and earlier) that you have covered previously (see Figure 1.20) you should get the scatterplot shown in Figure 6.10.

As can be seen, the relationship is sufficiently linear for us to continue with the Pearson correlation. To do this run the **Analyze → Correlate → Bivariate. . .** procedure as shown previously (see Figure 3.11), ensuring that you have selected "Pearson" and this will give you the results shown in Output 6.14. The two pieces of information to derive from this output are the correlation coefficient (".771") and the statistical significance of this (".000"

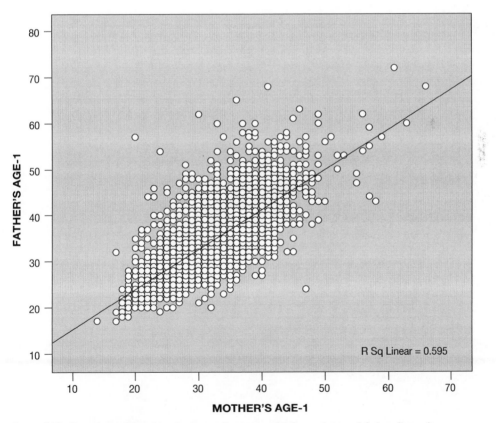

Figure 6.10 Correlation between the ages of a young child's mother and father from the earlychildhood.sav dataset

or p<0.001). Also, from Chapter 3, it will be remembered that this correlation coefficient can be used to calculate the percentage of variance shared by the two variables (i.e. 0.771 × 0.771 = 0.594 = 59.4 percent). This is also a useful bit of information to share. This can then be reported simply as:

> A fairly strong and positive correlation was found between the ages of the child's mother and father (r_p = 0.771, p<0.001). This indicates that the mothers' and fathers' ages in the sample share 59.4 percent of their variation in common.

The key point to draw from this is that even though the correlation coefficient suggests a fairly strong relationship between the two variables, it can be seen from the scatterplot in Figure 6.10 that there is still a fair amount of variation. This is why it is always useful to display your findings graphically wherever possible. This is particularly true should you ever find statistically significant correlations of 0.2 or 0.1 where it is tempting to emphasize the correlation that exists and yet a scatterplot would just tend to show a largely indiscernible mass of points. In this case, while statistically a relationship may be detectable, in reality the relationship is barely visible (and thus negligible in practical terms).

EXERCISE 6.6

Using the **international.sav** dataset explore the extent of the correlations and their statistical significance between some of the indicators used. Check your method and findings on the companion website.

Output 6.14

Correlations

		MOTHER'S AGE-1	FATHER'S AGE-1
MOTHER'S AGE-1	Pearson Correlation	1	.771**
	Sig. (2-tailed)		.000
	N	3556	2897
FATHER'S AGE-1	Pearson Correlation	.771**	1
	Sig. (2-tailed)	.000	
	N	2897	2959

**Correlation is significant at the 0.01 level (2-tailed).

> The two pieces of information required can be found here: the correlation coefficient ("0.771") and the statistical significance of this ("0.000")

If you were conducting a Spearman correlation (because one or both of your variables is ordinal) then it is exactly the same procedure to follow as set out above, except that you would select "Spearman" rather than "Pearson" in the **Bivariate Correlations** window.

Wilcoxon test

For the rest of this chapter we will use the **experiment.sav** dataset. This is a fictitious dataset relating to a scenario involving an elementary/primary school that runs an after-school Reading Club that 60 children aged 6–7 currently attend. The club runs for one afternoon a week and involves the children visiting the local library, borrowing books and listening to a story being read aloud. Now, let's suppose that one of the teachers has devised a modified program whereby the story read aloud is followed by role play and drama in which the children are encouraged to re-enact parts of the story and also to explore different endings.

The school principal was very interested in this new program, which we will call the Reading and Drama Club, and decided to set up a small experiment to assess whether it was more effective than the existing Reading Club in terms of improving the children's reading skills and attitudes towards reading. To do this it was decided to randomly allocate the 60 children into two groups of 30. One group would continue to attend the existing Reading Club for a whole school year and the other group would attend the new Reading and Drama Club for the same period. All of the children were asked to take a standardized reading test at the start of the school year and also at the end of the year. They were also asked a simple question at the start and end of the year concerning how much they liked reading. For this question they could choose from five responses: "a lot"; "quite a lot"; "a little"; "not very much"; or "not at all."

The first thing we will do here is to assess whether the children who attended the Reading and Drama Club did actually increase their liking of reading over the year or not. In this case the alternative and null-hypotheses are:

- H_1: The children's liking of reading was higher at the end of the school year compared to the beginning.
- H_0: There was no difference between the children's liking of reading at the beginning and the end of the school year.

As can be seen, in this case we are working with a directional (one-tailed) hypothesis. The two variables we will use in this case from the **experiment.sav** dataset are "attitud1" and "attitud2" which relate the children's responses to the question "How much do you like reading?" asked at the beginning and then again at the end of the year, respectively. Here, therefore, we are dealing with two ordinal variables that represent the same measure taken at two different points in time from the same pupils. As such, as can be seen from Box 6.1, this suggests that we use the Wilcoxon test.

Before we run the test we need to use the **Data → Select Cases. . .** procedure to select only those in the Reading and Drama Club (i.e. "group = 1"). Once done you run the test by selecting **Analyze → Nonparametric tests → 2 Related Samples. . . .** This opens the **Two-Related-Samples Tests** window shown in Figure 6.11. Click on "attitud1" and then "attitud2" so that both are selected together and then click on the arrow button to place them in the "Test Pair(s) List:" field as shown. Make sure that "Wilcoxon" is selected

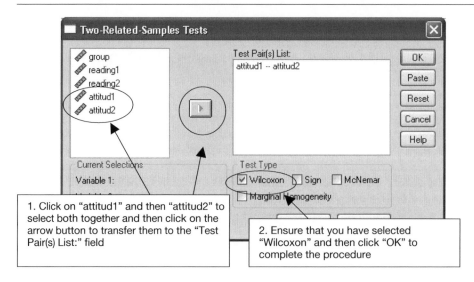

Figure 6.11 Two-Related-Samples Tests window in SPSS

before then clicking "OK" to complete the procedure. The output this produces can be seen in Output 6.15.

The first table provides information about the nature and extent of the changes in the children's responses. To interpret these it should be noted that the five responses were coded "1" to "5" with higher values indicating higher levels of liking reading. With this in mind it can be seen that of the children in the Reading and Drama Club, 22 actually increased their liking of reading over the year, five remained the same and only three decreased their liking. This would certainly suggest a positive difference and this is confirmed by the test statistics presented in the second table where the difference was found to be statistically significant (".000" or p < 0.001). As this is a one-tailed test, we would usually divide this probability by two but given that it is so low then this is not necessary on this occasion.

As for the effect size, we use the same formula as we did for the Mann-Whitney U test:

$$\text{Effect size, } r = \frac{Z}{\sqrt{n}} = \frac{3.858}{\sqrt{30}} = 0.704.$$

Pulling all of this together we can report the findings as follows. Here it is assumed that a clustered bar chart is used to compare the children's responses to the question at the beginning and end of the year:

As illustrated by the clustered bar chart, the children who attended the Reading and Drama Group rated their liking of reading much more highly at the end of the school year compared to the beginning (p < 0.001, Wilcoxon Test, Z = 3.858). While 36.7 percent stated that they liked reading "a lot" or "quite a lot" at the beginning of the

Output 6.15

Ranks

		N	Mean Rank	Sum of Ranks
'How much do you like reading?' (Post-Test) - 'How much do you like reading?' (Pre-Test)	Negative Ranks	3[a]	7.50	22.50
	Positive Ranks	22[b]	13.75	302.50
	Ties	5[c]		
	Total	30		

a. 'How much do you like reading?' (Post-Test) < 'How much do you like reading?' (Pre-Test)

b. 'How much do you like reading?' (Post-Test) > 'How much do you like reading?' (Pre-Test)

c. 'How much do you like reading?' (Post-Test) = 'How much do you like reading?' (Pre-Test)

Test Statistics [b]

	'How much do you like reading?' (Post-Test) - 'How much do you like reading?' (Pre-Test)
Z	−3.858[a]
Asymp. Sig. (2-tailed)	.000

a. Based on negative ranks.

b. Wilcoxon Signed Ranks Test.

1. This information suggests that there was a positive change overall with 22 children increasing the rating they gave to reading, 5 remaining the same and only 3 decreasing their rating

2. The two pieces of information we need to report the results of the test are the significance level of the difference (".000") and the Z score ("−3.858"). As can be seen, this indicates that these changes are statistically significant

year this had risen to 73.4 percent at the end of the year. This change in attitudes was found to be relatively strong (r = 0.704).

Of course the big question here is whether we can assume from these findings that the Reading and Drama Club was a success. Is this evidence of the positive effects on children of attending this particular club? We will answer this question shortly.

EXERCISE 6.7

Create frequency tables to check the percentage figures quoted above. Also, see if you can create a clustered bar chart to illustrate the change in children's attitudes from the beginning to the end of the year. Check your method and results on the companion website.

Related samples t-test

Alongside wanting to assess whether the attitudes towards reading of the children attending the Reading and Drama Club had improved, it was also decided to assess whether their actual reading skills had improved as well. This time, therefore, the alternative and null-hypotheses are:

- H_1: The children's reading skills were higher at the end of the school year compared to the beginning.
- H_0: There was no difference between the children's reading skills at the beginning and the end of the school year.

The two variables that can be used to test this hypothesis from the **experiment.sav** dataset are "reading1" and "reading2" which represent the children's scores on a standardized reading test taken at the beginning of the year and then again at the end. Both of these variables are scale and it can be seen from Box 6.1 that when we are dealing with two scales that actually represent the same measure taken at two different points in time from the same pupils then we should use the related samples t-test. Before we run this test, however, we need to be sure that the following two conditions are met:

- that we are dealing with a scale measure;
- that the scale measure is normally distributed.

The first assumption has been met and the second one can be checked visually by generating a histogram, and then more formally by using the **Analyze → Nonparametric Tests → 1-Sample K-S. . .** used earlier in relation to the independent samples t-test (see Figure 6.7). Before doing any of this make sure you have used **Data → Select Cases. . .** to select only those children in the Reading and Drama Club (i.e. "group = 1").

EXERCISE 6.8

Check the assumption of normality for yourself both for the pre-test reading scores ("reading1") and the post-test scores ("reading2"). You should find that the pre-test scores are sufficiently normally distributed ($p = 0.970$, Kolmogorov-Smirnov, $Z = 0.491$) as are the post-test scores ($p = 0.942$, Kolmogorov-Smirnov, $Z = 0.530$). Check to see where the results of the Kolmogorov-Smirnov tests as reported here were taken from in the SPSS output you generated.

As both assumptions have been met we can now run the related samples t-test. To do this, select **Analyze → Compare Means → Paired-Samples T Test. . . .** This opens the **Paired-Samples T Test** window shown in Figure 6.12. Click on "reading1" and then on "reading2" to select both together before then clicking on the arrow button to place them in the "Paired Variables:" field as shown. Click "OK" to complete the procedure. The output you should obtain is shown in Output 6.16.

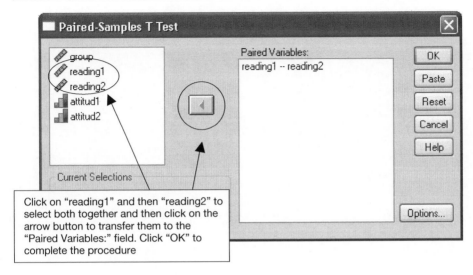

Figure 6.12 Paired-Samples T Test window in SPSS

It can be seen that the mean reading score achieved by the children in the Reading and Drama Club at the end of the year is higher than that achieved at the beginning of the year and the difference between these mean scores is statistically significant. As always, the one final piece of information we need to calculate is the effect size associated with this difference. The formula to use is the same as that for the independent samples t-test:

$$\text{Effect size, r} = \sqrt{\frac{t^2}{t^2 + df}} = \sqrt{\frac{(-24.390)^2}{(-24.390)^2 + 29}} = 0.976.$$

If only we could get effect sizes like this in real life! Pulling it all together we can report the findings as follows:

> The children who attended the Reading and Drama Group were found to have increased reading scores at the end of the school year (mean = 65.7, SD = 12.1) compared to the beginning of the year (mean = 46.4, SD = 10.2) (p < 0.001, t = 24.390, df = 29). The size of this difference in mean scores was found to be extremely strong (r = 0.976).

With such a huge effect size as found here, it is tempting to claim that we now have strong evidence of the particular effectiveness of this new Reading and Drama Club not only in dramatically increasing reading scores but also having a relatively strong and positive effect on the children's attitudes to reading as well. However, is it as simple as this? Have we proven beyond doubt that it is the Reading and Drama Club that is behind these effects? Unfortunately things are not that simple and this is why we need to turn, finally, to experimental research designs.

Output 6.16

Paired Samples Statistics

		Mean	N	Std. Deviation	Std. Error Mean
Pair 1	Reading Scores (Pre-Test)	46.37	30	10.159	1.855
	Reading Scores (Post-Test)	65.70	30	12.140	2.217

1. We can see from this table that the reading scores of the children at the end of the year (mean = 65.7, SD = 12.1) were higher than those achieved at the beginning of the year (mean = 46.4, SD = 10.2)

Paired Samples Correlations

		N	Correlation	Sig.
Pair 1	Reading Scores (Pre-Test) & Reading Scores (Post-Test)	30	.939	.000

2. This second table reports the Pearson correlation between the two reading scores. As can be seen, they are highly correlated (rp= 0.939, p < 0.001)

Paired Samples Test

		Paired Differences							
					95% Confidence Interval of the Difference				
		Mean	Std. Deviation	Std. Error Mean	Lower	Upper	t	df	Sig. (2-tailed)
Pair 1	Reading Scores (Pre-Test) – Reading Scores (Post-Test)	–19.333	4.342	.793	–20.955	–17.712	–24.390	29	.000

3. This final table indicates that the difference between the two mean scores is statistically significant (p < 0.001, t = –24.390, df = 29)

EXERCISE 6.9

Think about the changes found here in relation to the children's attitudes to reading and also their reading skills. Beyond the possible effects of the Reading and Drama Club, can you identify other potential explanations for these changes?

Analyzing experimental research designs

So why can't we just use the findings above as evidence that the Reading and Drama Club has been effective? The reason is simply that the increase in the children's reading scores and attitudes to reading may have been due to a range of other factors unconnected with the Reading and Drama Club. For example:

- We would expect the children's reading scores to increase anyway over the course of a year simply due to the fact that they are attending school.
- Similarly, the children's increased liking of reading may have also been due simply to the effects of attending school and possibly the influence of enthusiastic teachers.
- On top of their general attendance at school, the fact that the children are also participating in an after-school reading club may also improve their attitudes to reading as well as their reading skills. In this sense, we don't know whether the Reading and Drama Club has been any more effective than the original Reading Club.
- In addition to all of this there are likely to be other factors at play that are not easily identifiable but that could also have a positive impact on the children's attitudes to, and skills in, reading. These could relate to events in the local media or particular initiatives on literacy run by the local education authority or more widely on children's television.

The fundamental problem, therefore, is that with the simple one group pre-test and post-test designs outlined above with the Wilcoxon test and also the related samples t-test, we have no way of knowing what the factors were that actually caused the effects we identified. The only way we are able to isolate and measure the effects of the Reading and Drama Club specifically is through what is called an experimental design. At its simplest, an experimental design can take two main forms as illustrated in Figure 6.13. In both forms we see a process whereby pupils are allocated randomly to one of two groups—a treatment group (that gets the educational program being tested) and a control group (that does not get the program but continues with its existing activities). This is precisely how the current example was set up. It will be remembered that there were 60 children who were currently attending the existing Reading Club after school. These were randomly split into two groups so that 30 continued to attend the Reading Club and the other 30 attended the new Reading and Drama Club.

As the name suggests, the purpose of the control group is to control for all of the other potential factors that could have influenced the children's attitudes to, and skills in, reading. In this sense it is essential that the children in the control and treatment groups are exactly the same with the only difference between them being the type of after-school

Post-test only design

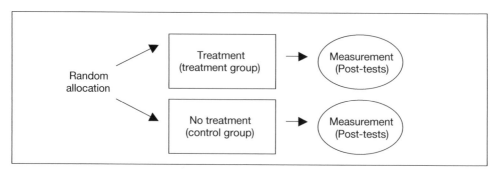

Pre-test / post-test design

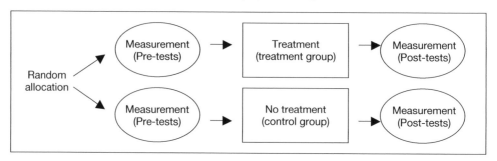

Figure 6.13 Examples of experimental research designs (or randomized controlled trials)

club they attend. This is why the random allocation is a central component to the research design. The fact that all children taking part in the study have an equal chance of being allocated to either the treatment or control group means that there will be no systematic differences between the two groups and any differences found will be due simply to random variation (which our statistical analysis can account for). Let's assume, for example, that we didn't have random allocation but instead we split the 60 children who were attending the current Reading Club into two groups by which class in school they attend. The problem here is that if we do find a positive effect for the children attending the Reading and Drama Club we are back to the problem of not knowing whether this was due to them attending the club or the fact that they have a different school teacher during the day.

In this present example the random allocation means that we have two matched groups in relation to pupils from the same school, of the same age range and who all already attend the after-school Reading Club. How this design works in practice is illustrated in Figure 6.13 and we will consider each design in turn.

Post-test only control group design

We will begin with the first of the two designs—the post-test only control group design. It can be seen that the children are randomly allocated to one of two groups, with one group receiving the specified treatment (in this case attending the Reading and Drama Club for a school year) and the other group not receiving this treatment (in this case just continuing to attend the existing Reading Club). Their attitudes to reading, and reading scores are then tested once at the end of the year. The focus for the statistical analysis is to see whether there is a significant difference between the two groups of children in relation to their attitudes to reading and also their reading scores. Because the two groups are the same (save for any differences occurring due to the random allocation process), if there is a difference between the two groups this can only be due to the difference in the types of after-school club they attended. All other potential influences on the children's attitudes to, and skills in, reading will have influenced both groups of children equally. Thus it may well be that the children's liking of reading and their reading skills will have increased simply by attending school for a year and also due to the fact that they are attending an after-school club as well. However, if this is the case then such an increase will be evident in the control group. What we are interested in here is assessing whether attending the Reading and Drama Club has led to an additional improvement in attitudes towards, and skills in, reading *above and beyond all of these other possible influences* (including, in this case, attending a traditional Reading Club).

The actual statistical tests we use to assess the differences between the control and treatment groups have already been covered in this chapter. If we are considering the ordinal variable representing children's liking of reading ("attitud2" in the **experiment.sav** dataset) then as we are comparing just two groups of a nominal variable ("group") Box 6.1 tells us that we should select the Mann-Whitney U test. Alternatively, if we are considering the scale variable representing children's reading skills ("reading2") then because we are still comparing just two groups, Box 6.1 indicates that we should use the independent samples t-test.

EXERCISE 6.10

Try running both of these tests to see whether there are any statistically significant differences between the two groups in relation to their liking of reading and also their reading skills. Check your method and results on the companion website.

If you have done Exercise 6.10 then you should find that there is a difference between the two groups in relation to both measures. More specifically:

- A difference was found in relation to the children's liking of reading (p = 0.010, Mann-Whitney U = 282.0, Z = 2.587). While 40 percent of those in the control group (attending the Reading Club) said they liked reading "a little" or "a lot," 73.4 percent said this in the treatment group (attending the Reading and Drama Club). This represented a moderate effect (r = 0.334).
- A difference was also found in relation to the children's scores on a standardized reading test (p < 0.001, t = 5.216, df = 58). While the mean score of those in the control group was 50.4 (SD = 10.6) it was 65.7 (SD = 12.1) in the treatment group. Moreover, this was found to represent a fairly strong effect (r = 0.565).

Overall, therefore, the differences found in relation to both measures are statistically significant and indicate that those children who attended the Reading and Drama Club had more positive attitudes to reading and higher reading test scores than those who just attended the Reading Club. Moreover, the results of the statistical tests confirm that these differences are unlikely to have been the result of random variation between the two groups (caused by the way they were initially randomly allocated). In this sense, therefore, this post-test only control group design has provided good evidence that attending the Reading and Drama Club has a positive effect on the children's attitudes to reading and their reading skills above and beyond what we would expect if they just attended the existing Reading Club.

Pre-test/post-test control group design (scale outcome measure)

While the above design is certainly adequate, it does suffer a little from the fact that the random allocation of pupils may result in initial differences between the control and treatment groups. Ideally, therefore, it would be good to identify and control for these differences if at all possible. This can be done through the second design shown in Figure 6.13—the pre-test/post-test control group design. As can be seen, it is very similar to the previous design but now it includes pre-tests as well. In our current example this simply means testing the children's liking of reading and also their reading scores at the beginning of the experiment as well as at the end. This way we can see if there is any difference between the groups on these two measures before they start and we can also control for these in our analysis.

This type of pre-test/post-test control group design tends to be used with outcome measures that are scale variables. This is to ensure that the experiment has sufficient statistical power, especially because the analysis required is a little more complex. We will, therefore, illustrate the basic method of analyzing the simplest of pre-test/post-test control group designs here using the scale measure representing reading scores. However, and for completeness, we will conclude by looking briefly at how we might best approach analyzing the data from such a design when the outcome measure is ordinal (in this case using the children's responses to the simple question asking them whether they like reading).

In psychology, such experimental designs tend to be analyzed using what is called a two-way mixed ANOVA. In educational research, however, there is a tendency to prefer the use of a slightly different technique—linear multiple regression—and so it is this technique that will be illustrated here. As it happens, both techniques are fundamentally doing the same thing, they just tend to go about it in different ways (Miles and Shevlin, 2001). The reason why linear multiple regression tends to be preferred in educational research is that it can be easily extended to include techniques such as multilevel modeling that help to account for the effects on children of attending different classes in different schools. Moreover, I also tend to think linear multiple regression is much easier to understand conceptually and also to run using SPSS.

The basic principle underlying linear multiple regression is that we are attempting to construct a statistical model that can help to predict the children's post-test scores ("reading2") using a range of variables. In our present analysis these will just include the children's pre-test scores ("reading1") and also whether they attended the treatment or control group ("group"). It is probably best to actually show you how to run the test and then to explain all of this more fully with the results that are produced. However, before we press ahead and run the test we need to ensure a number of criteria are met:

- The variable that we are wishing to predict (i.e. the post-test scores) needs to be a scale variable. In this case "reading2" is a scale variable and so that is fine.
- This variable also needs to be approximately normally distributed. We can test this in the usual way using a histogram (see Figure 6.14) and then more formally using the Kolmogorov-Smirnov test covered earlier (Figure 6.7). In this case, the test confirms that this distribution is not significantly different from a normal distribution ($p = 0.633$, Kolmogorov-Smirnov $Z = 0.747$).
- All other variables that we use for the analysis need to be either scale variables or simple dichotomous variables. Ordinal or nominal variables with three categories or more cannot be used unless they have been modified first (into a series of what are called dummy variables). For the current example, however, this condition has been met as the two variables concerned are scale ("reading1") and dichotomous ("group").
- The other scale variables need to be approximately normally distributed and to have a linear relationship with the variable that is to be predicted. The first of these conditions can be confirmed, as before, with a histogram and Kolmogorov-Smirnov ($p = 0.555$, Kolmogorov-Smirnov $Z = 0.793$). The second condition concerning the linear relationship can be confirmed using a simple scatterplot (see Figure 6.15).

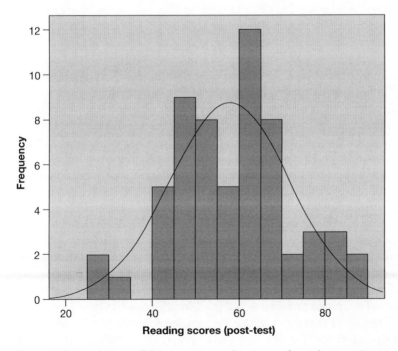

Figure 6.14 Distribution of the post-test reading scores from the experiment.sav dataset

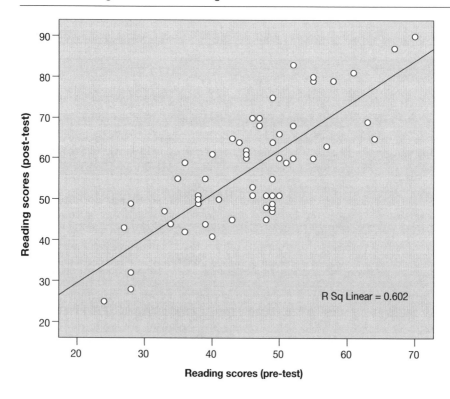

Figure 6.15 Relationship between pre-test and post-test reading scores in the experiment.sav dataset

With all of these conditions met we can now proceed to run the linear multiple regression analysis. Before actually running the analysis it is worth getting a feel for the data and this can be done by using the **Data → Split File. . .** procedure (splitting the file by "group") and then just calculating descriptive statistics for the two variables "reading1" and "reading2." The results are shown in Output 6.17. As can be seen, the mean scores for the control and treatment groups were actually very similar for the pre-tests (46.0 and 46.4 respectively). Moreover, the post-test scores certainly suggest that the Reading and Drama Club has had a positive effect on reading scores (mean = 65.7, SD = 12.1) above and beyond that achieved by the Reading Club (mean = 50.4, SD = 10.6).

However, before we take these findings at face value we need to test whether they are statistically significant. To do this we need to conduct the linear multiple regression analysis. To begin this, make sure you reset **Split File** and then select **Analyze → Regression → Linear. . .** which opens the **Linear Regression** window shown in Figure 6.16. Select the variable representing the post-test scores ("reading2") and place it in the "Dependent:" field as shown and then select the variables representing the pre-test scores ("reading1") and also the group to which the children belong ("group") and place these in the "Independent(s):" field. Click "OK" to complete the procedure. The output produced from this is shown in Output 6.17.

Output 6.17

Type of After-School Group = Reading Group (Control)

Descriptive Statistics[a]

	N	Minimum	Maximum	Mean	Std. Deviation
Reading Scores (Pre-Test)	30	24	64	45.97	9.507
Reading Scores (Post-Test)	30	25	69	50.37	10.578
Valid N (listwise)	30				

[a.] Type of After-School Group = Reading Group (Control)

Type of After-School Group = Reading and Drama Group (Treatment)

Descriptive Statistics[a]

	N	Minimum	Maximum	Mean	Std. Deviation
Reading Scores (Pre-Test)	30	27	70	46.37	10.159
Reading Scores (Post-Test)	30	43	90	65.70	12.140
Valid N (listwise)	30				

[a.] Type of After-School Group = Reading and Drama Group (Treatment)

While there is a lot of information here it is quite straightforward to follow if you do it step by step. Remember that the purpose of linear regression is to create a statistical model (or formula) that can be used to predict post-test scores ("reading2") using the two variables representing pre-test scores ("reading1") and which group the children belonged to—treatment or control ("group"). The first thing to do, therefore, is to check whether this model itself is statistically significant. If it is not then we need go no further and we would simply conclude that it is not possible to predict post-test scores using either of these two variables. To put it in other words, this would indicate among other things that there is no difference in the post-test reading scores between the control and treatment groups (and hence no evidence that the Reading and Drama Club had any effect above and beyond that achieved by the Reading Club). The information we need to check the statistical significance of the model is provided in the ANOVA table in Output 6.18. As can be seen, the significance level is ".000" indicating that the model itself is statistically significant ($p < 0.001$, $F = 266.628$, df = 2, 57).

Once we have confirmed that the model is statistically significant we can then check to see how good the model is as a whole in being able to predict post-test reading scores using the two variables "reading1" and "group." This information is provided in the first table—Model Summary—and under the column headed "Adjusted R Square." As can be

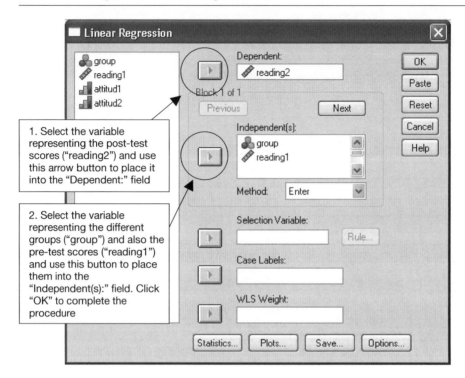

Figure 6.16 Linear Regression window in SPSS

seen, the value here is 0.900. Multiplying it by 100 tells us how accurate the model is, i.e. it is very accurate, being able to predict post-test scores with 90 percent accuracy.

The key information we are interested in can be found in the third table, headed Coefficients. What we are looking for here is whether the "group" variable (named: "Type of After-School Group") is statistically significant or not. If the value in the column headed "Sig." is 0.05 or less then we can conclude that the difference between the mean post-test scores of the treatment and control groups is statistically significant *once the pre-test scores have been controlled for*. In this case the difference is statistically significant (".000" i.e. $p < 0.001$) indicating that the Reading and Drama Club (treatment group) has had an effect on children's reading scores above and beyond that found in the Reading Club (control group) once the children's pre-test scores have been controlled for. Moreover, the value in the column headed "Standardized Beta Coefficients" is the effect size for that difference, again once pre-test reading scores have been controlled for. As can be seen, the effect size is also moderately strong ($r = 0.549$). Finally, the value in the column marked "B" indicates the difference between the mean post-test scores for the treatment and control groups once pre-test scores have been controlled for (in this case, 14.9 points).

With all of this information it is now possible to report the findings of the test. This would usually be done by including and making reference to a table as shown (see Table 6.2) and could be expressed as follows:

Output 6.18

2. If the overall model is statistically significant then we can use the Adjusted R Square finding to ascertain how well the children's post-test reading scores can be predicted from their pre-test scores and which group they attended. As can be seen, this figure suggests that we can use these two variables to predict post-test scores with a high degree of accuracy (i.e. 90.0 per cent accuracy)

1. We first need to check whether the overall model produced from the analysis is statistically significant. We do this using the findings from this ANOVA table which confirms that at least some of the findings are significant ($p < 0.001$, $F = 266.628$, df = 2, 57)

3. These figures tell us that after controlling for pre-test scores, there remains a statistically significant difference between the mean scores of the treatment and control groups ($p < 0.001$ in this case) and also the associated effect size is moderately strong ($r = 0.549$)

4. These figures tell us that there is also a statistically significant relationship between the pre-test and post-test scores ($p < 0.001$) once the group that the children are attending is controlled for and the effect size associated with this relationship is $r = 0.764$

Model Summary

Model	R	R Square	Adjusted R Square	Std. Error of the Estimate
1	.950[a]	.903	.900	4.326

a. Predictors: (Constant), Reading Scores (Pre-Test), Type of After-School Group

ANOVA[b]

Model		Sum of Squares	df	Mean Square	F	Sig.
1	Regression	9979.246	2	4989.623	266.628	.000[a]
	Residual	1066.688	57	18.714		
	Total	11045.933	59			

a. Predictors: (Constant), Reading Scores (Pre-Test), Type of After-School Group

b. Dependent Variable: Reading Scores (Post-Test)

Coefficients[a]

Model		Unstandardized Coefficients		Standardized Coefficients	t	Sig.
		B	Std. Error	Beta		
1	(Constant)	1.086	2.769		.392	.696
	Type of After-School Group	14.904	1.117	.549	13.341	.000
	Reading Scores (Pre-Test)	1.072	.058	.764	18.569	.000

a. Dependent Variable: Reading Scores (Post-Test)

5. These are the figures needed to construct the model used to predict post-test scores

It was found that the children attending the Reading and Drama Club achieved a post-test mean reading score of 65.7 (SD = 12.1) compared to 50.4 (SD = 10.6) for those attending the Reading Club. As the results from the pre-test/post-test control group experimental design indicate (see Table 6.2) this difference was found to be statistically significant. Moreover, once the children's pre-test scores were controlled for, it was found that a child attending the Reading and Drama Club for a year would, on average, achieve a reading score 14.9 points higher than a child who had attended the Reading Club for the same period. This effect was found to be moderately strong (r = 0.549).

It would be wrong not to just complete this example by actually showing you the model that has been calculated from this analysis. You will find this useful in helping to further develop your understanding of what is going on here. However, it is not essential and if you want to you can skip to the next section. For the rest of you, the actual statistical model is constructed using the values listed in the Coefficients table of the output under the heading "B." Using these, the model becomes:

Post-test score = 1.086 + 14.904 × (Group) + 1.072 × (Pre-test score)

As can be seen, it is no more than a simple formula that allows you to predict a child's post-test reading score by inputting details on the pre-test score and what group they belonged to. The pre-test score that is inputted is simply the score achieved by the child, while the value for the variable "group" is simply "1" if that child was in the treatment group (the Reading and Drama Club) or "0" if they were in the control group (i.e. the Reading Club). We can illustrate this using the mean scores shown in Output 6.17. Let's begin by using the example of a child in the control group whose pre-test score was actually the mean for that group (i.e. 45.97). In this case the value for the variable "group" is "0." With this information the formula becomes:

$$Post\text{-}test\ score\ = 1.086 + 14.904 \times (0) + 1.072 \times (45.97)$$
$$= 1.086 + 0 + 49.280$$
$$= 50.366\ (i.e.\ 50.37)$$

As can be seen, the formula predicts that the child's post-test score will be 50.37, which is actually the mean post-test score for the control group as shown in Output 6.17. If we

Table 6.2 Results of linear multiple regression from an analysis of the results of the pre-test/post-test control group experimental design (dependent variable = post-test reading scores)

Independent variables	Unstandardized coefficients		Standardized coefficients (Beta)	t	Sig.
	B	Std. error			
Constant	1.086	2.769		0.392	0.696
Type of after-school club	14.904	1.117	0.549	13.341	< 0.001
Pre-test reading scores	1.072	0.058	0.764	18.569	< 0.001

Model fit: p < 0.001, F = 266.628, df = 2, 57

now do the same but this time choosing a child from the treatment group who achieved a pre-test score the same as the mean pre-test score for the treatment group (46.37), then, noting that the value for "group" is now "1," this gives us:

$$\text{Post-test score} = 1.086 + 14.904 \times (1) + 1.072 \times (46.37)$$
$$= 1.086 + 14.904 + 49.709$$
$$= 65.699 \text{ (i.e. 65.70)}$$

Not surprisingly, this predicted value for the post-test score is actually the same as the mean post-test score for the treatment group. Overall, it can be seen that this statistical model gives a relatively simple picture of the contribution of each variable to the post-test score. Thus, irrespective of which after-school club they attended, we can expect that a child's reading scores will have increased over the year by a factor of 1.086 plus 1.072 times their pre-test score (i.e. $1.086 + 1.072 \times$ (pre-test score)). However, and this is the key point, above and beyond this general improvement, attending the Reading and Drama Club was found to increase the child's score by a further 14.904 points on average.

Of course, this present example reflects the simplest design of a pre-test/post-test control group experiment possible. However, it is possible to control for as many additional variables as one would like (i.e. sex, age, family income etc.) simply by adding these into the model, just as we have done with pre-test reading scores in the present example. In addition, multilevel modeling would also help to account, and thus control, for the effects of higher-level variables such as the classes that the children attend and then their schools and also, possibly, their local education authority. While the model can, therefore, get extremely complicated, the key approach remains the same—to ascertain whether the variable representing which group the child belongs to (treatment or control) is statistically significant in the model. If so then the standardized beta value will indicate the effect size associated with the treatment (when all other variables have been controlled for) and the unstandardized coefficient (B), as we have seen, will actually tell us precisely how much we can expect a child's score to improve, on average, as a result of belonging to the treatment group compared to the control group, again once all other variables have been controlled for.

Pre-test/post-test control group design (ordinal outcome measure)

Finally, we will look at how we can analyze a pre-test/post-test control group experimental design when we are dealing with an ordinal rather than scale outcome measure. In this particular example we will take the children's responses to the simple question "How much do you like reading?" to which they could choose from five response categories: "a lot"; "quite a lot"; "a little"; "not very much"; or "not at all." However, before we begin it is worth stressing that it is highly preferable to conduct an experiment of this type with a scale outcome measure. In fact, I would go as far as to suggest that you should always use a scale rather than an ordinal measure wherever possible. There are three reasons for this. First, because ordinal variables are less precise than scale variables, the statistical tests we can use with them will be less powerful (i.e. less likely to detect an effect in the sample even if one actually exists within the population as a whole). Second, while it is not impossible, it becomes much more difficult to conduct more complex and advanced analysis of the experimental data of the type mentioned at the end of the last section. Third, there will tend to be greater questions over the validity of a simple ordinal measure compared to a scale measure. If we take our present example, then it would have been preferable to have asked a number of questions about the different dimensions of reading and used these to create a summative scale measure, just as outlined in Chapter 2 (see Box 2.2). This way, not only would we have a scale outcome measure but it is likely to be more valid given that it taps into a range of dimensions of the variable we are interested in. Moreover, it is likely to be more reliable given that for the simple ordinal measure, a child may answer the question with one of many different types of reading in mind (i.e. comics, teen magazines, children's fiction or factual history). As such they could answer the question completely differently on another occasion simply because they are thinking of a different type of reading rather than because their underlying attitude has changed.

Overall, therefore, if you are going to go to all the trouble of designing and running a true experiment then it stands to reason that you should use the most appropriate and effective outcome measure(s) possible. While this will almost always involve choosing a good scale measure over an ordinal one, there may be occasions (because of the lack of opportunity or the nature of the variable that you are interested in) where you have no choice other than to use an ordinal variable. Moreover, if your scale outcome measure is not normally distributed (and cannot easily be transformed into one that is) then you will still need an alternative way of analyzing the data as if it is ordinal. This is what we will look at here.

To begin with, we need to develop some measure of the change that has taken place for each child in terms of their pre-test and post-test scores. This can then be used to compare the relative effects of the two after-school programs. One simple way of doing this is to subtract each child's post-test score from their pre-test score. It will be remembered that their scores vary from "1" to "5" with higher scores indicating that they like reading more. By subtracting the pre-test score from the post-test score we will get a measure that ranges from –4 to +4 and represents how many ranks they have changed from the beginning to the end of the school year and in which direction. Thus if the resultant figure is positive then this indicates that they have increased their rating of reading by one or more ranks. If it is zero then clearly they have not changed their rating and if the score is negative then they have actually reduced their rating by one or more ranks.

To do this, therefore, use the **Data → Compute Variable. . .** procedure covered previously in Chapter 3 (see Figure 3.20) to create a new measure that we can call "effect" and which will be computed using the formula "Attitud2 – Attitud1" which you need to enter into the "Numeric Expression:" field. It is important that you organize the two variables in this order so that you can interpret the new variable properly. Once done, use the **Data → Split File. . .** procedure also covered in Chapter 3 (see Figure 3.4) to organize your output by "group" and then use **Analyze → Descriptive Statistics → Frequencies . . .** to get some sense of how the children's attitudes in the treatment and control groups changed. The results are shown in Output 6.19. As can be seen, there certainly seems to be a difference, with 73.3 percent of children in the treatment group (i.e. attending the Reading and Drama Club) increasing their liking of reading compared to 40 percent in the control group (i.e. attending the Reading Club).

To test whether this is statistically significant we can simply run a Mann-Whitney U test comparing the treatment and control group scores on this new variable. Begin by resetting Select Cases and then run this procedure as shown earlier in this chapter (see

Output 6.19

Type of After-School Group = Reading Group (Control)

Change Between Pre-test and Post-test Scores[a]

		Frequency	Percent	Valid Percent	Cumulative Percent
Valid	−1	8	26.7	26.7	26.7
	0	10	33.3	33.3	60.0
	1	7	23.3	23.3	83.3
	2	4	13.3	13.3	96.7
	3	1	3.3	3.3	100.0
	Total	30	100.0	100.0	

a. Type of After-School Group = Reading Group (Control)

1. Use the cumulative percent total for all of the negative values to calculate what proportion of the group reduced their liking of reading (in this case 26.7 percent)

2. This valid percent figure for those with a value '0' will obviously tell you what proportion of the group did not change their ranking (in this case 33.3 percent)

3. The remaining proportion (100 − 26.7 − 33.3 = 40.0 per cent) thus increased their liking of reading

Type of After-School Group = Reading and Drama Group (Treatment)

Change Between Pre-test and Post-test Scores[a]

		Frequency	Percent	Valid Percent	Cumulative Percent
Valid	−1	3	10.0	10.0	10.0
	0	5	16.7	16.7	26.7
	1	11	36.7	36.7	63.3
	2	7	23.3	23.3	86.7
	3	3	10.0	10.0	96.7
	4	1	3.3	3.3	100.0
	Total	30	100.0	100.0	

a. Type of After-School Group = Reading and Drama Group (Treatment)

4. In a similar vein we can see that 10.0 per-cent of those in the treatment group reduced their liking of reading, compared to 16.7 per-cent who didn't change and thus 73.3 percent increased their rating

Figure 6.4) placing the new variable "effect" in the "Test Variable List:" field and "group" in the "Grouping Variable:" field (remembering that the two groups we are comparing are coded "0" and "1"). The results of the test are shown in Output 6.20. As can be seen, this difference between the control and treatment group was found to be statistically significant. Using the Z score, as also previously shown, the effect size from this can be calculated as $r = 2.601/\sqrt{(60)} = 0.336$ which represents a moderate effect.

In terms of reporting all of this, it would be useful to show a clustered bar chart illustrating how the children's liking of reading for the post-test compared between the treatment and control groups. You could then make reference to this, as well as reporting the findings derived above, in the following way:

> To test the relative effects that attending the clubs had on the children's liking of reading, the change in each pupil's rating of how much they liked reading at the beginning and end of the school year was calculated. It was found that while 40 percent of children in the Reading Club increased their rating over the year, 73.3 percent of children in the Reading and Drama Club did ($p = 0.009$, Mann-Whitney $U = 279.0$, $Z = 2.601$). The effect associated with this difference was found to be moderate ($r = 0.336$). The children's actual ratings of reading at the end of the school year are illustrated and compared in Figure X.

Dealing with weighting variables

At various points in this and previous chapters you have been asked to apply a weighting variable prior to analysis. You may remember that it was mentioned in Chapter 2 that weighting variables are used, among other things, to correct for any known biases in the final achieved sample caused by non-response and/or the particular sampling methods used. Weighting variables are often used in relation to large-scale datasets and so it is important that you have some understanding of what, precisely, they are meant to do and how you should use them in relation to your analysis. In this final section, therefore, we will begin by explaining the main reasons for using weighting variables. In most cases, weighting variables are used to do one or more of the following:

- To correct for any known biases that may exist in relation to the final achieved sample due to non-response or the particular sampling methods used.
- To "scale-up" frequencies calculated from the sample so that they represent estimates for the population as a whole.
- To correct for what are known as "design effects" arising from the particular sampling techniques used (especially cluster sampling but also the application of weights to adjust for non-response).

Having explained each of these in turn, advice will then be provided on how the different types of weighting variables should be used when analysing a dataset, especially in relation to the use of tests for statistical significance.

Correcting for non-response

As regards the first reason for using weights—to correct for any known biases in a sample —the best way to illustrate this is through the use of a simple example. Let's assume we

Output 6.20

Ranks

	Type of After-School Group	N	Mean Rank	Sum of Ranks
Change Between Pre-test and Post-test Scores	Reading Group (Control)	30	24.80	744.00
	Reading and Drama Group (Treatment)	30	36.20	1086.00
	Total	60		

1. Remember that higher ranks indicate more positive changes. In this case the mean rank for the treatment group (36.2) is higher than for the control (24.8) confirming that there has been a more positive change among children in the former

2. This difference is also statistically significant

Test Statistics [a]

	Change Between Pre-test and Post-test Scores
Mann-Whitney U	279.000
Wilcoxon W	744.000
Z	-2.601
Asymp. Sig. (2-tailed)	.009

a. Grouping Variable: Type of After-School Group

wish to undertake a survey of students at a university to find out what proportions of students tend to use the different facilities available in the library. Let's further suppose that we have selected a random sample of students for this purpose. We know from university records that the student population is evenly split with 50 percent being male and 50 percent female. However, for some reason our final achieved sample has a disproportionate number of female students (60 percent) compared to male students (40 percent).

Now, if we simply used this final achieved sample to generate statistics such as the percentage of students who tend to use the online databases in the library or who tend to use the newspaper archive then we run the risk of producing biased estimates as it may be that these facilities are disproportionately used by male or female students. In other words, if female students are much more likely to use the online databases then because they are over-represented in the final sample our estimate of how many students in general tend to use the online databases will tend to be a little higher than it should be. What is happening, in effect, is that by not correcting for the bias in the sample we are giving a greater weight to female students than male students. One way of dealing with this is to balance this out by giving slightly less weight to the female respondents and slightly more to the male respondents so that their respective contributions to any statistics generated tend to reflect their true proportions in the population as a whole.

In this particular example, we want both female and male students to be represented equally (i.e. both representing 50 percent of the sample). As female students currently represent 60 percent of the sample and male students 40 percent, we can achieve this by multiplying the responses of all female students by 50/60, i.e. 0.83333 and, similarly, multiply all of the male students by 50/40, i.e. 1.25000. The weighting variable to use would therefore consist of just two values, 0.83333 if the respondent is female and 1.25000 if the respondent is male. If we applied this weighting variable and then used **Analyze → Descriptive Statistics → Frequencies. . .** to calculate the proportions of male and female students in the sample we would find that these proportions have now been adjusted so that there would be 50 percent males and 50 percent females as required. We could then be more confident that any estimates we subsequently produce for students as a whole would not be biased (at least in relation to the over-representation of female students in the sample). Of course this is a very simple example. In reality, weighting variables tend to be used to correct for known biases in relation to a number of different factors. An example of this is the weighting variable used in the **youthcohort.sav** dataset ("s1weight") that attempts to correct for four factors known to be associated with non-response (i.e. respondents' sex, qualifications achieved, region in which they live and type of school attended). However, while the calculation of the weighting variable in this instance is a little more complex, the general principle remains the same.

Scaling up frequencies to create population estimates

The second purpose of using a weighting variable is to "scale up" the frequencies derived from a sample to those of the population as a whole. To explain why this might be useful let's continue with the last example. Suppose that the final achieved sample included 500 students and that the total student population at the university was 10,000. To "scale up" the sample we would simply create a weighting variable that had the same value for all respondents and that was equal to 10,000/500, i.e. 20. What this would do in effect would be to increase all of the frequencies calculated by a factor of 20. Thus, let's say that in the sample of 500, 15 students said that they used the newspaper archive. With this weighting variable applied, while the proportion of students using this service would remain the same (i.e. 3 percent), in terms of the actual frequencies we would now get the figure of 300 (i.e. 20×15) rather than 15 students. This is possibly a useful thing to do if we were primarily interested in estimating the actual demand for a particular service. Thus knowing simply that 3 percent of students are likely to want to use the newspaper archive is of little use in itself. However, by using the scaling up weighting variable we now have a much more useful estimate that 300 students at the university are likely to want to use the newspaper archive. If we also collected information on the number of times per semester these 300 students intended to use the archive then we could use this information to design the resource accordingly to meet this demand.

Of course, it is quite possible to calculate a weighting variable that not only corrects for any known biases but also then attempts to scale up the frequencies to generate population estimates. In the example above, it will be remembered that we already had a weighting variable to correct for sex biases in the sample that had just two values— 1.25000 for males and 0.83333 for females. If we now wanted to also scale this up so that we could generate estimates for the population of students as a whole we would simple multiply these two values by 20 so that the weighting variable would now consist of the values 25.00000 for male students (i.e. 20×1.25000) and 16.6666 for female students (i.e. 20×0.83333). You will notice that we tend to use values that have a number of decimal places. This is simply to reduce the errors that may occur due to rounding. This approach to using weighting variables not only to correct for non-response but also to scale up the sample is, in effect, what the two weighting variables "FEWT" and "FSWT" have been designed to do for the **earlychildhood.sav** and **afterschools.sav** datasets. Alongside correcting for known biases due to non-response they also scale up the frequencies to provide estimates for the United States population as a whole as we saw in Chapter 2 (see, for example, Figure 2.6 and Table 2.2).

Correcting for design effects

The final purpose of applying weights is to correct for any design effects associated with a particular sample caused by the sampling procedure used (most notably in relation to the use of cluster sampling). To understand the problem here we need to understand what the effects of a cluster sample are on the calculation of standard errors. In essence, cluster sampling is used most often in large-scale (often national) surveys where it would simply be too costly to select a simple random sample. Suppose, for example, that we needed to conduct a national survey of 10–11 year old pupils in schools. Assuming it is possible to create a full list of all eligible pupils in the country, then the selection of a simple random sample of 2,000 pupils from this list could easily result in a situation where we might have children to interview distributed across, say, 800 schools scattered throughout the country. Alongside the substantial costs involved in travelling the length and breadth of the country to visit these schools there would also be a considerable amount of time taken up in terms of having to initially contact and negotiate access with each school before then seeking the permission of the parents and children themselves.

It is with this in mind that researchers almost invariably tend to use some form of cluster sampling. A simple version of this would involve selecting, say, 100 schools randomly from a list of all eligible schools and then surveying all 10–11 year-old-children in each school. If we assume that an average of 20 pupils per school takes part in the survey then this would still give us the final sample of 2,000 pupils (i.e. 100 × 20) but at much less cost—having only to visit 100 schools rather than 800. However, the problem is that this clustered sample is now likely to underestimate the level of variation within the pupil population as a whole. The reason for this is that the pupils within each cluster (i.e. in this case within each school) are likely to be more similar to each other than they are to children outside of the school. As such we are likely to find less variation in our sample because of the existence of these clusters of pupils than if we had just selected a simple random sample of the same size. If we do not account for this clustering in our analysis then any estimates we produce from our analysis are likely to underestimate the level of true variation in the population. This, in essence, is what is referred to as the "design effect" of the sampling procedure used and will lead, in turn, to the production of standard errors that are smaller than they should be. The main consequence of this is that we will tend to over-estimate the precision of any estimates that we do generate from the sample and this will increase our risk of committing Type I Errors.

The best way to address this problem is to use an advanced statistical technique called multilevel modelling that can account for the clustering of respondents in a sample and thus that produces more accurate and less biased standard errors. Unfortunately, such modelling techniques are beyond the scope of this book and are actually not possible to run with SPSS without a specialist add-on module. A compromise position is to use a weighting variable that effectively reduces the overall size of the sample so that the standard errors calculated by SPSS are increased to account for the design effect. This is effectively what the "WTCORRCT" weighting variables do for the **afterschools.sav** and **earlychildhood.sav** datasets. In fact these two respective weighting variables not only correct for known biases introduced by non-response but also provide a correction for the effects of sampling.

EXERCISE 6.11

Using the earlychildhood.sav dataset, examine the effects of the "WTCORRCT" weighting variable on the calculation of standard errors. Do this by using the **Analyze → Descriptive Statistics → Explore...** procedure to examine the effects of this on the calculation of standard errors. Run the procedure for the mother's age ("momage1") both on the unweighted sample and also the weighted sample. You should find that the final achieved sample (based on the unweighted data) is 6,969 while the effective sample size for the weighted data is about half this (i.e. 3,556). Now, alongside the mean ages being slightly different (reflecting the fact that the weighting variable has been calculated to correct for non-response), you should also notice that the standard errors for both estimates of the mean are different. More specifically, for the unweighted sample the standard error is 0.076 whilst for the weighted sample it has been corrected and thus increased to 0.108.

Dealing with weight variables in the analysis of datasets

So, what are the implications of all of this in terms of how you should use weighting variables when analysing datasets? Unfortunately there is no universally agreed and definitive set of guidelines available. However, as an initial guide you could use the following steps:

1   Check whether the dataset you are using has a weighting variable. If not then simply run your analysis, including conducting tests for statistical significance, on the dataset as it is. However, check what sampling methods were used. If any form of cluster sampling was employed then you should bear this in mind when interpreting your findings. In particular, be careful when reporting any findings that are only just statistically significant and explain that these should be treated with caution given that they may not have turned out to be statistically significant if the effects of clustering had been accounted for in your analysis. Alternatively, you could use a stricter level of significance (possible $p \leq 0.01$) to be extra cautious.

2   If a weighting variable has been created, find out what type of weighting variable it is:
   • If it is a weighting variable that has been used to correct for design effects, then you should conduct all of your analysis (including tests for statistical significance) with this applied.
   • If it is a weighting variable used simply to correct for non-response then you should also conduct all of your analysis with this applied. However, you should also check what sampling procedure was used and if it involved cluster sampling then you need to be cautious in how you report findings that are only just statistically significant in the same way as argued above.
   • If it is a weighting variable used to scale up the frequencies to provide population estimates then you need to check if the weighting variable has also been calculated to correct for known biases caused by non-response. You then have two possible options:
     – If the weighting variable has been calculated solely to scale up the frequencies to create population estimates then just run all of your analyses on the unweighted dataset (unless, of course, you actually want to create population estimates in which case you should just use the weighting variable for this particular purpose). Again, however, you need to check what sampling procedure was used and, as before, if it involved cluster sampling then you need to be cautious in interpreting findings that are only just statistically significant.
     – If the weighting variable has been calculated to address known biases created by non-response as well as to scale up the dataset then you should use the **Transform → Compute...** function to adjust the weighting variable to remove the scaling-up element. The simplest way to do this is to calculate the total sample size for the unweighted dataset (X) and the weighted dataset (Y) in turn. You can then compute a new and adjusted weighting variable by multiplying the existing weighting variable by X and dividing it by Y. Thus, for example, suppose the original weighting variable is called "weight". If the unweighted sample size is 200 and the weighted sample size is 10,000

then you would calculate the adjusted weighting variable by using the formula: "(200 × weight)/10000." What you now have is an adjusted weighting variable that simply corrects for known biases due to non-response and/or the particular sampling procedure used. You should now conduct your analysis (including tests for statistical significance) with this adjusted weighting variable applied. However, you still need to check how the sample was selected and, as before, if this involved an element of cluster sampling then you need to be careful in interpreting any findings that are just found to be statistically significant.

One final and important point to note: *you should never conduct tests for statistical significance on data where a scaling up weighting variable has been applied*. Unless you adjust it as explained above to remove the scaling up element then this is likely to result in almost all of your findings being highly statistically significant. This is because SPSS will assume that your findings really are based upon a sample that is the size of the population (i.e. a sample of 20.7 million in the case of the weighting variable "FEWT" in the **earlychildhood.sav** dataset!).

Conclusions

In this chapter we have run through all of the main statistical tests you are likely to encounter and wish to use in the routine analysis of quantitative data in education. Alongside showing you how to choose the correct statistical test for the variables you are interested in we have also covered how you can run each of these tests and, moreover, how you should interpret the output. In each case you have been shown how to identify and interpret the relevant information in the output and also how you can then report these formally. Certainly until you get more experience undertaking statistical tests you should try to follow the style of reporting shown above. This will ensure that you provide the reader with the key information they need to understand and assess your analysis. As you will have seen, we have tried to be as efficient as possible in only providing essential information and then often trying to contain these in parentheses so as not to unduly distract from the key substantive findings. What you should certainly try to avoid doing is cutting and pasting SPSS output into the main body of your report. Not only will it confuse many readers but it is unnecessary.

Hopefully, the fact that we have applied the logic of hypothesis testing to each of the main tests covered has helped you to consolidate your understanding of the key concepts associated with hypothesis testing and how they relate together in practice. If you struggled at all with the last chapter then now is probably a good time for you to go back and read that chapter again. The key concepts should now make more sense with the examples in mind that you have just covered here. Beyond this (and assuming you have read and followed the examples covered in this book) you have now acquired the necessary knowledge and skills to enable you to do quantitative data analysis in education to a high level—congratulations! The only question remaining is where can you go from here? This is the subject of the last brief chapter.

Chapter 7

Where next?

Introduction

If you have worked through this book carefully, and have followed the examples and exercises suggested, then you should have gained a sound understanding and have also acquired the necessary skills to do routine quantitative data analysis to a high level. More specifically, you should now have the competence not only to undertake simple but effective statistical analysis, but also to be able to interpret the findings appropriately and to write them up to a standard fit for publication. Moreover, you should also now have a critical eye for quantitative data analysis and an ability to critically read and interpret the quantitative research of others.

If you are content to stop at this point then that's absolutely fine. After all, you now have the necessary grounding to deal competently and confidently with routine quantitative data and to critically assess the quantitative analysis of others. Moreover, the more you handle quantitative data yourself and also critically engage with other people's quantitative work, the more you will consolidate and build upon the knowledge and skills gained here. However, I am hoping that for some of you this book has helped you to look at quantitative data in a different way. More specifically, I am hoping that the book has helped to demystify quantitative research for you and thus given you the confidence and motivation to want to learn more. Hopefully you have also seen some of the potential that quantitative research has, if done properly, for providing new and important insights into the processes and practices of education. In this case, rather than seeing this book as an end point it can be seen simply as the beginning of a longer journey where you seek to consolidate and develop further your knowledge and skills in quantitative research. With this in mind, the purpose of this final, brief chapter is to set out what your next few steps could be in relation to this.

1 Develop your understanding of the nature of quantitative data and how they are generated

While the focus of this book has been on quantitative data analysis, it is clear that quantitative data cannot be considered in isolation from the methods that are used to generate them. For you to be able to meaningfully evaluate the work of others you therefore need to develop a proper appreciation of the key issues and debates surrounding the range of methods and approaches used in quantitative research. Moreover, you will certainly need to develop a good grasp of these issues should you want to begin collecting your own quantitative data and then to reflect upon the validity and reliability of the findings you derive from these.

There are certainly some excellent texts out there covering quantitative research methodology. As a starting point you may find it useful to consult a more general text to gain an overview of the differing methods associated with quantitative research and how they relate to qualitative methods and the research enterprise more broadly in education. Perhaps Cohen *et al.* (2007) provide the best starting point as they focus specifically on education. However you will also find any of the following more general texts by Bryman (2004), Robson (2002) and Somekh and Lewin (2004) useful as well:

- Bryman, A. (2004) *Social Research Methods*, Oxford: Oxford University Press.
- Cohen, L., Manion, L. and Morrison, K. (2007) *Research Methods in Education*, 6th edn, London: Routledge.
- Robson, C. (2002) *Real World Research*, Oxford: Blackwell.
- Somekh, B. and Lewin, C. (2004) *Research Methods in the Social Sciences*, London: Sage.

Beyond this there are some more detailed and accessible texts focusing on various aspects of quantitative research methods. Field and Hole (2003) and Robson (1994) provide very useful and accessible overviews of experimental methods while De Vaus (2001) and Sapsford (2006) cover the core issues relating to survey methods very well. Oppenheim (1992) remains the classic text on attitudinal measurement and is well worth consulting.

- De Vaus, D.A. (2001) *Surveys in Social Research*, 5th edn, London: Routledge.
- Field, A. and Hole, G. (2003) *How to Design and Report Experiments*, London: Sage.
- Oppenheim, A.N. (1992) *Questionnaire Design, Interviewing and Attitude Measurement*, London: Pinter.
- Robson, C. (1994) *Experiment, Design and Statistics in Psychology*, 3rd edn, London: Penguin.
- Sapsford, R. (2006) *Survey Research*, 2nd edn, London: Sage.

2 Face your demons and have a closer look at the statistics behind the concepts covered in this book

There does come a time when it is necessary to have a brief look "under the bonnet" to see what is actually going on with the statistical tests and analyses that you are performing with SPSS. Especially if you want to develop your knowledge and skills further, you will definitely benefit from developing your understanding of some of the core statistics that underpin quantitative data analysis. Fortunately there are now some excellent and accessible texts out there that cover the core statistical elements without recourse to complex mathematical formulae. Moreover, now that you have an intuitive grasp of what is going on this will help you considerably in terms of making sense of the statistics involved and what they are attempting to achieve.

You will find any of the books below useful in providing you with a grounding in the basics. Of these four I have personally found Hinton (2004) very useful for explaining in a clear and accessible way the underlying statistics behind most of the tests covered in this book:

- Clegg, F. (1990) *Simple Statistics: A Course Book for the Social Sciences*, Cambridge: Cambridge University Press.
- Coolidge, F. (2006) *Statistics: A Gentle Introduction*, 2nd edn, London: Sage.
- Diamond, I. and Jefferies, J. (2001) *Beginning Statistics: An Introduction for Social Scientists*, London: Sage.
- Hinton, P. (2004) *Statistics Explained*, 2nd edn, London: Routledge.

3 Move onto more advanced quantitative data analysis techniques involving three or more variables

The focus for this book has been on giving you a solid grounding in the analysis of relationships between two variables (called bivariate analysis). The next step in analysis terms is obviously to begin looking at ways of examining the relationships between three or more variables (known as multivariate analysis). While this is where the statistics can get incredibly complicated it is still quite possible to gain a good and intuitive grasp of what is going on and, moreover, to perform such analyses competently using SPSS. In fact, you may not have noticed it but I did slip in an example of multivariate analysis at the end of the last chapter in relation to the linear multiple regression. If you don't believe me have another look at that section, there were definitely three variables involved in the analysis ("reading1," "reading2" and "group"). Hopefully, you can see from this example that as long as you can gain an intuitive understanding of the particular multivariate methods involved then actually undertaking them with SPSS need not be difficult.

There is now a growing number of books that aim to provide this type of intuitive understanding of some of the most common multivariate techniques you are likely to come across in educational research including: linear and logistic multiple regression; loglinear analysis; and factor analysis. In my opinion, Field (2005) remains the best text in this area. Not only does it explain multivariate statistics in as clear and accessible a way as possible using plenty of examples, but it also shows you clearly how to perform the analysis and interpret the findings using SPSS. The books by Cramer (2003), Foster *et al.* (2005) and Spicer (2005) also provide accessible introductions to multivariate analyses and attempt to explain the core concepts in words rather than numbers. Finally, if you are feeling a little brave then you should have a look at Plewis (1997) and Miles and Shevlin (2001). They are a little more technical but are probably the best non-technical introductions you will find to the more advanced methods associated with multilevel modeling and structural equation modeling.

- Cramer, D. (2003) *Advanced Quantitative Data Analysis*, Maidenhead: Open University Press.
- Field, A. (2005) *Discovering Statistics Using SPSS*, London: Sage.
- Foster, J., Barkus, E. and Yavorsky, C. (2005) *Understanding and Using Advanced Statistics*, London: Sage.
- Miles, J. and Shevlin, M. (2001) *Applying Regression and Correlation*, London: Sage.
- Plewis, I. (1997) *Statistics in Education*, London: Arnold.
- Spicer, J. (2004) *Making Sense of Multivariate Data Analysis*, London: Sage.

4 If you're still keen for more, think seriously about enrolling on an advanced statistics course or program

I tend to like finding things out for myself and so for a number of years I taught myself statistics, working from the basics upwards. However, I reached a point where I really needed help in navigating my way around and trying to make sense of the heavier statistical texts that I was beginning to encounter. This was the point when I decided to take a part-time Master's degree in applied statistics. Of course you don't need to go that far (not yet anyway!). There are a range of statistics courses out there ranging from those that will provide you with excellent groundings in basic statistical theory to others that are much more practical and hands-on and focus on using statistical software packages such as SPSS. Moreover, if you don't fancy the commitment of a full course there are plenty of places that run short workshops on a range of specific topics within quantitative data analysis. With a little advice you could easily plan out a pathway through some of these short courses and workshops in order to build up your expertise in a more flexible manner.

In all of this, my only advice to you is to choose your courses carefully and seek advice from others who may have taken the courses you are interested in or can at least advise you on them. Different courses will adopt differing approaches to teaching statistics with some approaching it from a "first principles" mathematical standpoint and others from a more applied and intuitive position. You need to choose the courses that best fit with your own preferred style.

5 Above all, make sure that you enjoy yourself!

Finally, a simple point but an extremely important one; in whatever you choose to do make sure you enjoy yourself. One of the key things I have learnt on my own journey through quantitative data analysis and statistics is that it does not have to be the dry and turgid subject that held little relevance to me that I remember from school. Rather, and in my professional life as a researcher and academic, I have found quantitative research to be an extremely effective and empowering approach that has a direct and immediate relevance to my own interests and concerns. Moreover, it is exciting to discover new relationships and patterns within real-life data that then have direct implications for education policy and practice. Above all, what I hope this book has done is to give you not only a sound appreciation of the benefits and uses of quantitative research to education, but also at least some of the enthusiasm to learn and do more with quantitative methods that I have developed over the years.

Defining variables in SPSS Version 9.0 and earlier

SPSS Version 9.0 and earlier do not include the Variable View feature outlined in Chapter 1. Rather, the main window is as shown in Figure A1.1. As can be seen, this is an empty dataset with the variables having yet to be defined. To define a variable you need to double-click on the column heading as shown in Figure A1.1. This opens the main **Define Variable** window as shown in Figure A1.2. Let us work through the procedure for defining the variable "contint" from the **international.sav** dataset featured in Chapter 1.

To start with type in the shortened variable name "contint" in the field marked "Variable Name:" as shown. For these versions of SPSS, variable names can only be a maximum of eight characters. Next, define the type of variable we are dealing with here by selecting "nominal" from the list of three at the bottom of the window. Having done all this it is just a matter of then working round the four buttons in the middle of the window to define the remaining elements of the variable. Clicking on the "Type. . ." button opens the **Define Variable Type:** window as shown in Figure A1.3. Check that "Numeric" is selected (which is actually the default setting in SPSS) and then just change the number of decimal

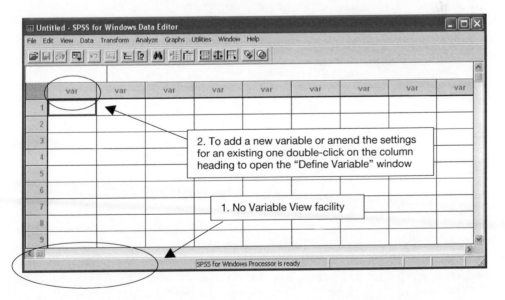

Figure A1.1 The main data view window as it appears in SPSS Version 9.0 and earlier

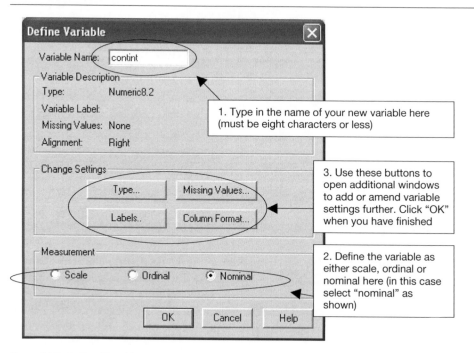

Figure A1.2 Define Variable window as it appears in SPSS Version 9.0 and earlier

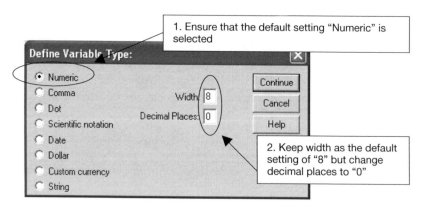

Figure A1.3 Define Variable Type: window as it appears in SPSS Version 9.0 and earlier

places to be displayed from the default setting of "2" to "0" as shown. Once complete, click "Continue" to return to the main window.

Next, click on the "Missing Values. . ." button to open the **Define Missing Values:** window shown in Figure A1.4. This is actually very similar to the window that appears in SPSS Version 15.0 (see Figure 1.16). In this case there are no missing values to define and so you can just click "Continue" to return to the main **Define Variable** window.

Next, clicking on the "Labels. . ." button opens the **Define Labels:** window as shown in Figure A1.5. This is also actually the same window as that which currently appears in

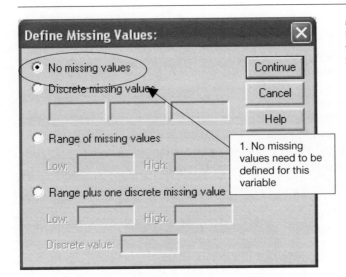

Figure A1.4
Define Missing Values:
window as it appears in
SPSS Version 9.0 and earlier

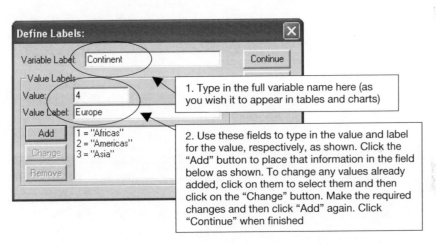

Figure A1.5 Define Labels: window as it appears in SPSS Version 9.0 and earlier

SPSS Version 15.0 (see Figure 1.15). In this window we need to give the variable a full label as you wish it to appear in tables and charts. Here we will just call it "Continent" and this needs to be typed into the field called "Variable Label:" as shown. We then need to define the values and labels of the four categories for this variable. This is done by entering the value in the "Value:" field and then its accompanying label in the "Value Label:" field as shown in Figure A1.5. Clicking on the "Add" button puts these settings in the bottom field as also shown. We can then do the same for the remaining three categories. If there is a need to edit one of the categories already entered this can be done by clicking on that category in the bottom window to select it. This puts the value and the value label back into the respective fields above and these can be edited as required before then clicking the "Change" button to make the changes. When complete, click the "Continue" button to return to the main **Define Variable** window.

Finally, clicking on the "Column Format. . ." button opens the **Define Column Format:** window shown in Figure A1.6. These settings basically alter the way the data is viewed in the main SPSS window in relation to the width of each column and how the text is aligned within it. The default settings for SPSS are as shown in Figure A1.6 and there is usually no need to amend these. Click on "Continue" to return to the main window and then click on "OK" in the main window to close it.

Once a variable has been defined, the shortened name for that variable will appear at the head of the column as shown in Figure A1.7. If there is a need to edit the variable settings further then this can be done by double-clicking on the variable name as shown in Figure A1.7 to open up the **Define Variable** window again.

Figure A1.6
Define Column Format:
window as it appears in
SPSS Version 9.0 and earlier

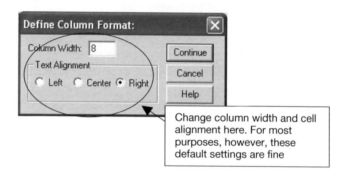

Change column width and cell alignment here. For most purposes, however, these default settings are fine

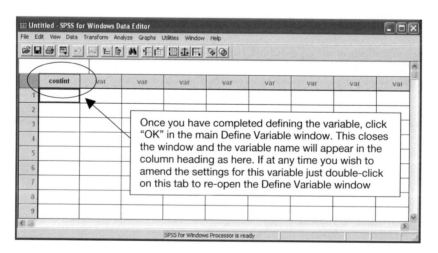

Once you have completed defining the variable, click "OK" in the main Define Variable window. This closes the window and the variable name will appear in the column heading as here. If at any time you wish to amend the settings for this variable just double-click on this tab to re-open the Define Variable window

Figure A1.7 The main screen showing a variable that has been defined as it appears in SPSS Version 9.0 and earlier

Editing charts in SPSS Version 12.0 and earlier

The Chart Editor in SPSS for Windows Version 12.0 and earlier (and also in SPSS Version 11.0 for Mac OS X and earlier) is slightly different to that illustrated in Chapter 4 in this book. To illustrate the differences we will follow the same example as used in Chapter 4 for generating and editing a clustered bar chart illustrating the school grades achieved by boys and girls from kindergarten through to Grade 8 in America (as reported by their parents) using the **afterschools.sav** dataset. To begin with, open the dataset and use the **Data** → **Weight Cases. . .** procedure to weight cases by the variable "WTCORRCT." Once done, generate the basic clustered bar chart as you were shown in Chapter 3 (see Figure 3.6) using the variables "SEX" and "SEGRADES."

The initial chart that you will generate with this procedure is shown in Figure A2.1. To edit the chart double-click anywhere on it. This opens the **Chart Editor** window as shown in Figure A2.2. All of the editing you will do in relation to the chart will be done in this window. When you have finished editing the chart all you need to do is to close it (by clicking the red cross situated at the top right of the window) to return to the main output window. In doing this you will see that the chart in this main output window will reflect the changes you have made. If you want to make any further changes you just need to double-click on the chart again to re-open the **Chart Editor** window. It is this main output window that you should use to save the chart (and any other output created). Once saved you can always return to, and re-open, this output file and continue editing the chart if you wish.

Adding a title to the chart

To begin with we need to add a title. Select **Chart** → **Title. . .** from the menu. This brings up the **Titles** window as shown in Figure A2.3. In this instance we will call the chart: "Figure 1. Sex differences in school grades attained by American children (Kindergarten through Grade 8) as reported by their parents in 2005." Type the first half of the title into the field "Title 1:" and the second half into "Title 2:". Next, use the drop-down menu as shown to ensure that the title is centered. Once done click "OK" to finish.

You will probably find that the size of the title is too large initially. To change the size of the text, click on the top line of the title to select it. A box will appear around the text as shown in Figure A2.4 to indicate that it is selected. Next, click on the Text Styles icon as also shown. This opens the small **Text Styles** window. Change the font to Arial Black and reduce the size to 9 point as shown and click "Apply" to change it. You will see that the style of the first line of the title changes accordingly but the **Text Styles** window stays

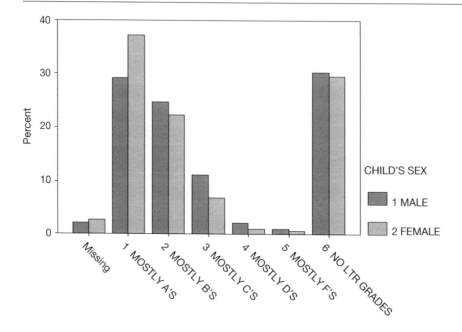

SE1-CHILD'S GRADES ACROSS ALL SUBJECTS

Cases weighted by WTCORRCT

Figure A2.1 The initial clustered bar chart as it appears in SPSS Version 12.0 and earlier

open. Click on the second line of the title to select it and change the style in the same way. While you have the **Text Styles** window open, work your way round the rest of the text in the chart and reduce it all to 8 points. Once finished you can click "Close" to close the Text Styles window.

Editing axis titles and value labels

The next thing to do is to remove the unnecessary detail from the title and labels on the *x*-axis. To do this, double-click on the *x*-axis title as shown in Figure A2.5. This opens the **Category Axis** window. To amend the axis title, click in the "Axis Title:" field as shown and amend the text. Here, we will just remove "SE1-" from the beginning and also change the text to lower case. Also, change the justification of the title to "center" using the drop-down menu as shown. Next, click on the "Labels" button to open the **Category Axis: Labels** window as also shown in Figure A2.5. Click on one of the labels listed and this brings it up in the "Label:" field. You can edit the label by clicking and typing in this field. In this case we just need to remove the numbers preceding the label names and also change the text to lower case. Once done, click the "Change" button to make the changes. Click on the next label and repeat the process until you have changed all labels. Finally, use the drop-down menu to change the orientation of the labels to vertical.

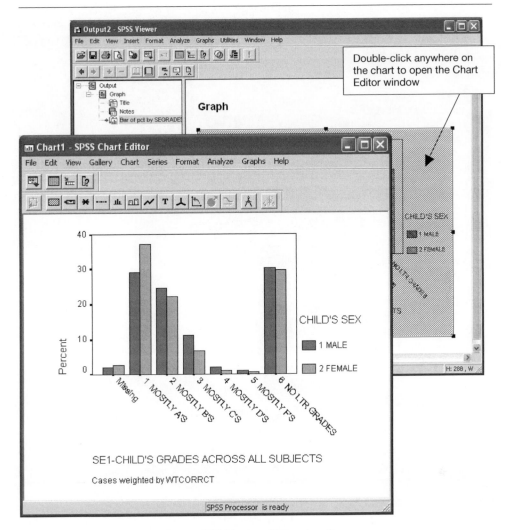

Figure A2.2 Chart Editor window in SPSS Version 12.0 and earlier

Once done click "Continue" to return to the **Category Axis** window and then click "OK" to finish the procedure.

Adding a footnote to the chart

Next, we need to add a footnote to explain the source of the data. Usually this can be done by selecting **Chart → Footnote...** from the menu. However, on this occasion SPSS has already added a footnote at the bottom of the chart ("Cases weighted by WTCORRCT"). As we do not need this particular footnote we can simply amend it to the one that we want. To do this, double-click on the footnote and this opens the **Footnotes** window shown

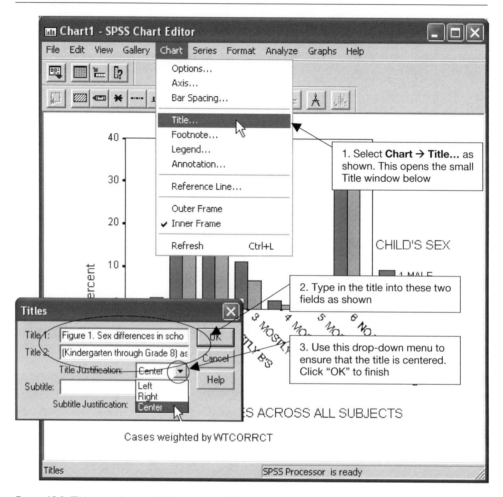

Figure A2.3 Titles window in SPSS Version 12.0 and earlier

in Figure A2.6. Click and type into the fields to add the footnote: "Source: Secondary analysis of the National Household Education Surveys Program of 2005 (After-School Programs and Activities Survey)." Click "OK" to finish.

Changing the colors of the bars in a bar chart

To change the colors of the bars click on one set of bars to select it. Little squares appear around the bars to indicate that they have been selected as shown in Figure A2.7. Once selected, click on the Colors icon and this opens the **Colors** window as shown. Click on the black square from the palette and then click on the "Apply" button to change the "Male" bars to black. Next click on the "Female" bars to select them and change these bars to white in the same way. Once finished click the "Close" button.

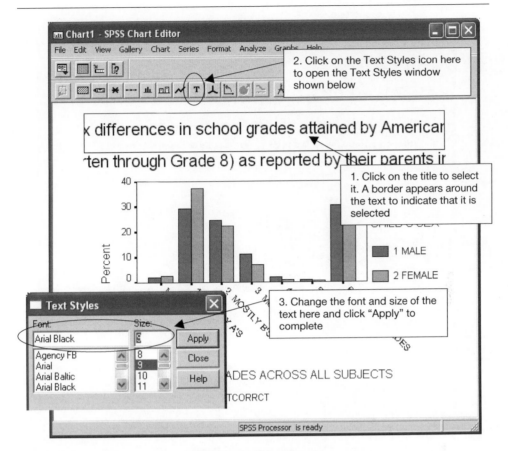

Figure A2.4 Text Styles window in SPSS Version 12.0 and earlier

Removing bars from a bar chart

The very last thing to do is to remove the bars representing missing values from the chart. To do this, double-click on any of the bars. This opens the **Bar/Line/Area Displayed Data** window as shown in Figure A2.8. Click on "Missing" from the list in the bottom "Display:" field and then click on the arrow button to place it into the "Omit:" field. Once done, click on "OK" to finish. You should see that the bars representing missing cases have now been removed. The final chart should now appear as shown in Figure A2.9.

As explained before, you can return to the main output window simply by closing the **Chart Edit** window. Once in this main output window you can click on the chart once to select it and then cut and paste it directly into your report just as you were shown with the tables (see Figure 4.6). This time, however, you can just choose **Edit → Paste** rather than **Paste Special. . .** as you are already dealing with an image. Once you have pasted the chart into your report you can select the chart and drag its edges to re-size it as you require.

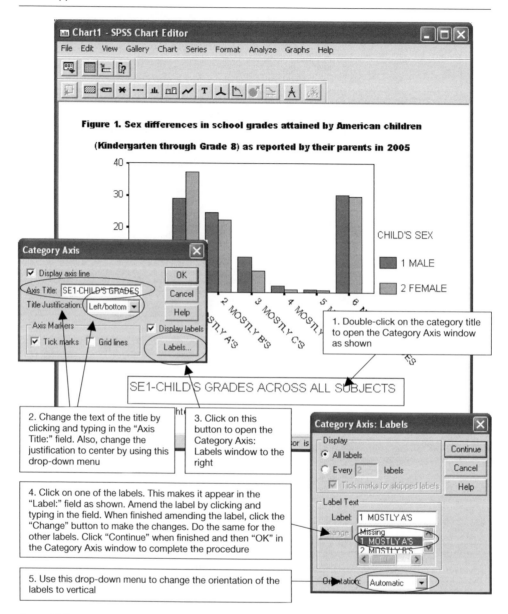

Figure A2.5 Category Axis window in SPSS Version 12.0 and earlier

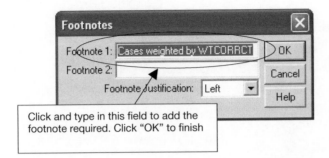

Figure A2.6 Footnotes window in SPSS Version 12.0 and earlier

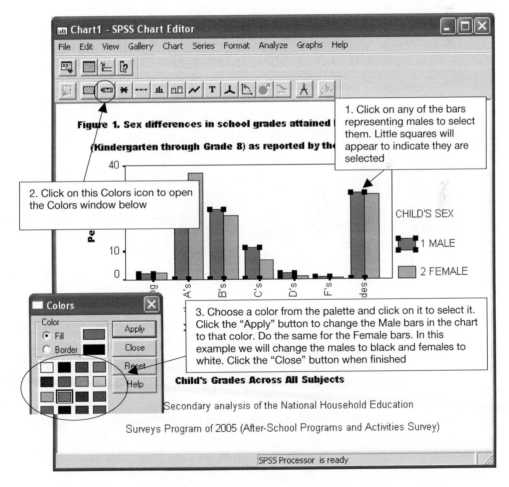

Figure A2.7 Colors window in SPSS Version 12.0 and earlier

Figure A2.8
Bar/Line/Displayed
Data window in SPSS
Version 12.0 and
earlier

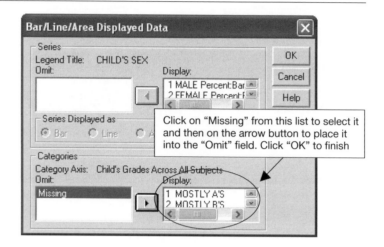

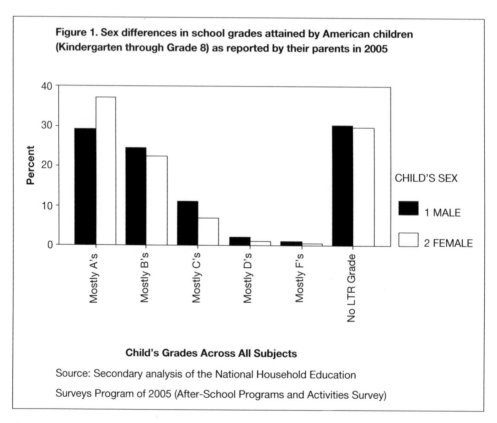

Figure A2.9 Final version of the clustered bar chart created using SPSS Version 12.0 and earlier

Editing other types of chart

Because of the range of charts available and the many different options to choose from within each type of chart, it is impossible to cover all aspects of how to edit charts here for SPSS Version 12.0 and earlier. However, in going through the example above you should have gained an intuitive feel for how to edit charts. In fact, whatever the type of chart you are working with the procedures are very similar. In this sense it is worth stressing two final points:

- Have a good look at the icons across the top of the **Chart Editor** window. We have used some of them in the example above (i.e. adding a title and a footnote). However, there are many more that perform some useful functions. Click on each one to explore what it does. You will learn a lot more by experimenting with the **Chart Editor** window than you will by just reading this book.
- As a general rule, if you wish to alter some specific element of a chart (i.e. the text, the color, the style of lines etc.) then you need to either click on it once to select it and then use one of the icons from the top menu, or double-click on it to open a specific window.

References

Aboud, F. (1988) *Children and Prejudice*, Oxford: Basil Blackwell.

Connolly, P. (1996) "Seen but never heard: rethinking approaches to researching racism and young children," *Discourse: Studies in the Cultural Politics of Education*, 17(2): 171–185.

—— (1997) "In search of authenticity: researching young children's perspectives," in: A. Pollard, D. Thiessen and A. Filer (eds) *Children and their Curriculum: The Perspectives of Primary and Elementary School Children*, London: Falmer Press.

—— (1998) *Racism, Gender Identities and Young Children: Social Relations in a Multi-Ethnic, Inner-City Primary School*, London: Routledge.

—— (2001) "Qualitative methods in the study of children's racial attitudes and identities," *Infant and Child Development*, 10(3): 219–233.

—— (2004) *Boys and Schooling in the Early Years*, London: Routledge.

—— (2006a) "Keeping a sense of proportion but losing all perspective: a critique of Gorard's notion of the 'Politician's Error'," *British Journal of Educational Studies*, 54(1): 73–88.

—— (2006b) "No new perspectives, just red herrings: a reply to Gorard," *British Journal of Educational Studies*, 54(4): 476–482.

—— (2006c) "Summary statistics, educational achievement gaps and the ecological fallacy," *Oxford Review of Education*, 32(2): 235–252.

Dahlberg, G., Moss, P. and Pence, A. (1999) *Beyond Quality in Early Childhood Education and Care: Postmodern Perspectives*, London: RoutledgeFalmer.

Delgardo, R. and Stefancic, J. (eds) (1998) *The Latino/a Condition: A Critical Reader*, New York: New York University Press.

DfES (Department for Education and Skills) (2005a) *DfES School and College Achievement and Attainment Tables*, www.dfes.gov.uk/performancetables/ (accessed: August 12, 2006).

—— (2005b) *Value Added Technical Informations*, www.dfes.gov.uk/performancetables/ schools_04/sec3b.shtml (accessed: August 12, 2006).

Field, A. (2005) *Discovering Statistics Using SPSS*, London: Sage.

Gillborn, D. and Mirza, H. (2000) *Educational Inequality—Mapping Race, Class and Gender: A Synthesis of Research Evidence*, London: Office for Standards in Education.

Gorard, S. (1999) "Keeping a sense of proportion: the 'politician's error' in analysing school outcomes," *British Journal of Educational Studies*, 47 (3): 235–246.

—— (2001) *Quantitative Methods in Educational Research: The Role of Numbers Made Easy*, London: Continuum.

—— (2006a) *Using Everyday Numbers Effectively in Research*, London: Continuum.

—— (2006b) "Yet another perspective: a response to Connolly," *British Journal of Educational Studies*, 54(4): 471–475.

—— with Taylor, C. (2004) *Combining Methods in Educational Research*, Buckingham: Open University Press.

Hammersley, M. (1992) *What's Wrong with Ethnography?*, London: Routledge.

Hartwig, F. and Dearing, B. (1979) *Exploratory Data Analysis*, Sage University Paper Series on Quantitative Applications in the Social Sciences, 16, Beverley Hills, CA: Sage.

Hoaglin, D., Mosteller, F. and Tukey, J. (eds) (1983) *Understanding Robust and Exploratory Data Analysis*, New York: John Wiley & Sons.

Marsh, C. (1988) *Exploring Data: An Introduction to Data Analysis for Social Scientists*, Cambridge: Polity Press.

Miles, J. and Shevlin, M. (2001) *Applying Regression and Correlation*, London: Sage.

Milner, D. (1983) *Children and Race: Ten Years On*, London: Ward Lock Educational.

NCSR (National Centre for Social Research) (1999) *Youth Cohort Study: Cohort 9 Sweep 1 Technical Report*, London: NCSR.

ONS (Office for National Statistics) (2005) *The National Statistics Socio-Economic Classification: User Manual*, 2005 Edition, London: ONS.

Pell, T. and Jarvis, T. (2001) "Developing attitude to science scales for use with children of ages from five to eleven years", *International Journal of Science Education*, 23(8): pp. 847–862.

Sylva, K., Siraj-Blatchford, I. and Taggart, B. (2006). *Assessing Quality in the Early Years. Early Childhood Environment Rating Scale Extension (ECERS-E). Four Curricular Subscales*, Stoke-on-Trent, UK: Trentham Books.

Troyna, B. (1984) "Fact or artefact? The 'educational underachievement' of black pupils," *British Journal of Sociology of Education*, 5: 153–166.

Tukey, J. (1977) *Exploratory Data Analysis*, London: Addison-Wesley.

Index

Pages containing relevant illustrations are indicated in *italic* type.

abbreviated variable names 13, 17
afterschools.sav 10, 122–3, 189, 194, 251; analyzing relationships between variables 69, 72, 76, 82, 91
age variable 39, 41
alpha (α) 165
alternative hypothesis 163–4, *166*, 167
analyzing relationships between variables 68, 111; nominal and ordinal variables 81–2, *83–6*; nominal and scale variables 87, *88–90*; ordinal and scale variables 96, *97*; two nominal variables 76–7, *78–9*, 80, *81*; two ordinal variables *91*, 92, *93–4*, *95–6*; two scale variables 98, *99*, 100, *101–2*, 103
analyzing trends over time 103, *104–10*
ANOVA *see* one-way ANOVA (one-way analysis of variance)
attention deficit disorder (ADD or ADHD) 181–5, *182, 183, 184*
attitudinal measurement 244
averages 48, *49*, 51, 57; *see also* means
axis titles 126, *127*, 252–3, *256*; *see also* titles, editing

bar charts 23–4, 63, *64*, *66*; changing the colors of bars 128, *129*, 254, *257*; clustered 83–4, *85–6*, 123; *see also* charts, presentation of
beta (β) *166*, 206
biases 142, 143–4, 171–2, 236, 238, 241–2; *see also* unbiased estimates
bivariate analysis 76, 245; *see also* analyzing relationships between variables
Bivariate Correlations window in SPSS *93, 94*

Bonferroni Correction 197
boxplots 60, *61–2*, *89–90*, *97*, 154
Bryman, A. 244
bullying *23*; and gender 155, *156*, 157, *158*, 178–81, *179, 180*
bullying.sav 10, 13, 40, 155, 178

cases 15; selecting 72, *73*, 74, *75*; weighting *52*, 53
central limit theorem 148
chance 160–1, *162*, 171; *see also* probabilities
changing default settings in SPSS 17, *20*
Chart Builder 134, *135–9*; *see also* charts, presentation of
charts, presentation of 122, *123*, *124*, 134, 140, *141*; changing colors of bars 128, *129*, 254, *257*; editing axis titles and value labels and removing text 126–7; footnotes 125, *128*; removing bars and changing their order *130, 131*, 132, *133*, 255, *258*; titles 125, 126, *127*; in SPSS Version 12.0 and earlier 251, *252–8*, 259; *see also* Chart Builder
Chi-Square test *177*, 178–89; ADD or ADHD and race/ethnicity example 181–5, *182, 183, 184*; bullying and gender example 178–81, *179, 180*; gender and educational attainment example 185–9, *187, 188*
Clegg, F. 245
closed questions 16
clustered bar charts 83–4, *85–6*, 123; *see also* charts, presentation of
cluster sampling 239–40, 241–2
Cohen, L. 244

colors of bars of bar charts, changing the 128, *129*, 254, *257*

columns and rows, changing the order of *120, 121, 122*

companion website for book 8–9, 206

confidence intervals for means *145–9, 153*; 95% confidence intervals 150, *151*, 152, *154*; *see also* confidence intervals for proportions; 95% confidence intervals

confidence intervals for proportions 155, *156–8*; *see also* confidence intervals for means

contingency tables 77; ADD or ADHD and race/ethnicity *182*; and effect sizes 181, 186, *188*, 189; out-of-school suspensions and race/ethnicity 79, 80, *81*; school grades 82, *83*, 91–2, *93*; 2 × 2 186, *187*

control groups 223, *224*; post-test only control group design 224–6; pre-test/ post-test control group design (ordinal outcome measure) 233–7, *235, 237*; pre-test/post-test control group design (scale outcome measure) 226–33, *227, 228, 229, 230, 231, 232*

Coolidge, F. 245

correcting for design effects 239–40

correcting for non-response 236, 238

correlation coefficients 92–3, 95–6, 97, 98, 102–3, 207, 214–16

Cramer, D. 245

Cramer's V 181, 186

creating datasets: Data View *31*; defining variables 25, *26–7*, 28, *29–30*; entering data 30; scatterplots *32–3*

critical approach to quantitative data analysis 3–4

critical regions 169

cross-product ratios 107–8, *109, 110*

Crosstabs window in SPSS *78*

cutting and pasting tables and charts 118, *119*, 132; *see also* charts, presentation of; tables, presentation of

datasets: understanding 13, *14–15*, 16; used in this book 8, *10–11*; and weight variables 241–2; *see also* creating datasets; opening exisiting datasets

Data View 30, *31*

Dearing, B. 7

default settings in SPSS, changing 17, *20*

defining variables 25, *26–7*, 28, *29–30, 247–50*

degrees of freedom (df) 176, 180–1

Descriptives window in SPSS *54*

design effects, correcting for 239–40

De Vaus, D.A. 244

Diamond, I. 245

differing versions of SPSS 9; defining variables in Version 9.0 and earlier *247–50*; editing charts in Version 12.0 and earlier 251, *252–8*, 259

directional hypotheses (one-tailed) 167–70, *168*, 189, 217

displaying and summarizing nominal and ordinal variables 62–3, *64–7*

displaying and summarizing scale variables 43–62; 67; boxplots 60, *61–2*; histograms 43, *45*, 46; mean and standard deviations 48–50; medians and interquartile ranges *56–7*, 58, *59*, 60; standardized scores (Z scores) *51–5*; stem and leaf display *46–7*, 48

"don't know" category 40

early childhood care 6, *53, 64*; *see also* earlychildhood.sav

earlychildhood.sav 10, 52, 63, *66*, 181, 214

East Riding of Yorkshire *211*, 212, *213*

editing charts *see* charts, presentation of

editing tables *see* tables, presentation of

educational and economic indicators for 20 countries *26*

effect sizes 173, 178, 194, 196; and Chi-Square test 179, 181, 186–7; formulas for calculating 193, 206–7

Element Properties window in SPSS 137, *138*

error bars 150, *151*, 152, *153–4, 157–8*

errors *see* error bars; sampling errors; sampling errors; standard errors; Type I and Type II errors

ethnicity 1, 69, *70–1*; and attention deficit disorder (ADD or ADHD) 181–5, *182, 183, 184*; charts illustrating racial and ethnic breakdown 63, *65, 66*; and school grades 194–9; and school-leaving attainment 87, *88*, 89, 90, 152, *154*; and suspensions from school 76–7, *79*, 80, *81*

experimental research designs 223, *224*;
    post-test only control group design
    224–6; pre-test/post-test control group
    design (ordinal outcome measure)
    233–7, *235, 237*; pre-test/post-test
    control group design (scale outcome
    measure) 226–33, *227, 228, 229, 230,
    231, 232*
experiment.sav 10, 217, 220
exploratory data analysis (EDA) 6–7, 138
Explore window in SPSS *31*
extreme values 61, *62*

factor analysis 245
father's age 214, *215–16*
female illiteracy *26, 33*, 98, *99, 102*
Field, A. 210, 244, 245
footnotes 114, 125, *128*, 253–4, *257*
Foster, J. 245
Frequencies window in SPSS 22, *23*
frequency tables 63, *64*, 83

Gabriel 210
Games-Howell 212
GCSE Benchmarks 100, *101, 105, 145*;
    and gender 103, 105, *106–9*, 138, *139*,
    185–9, *187, 188*; and racial/ethnic
    groups 87, *88*, 89, 90, 152, *154*; and
    truancy 97; *see also* local education
    authorities (LEAs)
"Gee Whizz" chart *141*
gender 74, 76, 159–60, *161–2*; and bullying
    155, *156*, 157, *158*, 178–81, *179, 180*;
    and GCSE Benchmarks 103, 105, *106–9*,
    138, *139*, 185–9, *187, 188*; and school
    grades 81–2, *83–6*, *123, 124*, 189–94,
    251, *252–8*; *see also* female illiteracy;
    male illiteracy
generalizations 142–3
Gorard, S. 98, 100, 106–7
G*Power 167, 206
gross domestic product (GDP) *56–7, 58,
    59, 62, 102*

Hartwig, F. 7
"highly significant" 172, 186
Hinton, P. 244–5
Hispanic boys 72, *73*, 74
histograms 43, *45*, 46
Hochberg's GT2 212
Hole, G. 244

hypothesis testing 163–5, *166*, 167,
    170–2
hypotheses, directional and non-directional
    167–70, *168*, 178, 189, 217

independent samples t-test *177*, 200–8,
    201–4, 207
inferential statistics 8
international.sav 10, 25, 43, 56, 98, 102,
    247
interquartile ranges (IQR) 58, *59*, 60
interval variables 41, *42*, 111
interviewer effects 5

Jarvis, T. *42*
Jefferies, J. 245

Kolmogorov-Smirnov test 201, *202*
Kruskal-Wallis test *177*, 194–9, *195, 196,
    199*

labels *see* value labels
Leeds local education authority (Leeds
    LEA): compared with York LEA 200,
    201–4, 205, *207*, 208; compared with
    York, East Riding of Yorkshire and
    North Yorkshire LEAs 208–14, *211,
    213*
legends 131, *132*
Levene's test 205, 210
Lewin, C. 244
likert scales 41, *42*
linear multiple regression 226, 228, *229,
    230, 232*, 245
line graphs *104, 105, 106, 107, 110*
"line of best fit" 102–3
local education authorities (LEAs):
    comparison of York and Leeds 200,
    201–4, 205, *207*, 208; comparison of
    York, Leeds, East Riding of Yorkshire
    and North Yorkshire 208–14, *211,
    213*
logilinear analysis 245

Mac versions of SPSS 9
male illiteracy 98, *99*
Mann-Whitney U test *177*, 189–94, *190,
    191, 192*, 197
margins of error 149, 150, 155, 157; *see
    also* confidence intervals for means;
    confidence intervals for proportions

means 48, *49–50*, 51, 54; confidence
    intervals for *145–9, 153*; trimmed
    57–8
medians *56–7*, 58, *59*, 60
Miles, J. 245
missing values 28, *29*, 40, 43
mothers: age of *53–5*, 214, *215–16*;
    educational achievements of 91–6, *91,
    93, 94*
multilevel modelling 240
multivariate analysis 245

names, abbreviated variable 13, 17
negatively skewed 56
nominal variables 36, *44*, 111; displaying
    and summarizing 62–3, *64–7*;
    relationships between ordinal variables
    and 81–2, *83–6*; relationships between
    scale variables and 87, *88–90*;
    relationships between two 76–7, *78–9*, 80,
    81; statistical tests for *177*
non-directional (two-tailed) hypotheses
    167–70, *168*, 178, 189
non-response 52, 144, 157, 170–1, 236,
    238–42
normal distributions 48, *49–50*
Northern Ireland Young Life and Times
    Survey *14, 23*
North Yorkshire *211*, 212, *213*
null-hypotheses 163–4, *166*
numeric variables 27

odds ratios 107–8; *see also* cross-product
    ratios
one- and two-tailed tests 167–70, *168*
one-sample Kolmogorov-Smirnov test
    201, *202*
one-way ANOVA (one-way analysis of
    variance) *177*, 208–14, *209, 211,
    213*
open-ended questions 16
opening existing datasets 16, *17–24*, 25;
    saving output 25; value labels icon 18,
    20; variables icon 18, *21*
opinion polls 155
Oppenheim, A.N. 244
opportunistic sampling 144
ordinal variables 37–40, *37, 44*, 111, 233–4;
    displaying and summarizing 62–3, *64–7*;
    relationships between nominal variables
    and 81–2, *83–6*; relationships between

scale variables and 96, *97*; relationships
    between two *91*, 92, *93–4*, 95–6;
    statistical tests for *177*
outliers 56–7, 61, *62*
Output window 23, *24*, 25

parentheses 74, *75*
Pearson Chi-Square statistic 180
Pearson correlation coefficients 98, 102–3,
    207, 214; *see also* correlation
    coefficients
Pearson correlation test *177*, 214,
    215–16
Pell, T. *42*
percentages *78–9*, 80, 155–6
Phi 181, 186–7
pie charts 63, *65–6*; *see also* charts,
    presentation of
Plewis, I. 245
point biserial correlations 207
population estimates 238–9
population means *147–8*, 149–50, *151*,
    152, 153
population pyramids *136–9*; *see also* charts,
    presentation of
positively skewed *56*, 58
post-hoc tests 210, 212, 214
post-test only control group design
    224–6
power, statistical 166–7, 206, 208
precoding 16
preparing variables and the dataset for
    analysis: recoding variables 68–9, *70–1*,
    92; selecting cases 72, *73*, 74, *75*; split
    file procedure 74, *75*, 76
presentation of findings 112; *see also* charts,
    presentation of; reporting findings; tables,
    presentation of
pre-test/post-test control group design *224*;
    ordinal outcome measure 233–7, *235,
    237*; scale outcome measure 226–33, *227,
    228, 229, 230, 231, 232*
probabilities (p) 161, *162*, 169, 176, 181; *see
    also* chance
proportions: analyzing 106–7; confidence
    intervals for 155, *156–8*
purposive samples 171

qualitative research 1, 4
quantitative data analysis, critical approach
    to 3–4

quantitative research methodology, texts on 244–5

quantitative versus qualitative research 4

questionnaires 5, 13, *14–15*, 16

race 1, 69, *70–1*; and attention deficit disorder (ADD or ADHD) 181–5, *182, 183, 184*; charts illustrating racial and ethnic breakdown 63, *65, 66*; and school grades 194–9; and school-leaving attainment 87, *88*, 89, 90, 152, *154*; and suspensions from school 76–7, *79*, 80, *81*

random allocation 223, *224*, 226

random samples 142, 143, 144, *146*, 147, *148*; and statistical significance 159–61, 171

random variations 171–2

ranges 58, *59*, 60

ratio variables 41, 42

Reading and Drama Club: related samples t-test 220, *221, 222*; Wilcoxon test 217, *218, 219*; *see also* experimental research designs

reading to young children, frequency of 63, *64*

recoding variables 68–9, *70–1*, 92

recommended texts for further study 244–5

related samples t-test *177*, 220, *221, 222*

relationships between variables 68; *see also* analyzing relationships between two variables; analyzing trends over time; preparing variables and the dataset for analysis

reliability 5, 82

removing bars from bar charts *130, 131*, 132, *133*, 255, *258*

reporting findings 198, 208, 212, 216, 218, 221; and experimental design 232, 236; not statistically significant 181, 185; use of terms "statistically significant" and "highly significant" 172–3, 186–8, 193

Robson, C. 244

routine quantitative data analysis 3

rows and columns, changing the order of *120, 121, 122*

sample sizes 159–61

sampling errors 144, 147, 148, 153, 161, 172

Sapsford, R. 244

saving: datasets 30; output 25

scale variables 40–3, *44*, 233–4; relationships between nominal variables and 87, *88–90*; relationships between ordinal variables and 96, *97*; relationships between two 98, *99*, 100, *101–2*, 103; statistical tests for *177*; *see also* displaying and summarizing scale variables

scaling up frequencies to create population estimates 238–9, 242

scatterplots *32–3*, 98, *99*, *101–2*

school grades: and gender 81–2, *83–6*, *123–4*; 189–94, 251, *252–8*; and mother's education 91–6, *91, 93, 94*; and race/ethnic background 194–9

school life expectancy 26, 30, *31–3*, 45, *46–7*, 98, *99*

selecting cases 72, *73*, 74, *75*

sex *see* gender

Shevlin, M. 245

"Sig." (statistical significance of the finding) 176

significance *see* statistical significance

"significant", use of term 172–3, 186, 193

socially constructed nature of quantitative data 4–6

socio-economic backgrounds of respondents 38–9

Somekh, B. 244

Spearman correlation coefficient 97, 103, 214; *see also* correlation coefficients

Spearman correlation test *177*, 214, *215–16*

Spicer, J. 245

split file procedure 74, *75*, 76

SPSS, differing versions of 9; defining variables in Version 9.0 and earlier *247–50*; editing charts in Version 12.0 and earlier 251, *252–8*, 259

SPSS, opening 17, *18*

stacked bar charts *123*; *see also* charts, presentation of

standard errors 148, *149*, 150, 155–6, *157*

standard deviations 48–9, *50*, 51, 54, 148

standardized scores (Z scores) *51–5*, 193

statistical power 166–7, 206, 208

statistical significance: Bonferroni Correction 197; concept of 158, *159–62*, 172–4; reporting 181, 185, 186–8, 208; testing for 163–70, *166, 168* statistical tests, selecting appropriate 175–8, *177*; *see also* Chi-Square test; independent samples t-test; Kolmogorov-Smirnov test; Kruskal-Wallis test; Mann-Whitney U test; one-way ANOVA; Pearson correlation test; related samples t-test; Spearman correlation test; Wilcoxon test

statistics, test 169, 176, 180

statistics courses 246

statistics texts 244–5

stem and leaf displays *46–7*, 48

string variables 27

student versions of SPSS 9

styles 117, *118*

summary statistics 6–7; means and standard deviations 48–50; standardized scores (Z scores) *51–5*, 193

suspensions, out-of-school 76–7, *79*, 80, *81*

systematic biases 143–4, 171–2; *see also* bias; unbiased estimates

tables, presentation of 112, *113*, 140, *141*; changing the appearance of data and text 121, *122*; changing the order of rows and columns *120, 121, 122*; changing the style 117, *118*; cutting and pasting into Word documents 118, *119*; footnotes 114; removing columns and rows 115, *116, 117*; titles 114; *see also* contingency tables

testing for statistical significance 163–70, *166, 168*

tests *see* statistical tests, selecting appropriate

test statistics 169, 176, 180

time *see* analyzing trends over time

timeseries.sav 10, 103–4, 107

titles, editing 114, *115*, 125, 126, *127*; in SPSS Version 12.0 and earlier 251–3, *254, 255, 256*

treatment groups 223, *224*; *see also* control groups

trends *see* analyzing trends over time

trimmed means 57–8

truancy *97*

Tukey 210

Tukey, John 6–7

Type I and Type II errors 165, *166*, 197, 206

unbiased estimates 147

validity 5–6, 23, 82, 90, 193

valueadded.sav 11, 98, 100, *101*, 200, 208

value labels: editing 126–7, 252–3; icon 18, *20*; window in SPSS 22, 28, *29*

values 13

variables: defining 25, *26–7*, 28, *29–30, 247–50*; displaying and summarizing nominal and ordinal 62–3, *64–7*; guide for distinguishing between types of *44*; icon 18, *21*; names of 13, *15*, 17; nominal 36; ordinal 37–40, *37*; scale 40–3; three or more 245; weighting 236, 238–42; *see also* displaying and summarizing scale variables; analyzing relationships between variables

variances 205, 209–10

versions of SPSS *see* differing versions of SPSS

website for book, companion 8–9, 206

weighting cases *52, 53*

weighting variables 236, 238–42

Wilcoxon test *177*, 217, *218, 219*

York local education authority (York LEA): compared with Leeds LEA 200, *201–4*, 205, *207*, 208; compared with Leeds, East Riding of Yorkshire and North Yorkshire LEAs 208–14, *211, 213*

youthcohort.sav 11; analyzing relationships between variables 87, 97; Chart Builder 134; confidence intervals 145, 152; non-response 144; tables 112, 120; test statistics and effect sizes 186; *see also* 20 samples.sav

Z scores *51–5*, 193

2 × 2 contingency table 186, *187*

5 percent cut-off point 162, 164–6, 169, 173–4

20samples.sav 11, 148, 150

95% confidence intervals 150, *151*, 152, *154*, 155, *157–8*, 162; *see also* confidence intervals for means; confidence intervals for proportions

An environmentally friendly book printed and bound in England by www.printondemand-worldwide.com